DEATH
ON
THE
DON

DEATH
ON DON
THE
DON

THE DESTRUCTION OF GERMANY'S ALLIES ON THE EASTERN FRONT, 1941–44

JONATHAN TRIGG

The
History
Press

Other books by this author also published by The History Press:

Hitler's Legions series
Volume I – *Hitler's Gauls: The History of the French Waffen-SS*
Volume II – *Hitler's Flemish Lions: The History of the Flemish Waffen-SS*
Volume III – *Hitler's Jihadis: The History of the Muslim Waffen-SS*
Volume IV – *Hitler's Vikings: The History of the Scandinavian Waffen-SS*

Battle Stories series
Hastings 1066

Cover illustration, front: Romanian infantry in Russia 1942. The corporal in the middle wears a winter tunic and is armed with a home-manufactured Orita submachine gun. His two comrades are in summer uniform.

First published 2013 by Spellmount
This paperback edition published 2017
Reprinted 2020

The History Press
97 St George's Place, Cheltenham,
Gloucestershire, GL50 3QB
www.thehistorypress.co.uk

British Library Cataloguing in Publication Data.
A catalogue record for this book is available from the British Library.

ISBN 978 0 7509 7946 7

Typesetting and origination by The History Press
Printed and bound by TJ International Ltd, Padstow, Cornwall.

CONTENTS

PROLOGUE

After studying history at university and then going on to a career in the British Army in a first-rate infantry regiment, it is perhaps surprising that I came to actually writing military history rather later than people might imagine. Examining the reasons for this seeming mystery, I am quite sure that it was my experience in the army that effectively mothballed any nascent desire to become a serious student of war. At the Royal Military Academy Sandhurst (RMAS), in the (now defunct) compressed seven-month Standard Graduate Course for young officers, the few lessons in military history with extremely well-read civilian tutors were gratefully accepted opportunities for cadets, like myself, to snatch a few minutes of extra sleep to make up for the hours lost each and every night polishing boots and ironing every piece of clothing we possessed.

Arrival at my battalion, then, was like escaping purgatory, but as regards the study of war, it was no better. Infantry work is hard, physically demanding and all about detail, and an officer's mess tends to reflect this. My own was, I am sure, pretty similar to most others, being filled with the same dedicated professionals who characterise the British Army and make it, rightly, envied and admired across the world. Physical fitness, integrity, knowledge of the job, commitment to your men and the regiment – and playing hard – were what we all strived for, and in that atmosphere a more cerebral reflection on conflict, its past and potential future, was anathema. At only one point did a relatively new commanding officer insist that his junior officers, including myself, write an essay on a military topic selected by him. I swear you could have heard the collective groans miles away – the project was not a success. My own treatise on the other European Union nations moving to a position of 'paying' the British Army in terms of providing logistics, supplies, intelligence, etc., as a form of 'foreign legion' to intervene in conflicts where they had no wish to place their own nationals in danger, did not play well.

Then, by some miracle, I was selected to attend the Junior Division of the British Army's prestigious Staff College (JDSC) as the third youngest student on my course. This was a real opportunity for young officers like myself to reassess mankind's addiction to war and where studying our trade was suddenly paid more than lip service. For the first time since I had joined the army six years earlier, I now became involved in earnest conversations with other officers discussing the endless tours of duty in our undeclared war in Northern Ireland and the lessons we could learn from the Falls Road and Crossmaglen, East Tyrone, the Short Strand, Divis Flats and the Bogside. Added to this was grave dissatisfaction and shame at the impotence of United Nations (UN) forces in Croatia and Bosnia – it was while I was at JDSC that I met some fellow officers who had been left powerless and unsupported in the face of horrendous brutality by all sides involved in those vicious civil wars, the get-out clause for both officialdom and senior command being 'we have no UN mandate' to intervene. It is to the eternal credit of my own Commanding Officer at the time of our tour in Croatia and Bosnia (even now I will not name him, just in case) that he gave every single one of us crystal-clear instructions that, UN mandate or not, we should be governed by our consciences and a solid sense of right and wrong. If we thought innocent lives were in danger, we were to act as those same consciences dictated. Our colonel was a good man and a great officer.

However, events on these operations resulted in a distinct sense of discomfort among some senior officers that they now possessed a generation of young commanders who were beginning to look beyond the Cold War and its certainties and wanted to begin to prepare for an altogether different era. I will never forget one senior officer in particular who came to see us at JDSC. After what had clearly been a good lunch, he proceeded to lecture an audience of young captains with the usual balderdash senior officers come out with when they had not bothered to think very much about what they were going to say beforehand. Well, it was a hot summer's day; we had all been working extremely hard, and tempers were somewhat short. At one point, I seriously thought he was going to start screaming in rage as officer after officer demanded answers to pertinent questions – a solution to Ulster, the primacy of politics over the military and the future of BAOR (The British Army on the Rhine – the UK's military commitment to NATO in mainland Europe and for decades the largest concentration of British forces). This was followed by questions on the nightmarish operational-tour system. In the end, he insisted that it was not 'the place of young officers to ask questions or try to understand issues above their pay grade'.

It was at that point that I realised that if I was to become a serious student of history, and the wars that dominate so much of that same history, then it was unlikely to be within the ranks of the British Army. Having said that, one of the few positives to come out the recent, and still unfinished, wars in Iraq and Afghanistan is a real awakening among whole classes of young officers of the importance of military history to their own current situations and its relevance to finding a way to win with honour – long may that resurgence continue.

As for me, this is now the sixth military history book I have written and the fifth on the Second World War. Subject-wise, this volume is a significant departure personally, having focused, up until now, almost exclusively on the exploits and battles of Nazi Germany's 'second army', the Waffen-SS, especially the large numbers of non-German nationals who, for a variety of reasons, ended up fighting in its ranks. Having written about the French, Belgian Flemish, Muslim and Scandinavian volunteers, I feel I have covered large tranches of that particular subject – perhaps the largest one left to me would be a volume on the hundreds of thousands of ethnic Germans from Eastern Europe who served in the ranks of the Waffen-SS.

As it is, my work has mainly focused on the fighting in the Soviet Union as that is where, to a large degree, the Waffen-SS fought their war. Writing on that mammoth campaign I have not touched on the Soviet victory at Stalingrad and the Don River offensives in anything more than a cursory manner – the SS were not involved – and it always seemed to me that this monumental battle had been covered and covered again by historians of the utmost skill, among whom Antony Beevor, for me, stands at the pinnacle. As ever, though, with history, certain stories draw you in remorselessly, and for me one such subject was the fate of Germany's allies – among them the Romanians, Hungarians, Italians, Croats and Slovaks.

Before beginning this journey, I confess I knew little of them, and what I did know was the usual generalisations – that is, they were bit players in a Russo-German war, what forces they did have were throwbacks to a bygone age (all pitchforks and peasants) and when faced with real soldiers firing guns, they invariably took to their heels in an instant. This, according to the legend, was what happened at Stalingrad, and it sealed the fate of the German Sixth Army trapped in the city. The utter dreadfulness of the Axis allies was compounded by Hitler's megalomania, as he continually refused to listen to the reasoning of his professional military advisers.

Then, following Paulus' surrender, these allied forces disappeared from view, only to briefly reappear as the victorious Red Army rolled over their borders and imposed Soviet Communism on almost all of them. Needless to say, as

I researched more, these myths began to fray and crack, and most ended up being shattered. That is not to say that there aren't elements of truth in most of the suppositions that surround the war they fought – that, after all, is how legends usually start – but it is also clear that time and cliché have done their work of obfuscation well. I hope that this book, perhaps, goes a little way to shining a light on the tragedy of hundreds of thousands of young men, most flung into a war they neither understood nor really wanted, and in which so many of them found nothing but a cold, dark grave in the rich, black earth of the Soviet Union.

NOTES ON THE TEXT

As with every profession on the planet, that of arms has a language of its own – with acronyms and ways of thinking that are a closed world to everyone else. That, indeed, is partly the intent. Therefore, when trying to write about the armed forces of not one nation but nine there is an absolute need for a common baseline, and as a former officer I have opted to use what I know. I have used British Army military ranks and their spellings throughout for all personnel, including German and other Axis forces. Many readers might be used to reading *Hauptmann* and understanding it is a Captain in the German Army, but others might not.

On equipment and some (what I would think of as) common military terms, I've taken another path. In my view, words like 'Blitzkrieg' and 'Panzer' are well understood by more or less everyone who might read this book. So I have used them where appropriate. However, I have purposefully steered away from an over-reliance on obscure military terminology and, where possible, tried to 'translate' matters into understandable words and phrases; if this offends purists, I ask their indulgence.

One vexing issue is that of unit designation; i.e., when is an army not an army, and is '2nd' correct or should it be 'Second'? The latter is an issue of description, nothing more, and I have decided on German formations being numbered up to divisional level and then Roman numerals and written for corps and army. Soviet formations are numbered at all levels, and the same applies to the Axis. The former issue, though, is of great importance and one that requires clarity in order to fully understand the battles described in these pages. For example, if a Soviet Army 'rifle division' is attacking a Hungarian 'light infantry division', it might be thought that they were evenly matched, but that would be wrong. A Soviet rifle division would have an average strength of about 3,000 to 5,000 men – around the same size as a British Army brigade or a German regiment – while the Hungarians would number as many as 12,000 men. For this reason, I have included some detail about the orders of battle for opposing forces, and while this may seem tiresome at times, it is intended to highlight how many were facing how many and with what, so that an informed judgement can be made about their relative performance.

For measurements, I have opted for imperial when describing distances, but weapon calibres are given in British Army–standard metric form (i.e. 76mm).

All of the fighting described in the following pages occurs in what was once the Soviet Union and mostly in what are now the independent sovereign countries of the Ukraine and the Russian Federation. Given that the Cyrillic alphabet is different from the European alphabet, the translation of place names can be anomalous. There can be several to describe the same town, e.g. Nikolaweski, Nikolajewski, Nikolayevka. I have tried to use the name that is in most common usage to aid the reader in following the ebb and flow of campaigns on any present-day maps.

On the subject of the Soviet Union, I am aware that not all members of the Soviet armed forces were Russians; there were well over one hundred different nationalities and ethnic groups that fought with distinction alongside the Russians. But for ease, I have occasionally used the term to cover everyone. The same applies to the campaign. I have referred in the book to the 'Russian Front' when the fighting was in the Ukraine, Belarus or the Baltic States; again, I have done this for ease of understanding and to aid the flow of the text. Finally, a note on language: French has accents; German has the umlaut; and Romanian, Hungarian, Bulgarian, Croatian and Russian have their own unique linguistic intonations. I have tried to get these right; if I have failed, I apologise. Also, I have chosen to use popular spellings rather than strictly correct ones where I have deemed it appropriate – so I have spelt the name of the head of the *Luftwaffe* (German Air Force) as Hermann Goering rather than Hermann Göring but used *Führer* (Leader) rather than *Fuehrer* as Adolf Hitler's common title. One last time, I crave the reader's indulgence.

ACKNOWLEDGEMENTS

I have been very fortunate in being able to build up a network of individuals, many in far-flung places, who are willing to help me in any way they can, be it with research, photographs, translations or, indeed, sound advice and critical commentary. They have been invaluable in bringing this book to fruition and helping this subject be exposed to the cold light of day after so long in the shadows. Hope Hamilton is one such individual. An excellent writer herself, she has been more than generous with her time and expertise, and I recommend to readers her own book on the tragic fate of the Italian Army's famed *Alpini* Corps during the Don battles: *Sacrifice on the Steppe*. Some of her own relatives served and suffered in the *Alpini*, and the first-hand accounts she relates are vivid and absorbing. I have liberally quoted from the book and extend my gratitude to her. As usual, I also did a lot of background reading, and yet again both Antony Beevor and the incomparable Paul Carell, whose pioneering work from the 1960s, *Hitler's War on Russia*, which examined the war with the Soviet Union from a German viewpoint, should be required reading for everyone studying the period.

Eyewitness testimony is still the 'holy grail' of this type of work, and the growing power of the Internet is an incredible tool in reaching out and contacting people who otherwise would stay unknown and unappreciated. As usual, Jimmy McLeod has been an enormous help both in this regard and with his 'little black book' of contacts, and on many occasions these conversations led to written primary sources – in this context, usually in the form of fading unit diaries, after-action reports and citations. Dry on the page, they speak volumes if you read between the lines.

As ever, several people helped me with proofreading and with the text. They have also made suggestions and amendments and corrected mistakes – my father, Robert, has a particular eye for this allied to a very patient demeanour — to improve the flow of the writing. I thank them all for their assistance. While, I have, of course, made every effort to achieve absolute accuracy, if there are any errors then they are entirely of my own making.

With regard to my immediate family, my wife, Rachel, has been far too busy with work, family and a new kitchen to be involved with another of her husband's odd 'projects', while sport, school and various technical devices have taken over the lives of our children. Nevertheless, I will persevere with them and leave a copy of this book in each of their rooms in the hope that out of sheer desperation and/or boredom they will flick through a few pages and maybe an arrow of interest will strike home!

INTRODUCTION

At 3.15 a.m. on 22 June 1941, Adolf Hitler, the Austrian-born founder and dictator of Nazi Germany, launched the greatest invasion force ever assembled in world history against the only Communist state on the face of the planet in an operation code named *Fall Barbarossa* (Case Barbarossa). These two giants of state repression – Hitler's Third Reich and Joseph Stalin's Soviet Union, hitherto bound together for two years by an unlikely Non-Aggression Pact – would now fight to the death in a war that would write a whole new chapter on the bestiality of mankind as well as come to define the future course of world history for well over half a century. Hitler's war – and this was one man's war – was also a new type of conflict. Europe and Asia were used to wars of conquest, fought for land, resources, power and prestige, but in the Russo-German struggle these factors were secondary. This war was fought for one reason and one reason only: race. Hitler's world view, his *Weltanschauung* (Belief), was clearly expressed by his acolyte Heinrich Himmler, the sociopathic head of the SS, in a pamphlet he wrote entitled *Die SS*:

> … as long as humans have existed on earth, war between humans and subhumans has become a rule of history. As far back as we can see this Jewish-led battle has become the natural course of life on this planet.

In other words, whereas Karl Marx saw all history as a struggle between different classes, the Nazis saw all history as a war between races – a *Rassenkrieg* (Race war). The prize for the victor was world domination and all that came with it – power and riches for eternity – while for the losers the abyss of total genetic extinction beckoned. By 1941, Hitler had spent almost a decade convincing the German people that they were the standard bearers of the

'Aryan race' and were destined to be the masters of the globe – the *Herrenvolk* (Chosen People). Most other north-western Europeans were also members of Hitler's imaginary Aryan people – the Scandinavians, the Dutch, the Flemish, the English (not the Celtic British, though) – while ranged against them were the Slavs and Asiatics (inhabitants of the Soviet Union and Poland). Most dangerous of all were the Jews. In Hitler's fevered imaginings, it was the Jews who were the spiders at the centre of a worldwide web that, through deceit, malevolence and the underhanded manipulation of capitalism and inferior races, was intent on the corruption of Aryan bloodlines and the eventual destruction of the race. The only way this racial extinction could be avoided was to take action and wipe out the enemy – not just defeat him but annihilate him; physically expunge his seed from the face of the earth. Hitler may well have sent his forces into the Soviet Caucasus to capture the oilfields of Baku and Grozny, but oil was not a goal in itself; rather, it was a means to an end, and that end was supremacy for one people – the Aryans – and the utter eradication of everyone else, the so-called inferior races. This meant that the driving force behind Nazism as a creed was not just thuggery but also violence at a genocidal level. Over time, this doctrine came to dominate the Nazi regime through what can be described only as an 'addiction to murder' as a direct tool of the state. No better example of this can be seen than in the *Generalplan Ost* (General plan East). This document, drawn up by Heinrich Himmler on the direct orders of Hitler himself, laid out a clear blueprint for the Soviet Union after its envisaged defeat by the German armed forces. In stark, bureaucratic terminology, it stated that 75 per cent of Belarusians and 64 per cent of Ukrainians were to be starved, worked to death or forcibly expelled from their lands to make way for waves of Aryan German settlers. For the Poles, the figure was even higher, at 80 per cent. At a weekend party just before Operation Barbarossa, Himmler went so far as to publicly tell some fellow guests:

> The purpose of any future Russian campaign will be to decimate the Slavic population by thirty millions.

This was a monstrosity of such immense proportions that, even at the time, it could not be comprehended by most people as anything other than rabid talk and hyperbole. But over time, and so often repeated, it became a mantra and created an ideological basis for the Russo-German conflict. This enabled Hitler and his henchmen to convince the German people into uniting behind his megalomaniac vision so that the forces positioned on the Soviet

Union's borders on the eve of Operation Barbarossa were in no doubt as to the rightness of their cause and the justice of their mission. That the mission would lead to racial slaughter was not even a point of discussion. The basic, and rather frightening, fact that Hitler was committing a nation of 80 million people to a do-or-die struggle with a country of almost infinite space and resources peopled by some 190 million and with the largest armed forces in the world, could therefore be conveniently forgotten. Without doubt, this system of belief, coupled with the immense internal power of a totalitarian state, helped sustain the German people when Hitler's promised victory of 1941 did not materialise and the casualty lists from the fighting during that first horrendous winter began to grow.

However, this utter fanaticism regarding the politics of race may have been good news in propaganda terms at home – every nation wants to be told it's special and one-of-a-kind – but was clearly going to be a massive handicap in any Nazi attempt to build a major global alliance of friendly states with which to win the war. It was going to be incredibly difficult to shake hands with a nation that you also trumpeted as being 'racially inferior' and of lower standing. Occasionally, this paradox would be circumvented with utter farce, such as the intellectual 'licence' that allowed the Nazis to claim the Japanese and Nepalese were in reality Aryans and that the Muslim Albanians were descended from Dark Age Ostrogoth cavalrymen. But this skill in alliance-building was something the Allies, brilliantly led by British Prime Minister Winston Churchill, succeeded at superbly. Churchill, a fervent anti-communist, was even prepared to ally himself with Stalin, a dilemma on which he famously commented:

> If Hitler invaded hell I would make at least a favourable reference to the devil in the House of Commons.

However, it would not be true to say that the Germans were alone as they stormed the western frontiers of the Soviet Union in the summer of 1941. Alongside the *Wehrmacht* as it streamed eastwards were troops from no fewer than six allied nations, plus contingents from six other non-belligerent nations. In this latter category, Heinrich Himmler's armed SS – the Waffen-SS – managed to recruit a few thousand men from across occupied Scandinavia and the Low Countries, and Franco's fascist Spain sent a full division of volunteers, nicknamed the *Blau Division* (Blue Division) on account of the colour of the shirts they initially wore.

But it was Germany's allied nations, the 'Axis' powers, that made by far the greatest contributions, although from the start those contributions were

unequal. Finland, for example, joined only as an attempt to recover the territories it had lost to the Soviets in the Winter War of 1939–40. The Finns
advanced to their old borders and then dug in and waited, refusing to invade
the Soviet Union just in case events did not turn out as they hoped.

As for the Bulgarians, they weren't enthusiastic about attacking their traditional Russian allies either and didn't even officially declare war on the Soviets.
The Bulgarian Army subsequently marched south and not east as it captured
disputed lands from the defeated Greeks and fought a fierce anti-guerrilla war
across Thrace and Macedonia. As far as Bulgaria was concerned, the country's
national interests were best served by territorial expansion at the expense of its
neighbours and not by arousing the wrath of its powerful Slavic cousin.

It would be in the south, though, where the vast majority of Germany's Axis
allies would make their mark. During the vast campaigns in the Ukraine and
southern Russia, the armies of Romania, Hungary, Italy, Slovakia and Croatia
would fight against an enemy with a long memory and a developed taste for
revenge. Soldiers from these latter states, often hating one another far more
than the Russians they faced in battle, initially made up less than 10 per cent
of the entire invasion force. They were usually given nothing more than secondary tasks by German commanders, the major exceptions to that rule being
the immensely costly victories by Romanian forces at Odessa and Sevastopol.
However, the failure of Operation Barbarossa at the very gates of Moscow,
and the subsequent massive Soviet winter counter-offensives, changed all that.
The *Ostheer* (German Army East) did manage to stand firm in the blizzards
and ice and fight the Red Army, but the losses were breathtaking, with over
1 million men killed, wounded or missing. In essence, the original *Wehrmacht*,
the conquerors of Denmark and Norway, France, the Low Countries and the
Balkans, died in Russia in 1941.

The beginning of 1942 brought Hitler another chance to finish the assault
in the East, but all the reports from the military planners of the *Oberkommando
der Wehrmacht* (Supreme High Command – OKW) made uncomfortable
reading for the *Führer*. The best brains the German staff had all agreed: Nazi
Germany was physically unable to repeat the scale of the original three-
pronged offensive of 1941 and would even struggle to adequately assemble
a single major assault force. Searching for a solution, Hitler's answer was to
belatedly turn to his allies and demand they commit totally to the war in the
Soviet Union. The result was a major influx of troops from Romania, Italy
and Hungary, as all together the 'Axis big three' committed 750,000 men to
that summer's drive to conquer the oil-rich Soviet Caucasus. The offensive,
code named *Fall Blau* (Case Blue), failed, and another Russian winter would

find the ill-equipped Axis allied armies stretched thin and shivering on the banks of the River Don to the north and south of Stalingrad, where the German Sixth Army was being ground into meat.

Then, under the direction of General Zhukov, the defender of Moscow, the Red Army prepared for its winter counter-offensives, its target nothing less than the complete annihilation of the allied armies and all of Germany's forces in southern Russia. With under-strength units holding impossibly long sections of front, short of heavy weapons, ammunition and all manner of modern military kit, the only hope of salvation for the Romanians, Hungarians and Italians if the Soviets did attack was the existence of powerful mobile reserves. Two corps – the XXXXVIII Panzer Corps and *Corps* Kramer – fulfilled this role, and in the vanguard were the elite of the Romanian and Hungarian armies, the 1st Romanian Panzer Division and the 1st Hungarian Armoured Field Division. On the shoulders of these men lay the burden of victory or defeat. They would fail. When the blows came, first against the Romanians in Operation Uranus and then against the Italians and Hungarians, the front line was shattered and the armoured pride of the Axis allies rode to its death and destruction. The defeat of the Romanian and *Magyar* tankers, and their German allies, sealed the fate of all four Axis allied armies on the Don. With no reserves left and Soviet troops pouring through to the rear, the Romanians, Hungarians and Italians disintegrated as the survivors retreated pell-mell to the west. In a little over ten weeks, the military might of Nazi Germany's allies was put to the sword as all of them suffered the worst ever defeats in their nation's histories.

The loss of hundreds of thousands of men and vast amounts of scarce equipment sent shock waves through the Axis. The Italians, Croatians and Hungarians effectively abandoned the Eastern Front, and the Romanian and Slovak contribution was greatly reduced. Only in late 1944, as the by now all-conquering Red Army approached their homelands, did they rouse themselves to one final military effort. It would not be enough. With defeat staring them in the face, they deserted Nazi Germany and switched sides; Italy had already done so a full year earlier. In the last months of the war, Romanians, Slovaks, Bulgarians and even Finns found themselves fighting their old comrades-in-arms, but even this last-ditch conversion did not save them, as Stalin had absolutely no intention of letting off the hook his all-too-recent enemies. Peace brought occupation, retribution and the advancement of Soviet Communism as monarchies and governments fell one by one to be replaced by pliant dictatorships, all controlled from the Kremlin – the spider in the communist web. Only Finland and Italy escaped the shadow of the

Iron Curtain, more than anything else protected by their geography from the terrible fate of the rest.

So why did the likes of Romania and Hungary — mortal enemies far happier being at each other's throats than anyone else's and the former a strong ally of France — end up on the Axis hook? It was that same issue of geography that had dictated so much of their history. Caught as they were between the two giants of the totalitarian world, more or less every country in Europe had to choose sides as general war engulfed the continent. Politics, history and personality all played their parts in who chose whom, and it was Hitler who played the canniest hand, first dangling safety from possible Nazi aggression and then a share in the spoils of future victory to a clutch of nations still effectively reeling from the aftermath and perceived injustices of the First World War. Every one of those countries then took their own paths as they lined up with the *Ostheer* — or not, in the case of the Bulgars.

For Mussolini's Fascist Italy, it was little more than a distraction of resources from their main war effort in the North Africa theatre, while for Romania, Hungary and Slovakia, the Eastern Front was the focus of all their military activity. The Nazis' failure to defeat the Soviet Union in Operation Barbarossa was, therefore, as much a disaster for the Axis allies as it was for Germany. Drawn into a war of attrition across the vastness of the Russian landscape, the glaring weaknesses of the Axis armed forces were fully exposed as they were cajoled into pouring ever more military resources into the field for the huge gamble that was the *Wehrmacht*'s summer offensive of 1942. The reality, though, was that Hitler had chosen his friends poorly. The creaking monarchies and authoritarian states that made up the Axis in Europe were never militarily or economically powerful enough to tip the balance on the Eastern Front in the *Wehrmacht*'s favour, and the cataclysm on the Don in the winter of 1942/43 — alongside the loss of their own Sixth Army — condemned the Germans to eventual defeat in the war.

Often overshadowed by that latter horror of Stalingrad, the disaster on the Don that befell the hundreds of thousands of frozen Romanian, Hungarian, Italian and Croatian conscripts and volunteers was every bit as dramatic and bloody as the battle for that stricken city on the Volga River and just as full of consequences for Europe for the next sixty years and more.

This, then, is the story of that momentous campaign and the men who fought it.

CHAPTER 1

THE POLITICS OF THE AXIS

The aftermath of the First World War – winners and losers

As with so much to do with the Second World War, the genesis of Hitler's 'unlikely alliance' on the Don in 1942 lay in the maelstrom of the First World War. Caught up on both sides of that horrendous conflict, the countries that would later become the Axis all suffered terribly, and each in its own way ended up a loser. For the Kingdom of Hungary, 1914 saw it as a co-partner in that gravity-defying relic of the Middle Ages, the Austro-Hungarian Habsburg Empire. Falling by accident into a war it was totally unprepared for, Hungary firstly lost hundreds of thousands of men on the battlefields of the East and was then utterly humiliated by the victors' justice of the Treaty of Trianon, Hungary's equivalent of the badly mishandled Treaty of Versailles that dealt with Imperial Germany.[1]

Signed on 4 June 1920, the Trianon Treaty was as much a recipe for future conflict as Versailles and St Germain had been. The warlike *Magyars* were stripped of their martial tradition as their army was capped at a miniscule 35,000 men; no aircraft, tanks or heavy artillery were allowed; and their new Regent, Miklos Horthy, became an admiral without a fleet as Hungary's access to the Adriatic Sea disappeared. This 'new army', the *Honved* (Home Army), now defended a nation shorn of an astonishing two-thirds of its former people and the lands on which they lived. Under the Habsburgs, different ethnicities moved, merged and intermingled across the rolling plains of the Danube basin and the adjoining territories, so it was impossible for

---

1 And the specifically Hungarian successor to the 1919 Treaty of St Germain, which initially broke up the Empire and created an independent Hungary, Czechoslovakia, Poland and Yugoslavia.

the cartographers of Trianon to separate the now-independent nationalities cleanly. The result was the worst of all outcomes. Ancient lands, long considered parts of historical Hungary, were parcelled out to her neighbours: 21,000 square miles of Transylvania went to the Kingdom of Romania, along with 1.7 million ethnic *Magyars*, and 600,000 others went with the province of Ruthenia to the newly created state of Czechoslovakia. In all, Trianon resulted in more than 2.5 million *Magyars* living outside their homeland's new, truncated borders. The inevitable result was a population and a government simmering with resentment and determined to take back what they had lost no matter the cost. Their chance would come with the rise of Nazi Germany and its willingness to act as a power broker in the region, but Berlin's help would come with a price.

In 1914, surrounded as she was by the Habsburgs and their allies the Bulgars, the Romanians played safe and stayed neutral. However, Romania was eventually persuaded to join the Allies by the seeming success of Tsarist Russia's Brusilov Offensives against the Austro-Hungarians in 1916 and presumptively declared war on the Central Powers of Germany and Austro-Hungary on 27 August 1916. Romania mobilised 750,000 men and sent the twenty-three divisions of her army into Hungarian Transylvania, expecting a quick and easy victory against a chastened enemy. Badly equipped and poorly led, they soon faced the might of no fewer than four German, Austrian and Bulgarian armies and were utterly routed. In just over four months, Bucharest had fallen, along with most of the rest of the country, as the remnants of the army fell back into Russia to escape annihilation. Saved by Germany's defeat and the Armistice, Romania counted the cost of victory – some 336,000 men killed and 120,000 wounded. As an ally of the victorious Allied powers, that blood price paid for the birth of *Romania Mare* (Greater Romania) as the country almost doubled in size overnight with Hungary's losses becoming Romania's gains. Vast new territories were added to Romania's Moldavian and Wallachian heartlands; Transylvania and its 5.5 million people (60 per cent of whom were in fact ethnic Romanians) came over, plus the former Imperial Russian provinces of Bessarabia and Bukovina (again mostly populated by Romanians) and, lastly, the ex-Bulgarian Dobruja region. Romania, now with a population 18 million strong, had become *the* regional power in the Balkans as it dwarfed its neighbours in Hungary and Bulgaria. As heady as this outcome was for Bucharest, it did not bring peace and prosperity, but instead fostered deep-seated hatreds with those same states that would plague Romania for the next twenty years or more and contributed in no small way to the disaster its armed forces suffered on the Don in 1942/43.

The United Kingdom of Italy, not even a half century old at the outbreak of the First World War, was initially a member of the Central Powers alliance alongside Germany and Austria-Hungary but very wisely decided to stay out of the conflict in 1914 as it snowballed out from the Balkans and engulfed most of Europe and Russia. Unfortunately for Italy, this outburst of political sanity did not last long, and in May 1915 Italy was persuaded by the Allies to abandon her neutrality and attack Austria-Hungary in return for the promise of future territorial gain once the war was won. The specific carrot that was dangled in front of Rome's nose was a juicy swathe of Austrian imperial provinces on Italy's northern border, starting with Trentino and Fiume and sweeping down Dalmatia on the eastern side of the Adriatic. In the same spirit of flag-waving nationalism that had burst forth across Great Britain, France, Germany and the other combatants the previous year, the recruiting offices in Italy were swamped as the country called up its youth to the colours. In all, some 5.6 million men would be mobilised – as it turned out, more than one million more than it managed to sign up in the Second World War. With disturbing echoes of what would happen some twenty-five years later, poorly trained, ill-equipped and often badly led Italian soldiers advanced bravely towards their enemy and were cut to pieces. In what would go down in Italian folklore as *Il Guerra Bianca* (The White War) – given that it was often fought in the snow among white limestone crags – a staggering 689,000 Italian soldiers were killed and 1 million more wounded at Caporetto and in other disastrous battles against the Austro-Hungarians. Winners though they were officially, the war left the nation traumatised and suffering a distinct sense of injustice as the victory of 1918 did not deliver all that was promised. The Trentino was indeed handed over, along with some other minor adjoining territories, but crucially, the major city and port of Fiume and the Dalmation coast were not. Instead, they went to the brand-new Kingdom of the South Slavs: Yugoslavia.

For Nazi Germany's other Axis allies of the early 1940s, the First World War was a mixed blessing. Bulgaria ended up on the wrong side and lost its province of Dobruja to Greater Romania and its Aegean coastline to Greece, leaving it landlocked and staring at Bucharest and Athens with ill-disguised loathing. Monarchist Spain stayed neutral throughout, and Finland (an Imperial Russian province beforehand) managed to break away from the disintegration of the Tsars and gain its independence after a nasty little war with newly born Communist Russia. The Slovaks, ever restless under Habsburg rule, managed to escape that yoke only to become second-class citizens in a new union with their Czech neighbours; Prague and Bratislava were not natural bedfellows. The Croats, too, although one of the *Kaisertreu* (most loyal) peoples in the Austrian Empire, gained their freedom from the Habsburgs only to mirror the Slovaks in being compulsorily tied into a new country – the Serb-dominated Yugoslavia in their case – where they were very much the junior partner and made to feel it.

Politics in the inter-war years

The response of the Croats, and to a lesser degree the Slovaks, to their new status was a surge in nationalist sentiment that bordered on ethnic bigotry and political extremism. The ethnic Croat and Bosnian-born lawyer Anté Pavelic founded the ultra-nationalist *Ustase* – the Croatian Revolutionary Movement – as a radical terrorist organisation committed to winning Croatian freedom through a campaign of bombings and assassinations, the most infamous of which was the murder of the Yugoslav king, the Serbian Alexander I, in Marseilles in 1934. The Serb-led Yugoslav reaction to Pavelic's terror tactics was one of often harsh oppression that fed a growing polarisation of opinion within the country throughout the late 1930s.

For the Slovaks, it was the often-heard put down 'the Czechs have culture whilst the Slovaks have agriculture' that fed a simmering resentment about Czech domination of the infant state and its institutions, including the professional and much-admired Czech Army. This tension led to calls for autonomy and self-government as the 1930s went on but did not give rise to the same sort of communal violence as was the case in Yugoslavia. Even after the Munich Conference gave the green light for Germany to effectively dissolve the Czech state, there was little in the way of mass agitation for independence. Never one to take no for an answer, Hitler ended up summoning the leaders of the nationalist Slovak Peoples Party to Berlin in March 1939 and told them that if they did not break away immediately and declare independence, he would allow the Hungarians to invade them. The Slovaks declared the followed day.

The inter-war years in the far north were overwhelmingly a time of peace, as the Finns got used to their newly won statehood and began to feel their way as a multi-party democracy. As a visible sign of their success at these endeavours, they even got to host the Olympic Games in 1940.

The same could not be said for Catholic Spain, which was engulfed from 1936 to 1939 by an incredibly vicious civil war between the age-old forces of right and left that tore the country asunder, killing hundreds of thousands in battle and retribution.

The kingdom of the Bulgars did not suffer Spain's horrendous fate, but the battle between the forces of tradition and those of social change that gripped most of Europe in the 1920s and 1930s also had its impact on clannish Bulgaria. The wartime Tsar Ferdinand's abdication (like their Russian counterparts, the Bulgars called their monarch a Tsar) ushered in the rule of his son, Boris III, and the beginnings of true democratic government. However, that path was far from smooth as attempted assassinations and coups became the norm, with even the Prime Minister, Aleksandur Stamboliyski, getting himself killed in June 1923.[1] Boris eventually stepped in and made himself dictator in April 1935, an act that ushered in a period of relative stability, albeit under authoritarian rule with no room for any opposition.

As for royalist Italy, its political system struggled in vain to respond to the bitter mood of the nation and satisfy popular grievances. A flurry of shaky coalitions came and went until, in 1922, through a combination of bluff and bluster that was very much his trademark, the populist ex-socialist agitator Benito Mussolini was offered power in Rome and a new political creed came to the world's attention – Fascism. Through the careful use of propaganda, political repression and actual reforms, Mussolini became the 'model dictator' of Europe, and even Hitler would look to emulate him until he realised, too late as it happened, that it was all a mirage created by a master of illusion. The signs were there though for all who had eyes to see. Committed to provide the Italian people with an outlet for their frustrated sense of national glory, Mussolini adopted a bombastic foreign policy that would all too often end in fumbling military intervention and subsequent humiliation. The result was a growing switch around in the previous 'big brother, little brother' relationship with the German leader, with Italy increasingly nothing but the tail of the German dog.

Expanding recklessly on the canine analogy, the two big dogs of the Balkan world in the inter-war years were Romania and Hungary – deadly enemies forever staring at each other over the much-disputed Transylvanian border, the former's large ethnic *Magyar* population acting as a latent 'fifth column' that caused Bucharest no end of sleepless nights. Romania needed friends, and given her past she naturally turned to her greatest ally from the First World War – France – and another state that had done well from Trianon – Czechoslovakia. Arms deals, often the progenitors of national alliances, were signed, and French and Czech aircraft and weapons became the mainstay of the Romanian armed forces. Diplomatic co-operation was close, but the rise of Nazi Germany drove a wedge between them as Paris, Prague and Bucharest struggled to formulate

---

1 He was brutally tortured, one of his hands was cut off and he was decapitated, with his head sent to Sofia in a biscuit box as proof of his death.

a response to the looming European superpower to the north. To a political intriguer and conspirator like Hitler, this complex web of enmity, deceit and fear was a home from home he sought to turn to his advantage.

1939–40 Alliances and war in the West

Hitler's attitude to alliances and international diplomacy changed dramatically over time. Never a man with a natural affinity for personal friends or political partners, at first for him it was about dictatorships with a common ideology sticking together as much for protection as anything else, hence his devotion to Fascist Italy. This view led to the establishment of the 'Pact of Steel' in May 1939 between Rome and Berlin, setting out joint co-operation on economic and military matters amongst other things, and then to the most eye-catching diplomatic coup of the inter-war era – the signing of the 'Molotov-Ribbentrop Non-Aggression Pact' on 23 August 1939 guaranteeing peace and friendship between Soviet Russia and Nazi Germany. Named after the two foreign ministers who negotiated it –Vyachelsav Molotov and Joachim von Ribbentrop – the Pact stunned the world, as these two avowed ideological enemies metaphorically smiled and hugged each other. What the world did not know was that the Pact contained a set of ultra-secret clauses that effectively divided up Eastern Europe and the Balkans between them into respective spheres of influence where each would have a free hand to do as they wished.

A week later, the clandestine protocol reared its head for the first time when Nazi Germany invaded Poland and ignited the Second World War. Not only did Moscow not utter a peep in protest: just a fortnight later, the Red Army rolled across Poland's eastern border, condemning Warsaw to defeat and partition. This was the first concrete manifestation of those secret clauses. Three months on, at midnight on 29 November, Berlin reciprocated by twiddling its thumbs, after the following statement from General Kirill Afanasievich Meretskov of the Red Army was read out to the 250,000 men he commanded:

> Comrades, soldiers of the Red Army, officers, commissars and political workers! To fulfil the Soviet Government's, and our great Fatherland's will, I hereby order that the troops in Leningrad Military District are to march over the frontier, crush the Finnish forces, and once and for all secure the Soviet Union's northwestern borders and Lenin's city, the crib of the revolution of the proletariat.

Finland, a nation of just 4 million people, was being invaded by the armed might of the Soviet Union. The rest of Scandinavia, and indeed the world, looked on horrified and transfixed as a supremely confident Red Army swept forward against an enemy it outnumbered many times over and who were equipped with little more than a handful of First World War anti-tank guns and obsolete aircraft. They expected an easy victory over the Nordic minnows. However, the courageous Finns stood their ground and inflicted devastating reverses on the ill-prepared Soviets – nowhere more so than the utter annihilation of the Red Army's 44th Division in the snow at Suomussalmi in late December. By the time hostilities ended on 13 March 1940, the Red Army had been forced to commit more than a million troops to the fighting and Stalin had been personally humiliated. Not that this stopped him from annexing Lithuania, Latvia and Estonia in June that year to fulfil another secret clause in the Pact.

The fall of France and the partition of Romania

When France fell on 22 June 1940, Romania was stripped of her only major ally and totally at the mercy of the vultures surrounding her. Moscow struck first, annexing Bessarabia, northern Bukovina and Hertza, the Red Army marching through Cernauti past sullen crowds of ethnic Romanians. Hungary and Bulgaria were the next beneficiaries, Ribbentrop and his Italian counterpart, Count Galeazzo Ciano, forcing Bucharest to accept the so-called 'Second Vienna Award' that gave 16,790 square miles of northern Transylvania to Budapest, and all of southern Dobruja to Sofia. Altogether, Romania lost 33 per cent of its land mass and population.

1940 – The Axis is born

Despite all of this, and the advantages the Pact brought Germany, Hitler was already set on the future destruction of the Soviet Union. His only real questions were 'when' and 'how'. These questions were partly addressed on 18 December 1940, when a top secret order – Directive No.21 – was sent out from Hitler's headquarters in Berlin to the most senior officers in the *Wehrmacht*[1] and was named after a twelfth-century, German-born, Holy Roman Emperor – Frederick Barbarossa. In the space of a single page, it laid out possibly the most audacious and risky military adventure ever planned – the invasion and destruction of the largest country on the planet, the Soviet Union:

---

1   The name given to the German armed forces, made up of the *Heer*, army; *Kreigsmarine*, navy; and the *Luftwaffe*, air force.

The German Armed Forces must be prepared to crush Soviet Russia in a quick campaign (Operation Barbarossa) even before the conclusion of the war against England.

It also included in section two the role envisaged for any German allies:

II. Probable Allies and their Tasks:

On the flanks of our operation we can count on the active participation of Romania and Finland in the war against Soviet Russia.

The High Command will, in due time, concert and determine what form the armed forces of the two countries will be placed under German command at the time of their intervention.

2. It will be the task of Romania, together with the forces concentrating there, to pin down the enemy facing her and, in addition, to render auxiliary services in the rear area.

3. Finland will cover the concentration of the redeployed German North Group (parts of the XXI Group) coming from Norway and will operate jointly with it. Besides, Finland will be assigned the task of eliminating Hangö.

This document, for the first time, acknowledged the need and desire for allies to assist Germany in its war plans, and the framework to deliver that assistance was the 'Tripartite Pact' and the 'Axis' – so-called because the alliances were often described in geographically directional terms. Despite this, Hitler had no real interest in bringing together a Napoleon-type multi-national army with which to destroy the Soviet Union, or of sharing out what he foresaw as the spoils of such a victory. This was incredibly short-sighted, especially given Japan's potential ability to attack the Soviet Far East and force Moscow into a war on two fronts. His main interests lay in little more than securing his flanks, especially in the south, and increasingly in safeguarding the economic raw materials needed to wage that self-same war, e.g. Swedish iron ore, Yugoslav bauxite and, above all, Romanian oil.

That oil was now in the safe-keeping of the Romanian Prime Minister, General Ion Antonescu. Antonescu, a short, dapper man, with a forceful character and strongly held views, at first governed with the support of the fascist 'Iron Guard' movement, or 'The Legion of the Archangel Michael' to give it its proper title, and on behalf of the young King Michael. However, the Iron Guard proved to be more of a problem than a solution for the head-strong general. The feeling was mutual, and in late January 1941 the Legion launched a coup to try to seize total power by force. With the support of the army, and the tacit accord of Hitler, Antonescu crushed the Iron Guard, arresting hundreds of them and killing any who resisted. The leaders fled to Germany where Hitler kept them in reserve in case Antonescu betrayed him. For the moment the Nazi dictator had chosen the general – or the *Conducator* (Leader) as he now styled himself – over the fascists.

Founded on the Pact of Steel, the Axis expanded at breakneck pace, being signed by Imperial Japan on 27 September 1940, Hungary on 20 November then Romania three days later, and Slovakia four days after that. Bulgaria fol-lowed suit, and Yugoslavia eventually joined in March 1941, only for the act to trigger a popular anti-German revolt that saw the *Wehrmacht* invade and conquer the country in a lightning two-week invasion. Carved up between the victors, the newly independent state of Croatia – now in the genocidal grasp of Pavelic and his *Ustase* – showed its gratitude by signing up in June.

The Axis was now a political fact, erected from nothing in less than a year. Berlin now sought to extract military and economic advantages from it.

CHAPTER 2

WAGING WAR
ECONOMICS AND THE MILITARY

War, and the making of war, has always been reliant on money and the equipment and resources that money buys. The industrialisation of war that really took hold with the 1914–18 conflict saw the increasing role of strategic raw materials and the factories that converted those inputs into the outputs needed for modern conflict, namely tanks, guns, aircraft and the whole paraphernalia of combat.

In this crucial regard, Nazi Germany could hardly have picked more unsuitable allies, while Churchill could not have picked any better.[1] Apart from Germany, none of the Axis nations were industrial powerhouses, indeed most were mainly rural and economically pretty backward. The almost total lack of military-industrial capacity in countries such as Italy, Hungary and Romania would directly contribute to the annihilation of their forces in Russia. Those same forces ranged along the Don River in the winter of 1942 relied utterly on a steady flow of supplies, ammunition and weaponry in order to hold the line against an increasingly capable Red Army, and that supply chain, which included necessities such as trucks, tanks, aircraft and artillery, was incredibly poor, as the Axis allies' home economies were unable to fulfil the needs of their frontline troops.

Italy was a relatively advanced European state, although as befits a football-mad nation the country was 'a tale of two halves'. In the north, clustered in the Po River valley and adjoining regions, were Italy's industrial heartlands. Here there was a potentially strong armament manufacturing infrastructure based on the automotive industries, such as Ferrari and Milan's Alfa Romeo, but as the names suggest these were niche producers, when Italy

---

1 The gross domestic product (GDP) of the United States of America at the outbreak of the Second World War was the same as the entire Axis put together, let alone the British Empire and the Soviet Union.

needed more mass manufacturers such as the giant Fiat works in Turin. But in the south of the country, it was a wholly different story. A soldier in the Sherwood Foresters Regiment, Private Whitmore, who fought in the 'boot' of Italy in 1943 with the Allied invasion force, said of the lower half of the country:

> Oh, terrible, terrible it was. It was worse than being in the Peak District of Derbyshire. The village people of southern Italy were very crude, no toilets, no nothing. What I can remember, there were houses they lived in, would have had a bed in that corner and a couple of nanny goats sleeping in this corner and a few chickens in that corner, and that would be it. The road would lead up into the hills out of the village, a lane sort of thing, and each side of this lane was absolutely swarming with flies all buzzing round piles of human excreta. I've never seen anything like it, there were no toilets anywhere and possibly I think that was why so many of us were sick.

Italy also had very limited access to natural resources that made it heavily dependent on imports, for example in 1940 its annual requirement for crude oil was 8.5 million tonnes, of which only a miniscule 100,000 tonnes was sourced by Italy, and the national reserves were only enough for a single year. In contrast, Germany produced 8 million tonnes and Britain 12 million tonnes in the same year. The figures for coal production were even worse. The vast underground coalfields of the Ruhr valley and German Silesia produced 365 million tonnes for Germany's ever-hungry furnaces, while the pits of Wales and northern England delivered not much less at 224 million tonnes. For Italy, home production stood at a paltry 4.4 million tonnes. That same coal was vital for the production of the steel which was the base component of most military equipment. Again Italy fell short as it had to import fully half of the 4.8 million tonnes of steel it needed in 1940. This shortfall meant that in the first year of the war Italy was only able to manufacture 250 tanks and just over 2,000 aircraft. In the same year, Britain produced 1,399 tanks and Germany 1,643, while the Nazis also turned out almost 11,000 aircraft and Britain an impressive 15,000. Mussolini would never admit it in public, but privately, as late as 1939 on the very eve of conflict, he was asking Hitler for the immediate delivery of no less than 170,000 tonnes of materiel in a desperate bid to re-equip the Italian armed forces in time for the coming war. Hitler had to decline, unable as he was to satisfy even his own generals' demands.

In fact, while the wartime economies of all the major combatants made huge strides in military production over the course of the war, those of the

Axis allies barely moved a jot. The figures are stark. Taking Italy for example as the most advanced of Germany's Axis partners, 2,473 tanks and self-propelled guns rolled off the production lines during the war, along with 7,200 artillery pieces and 83,000 trucks. By contrast, Germany was almost producing that number of tanks *every month* in 1944, and even Canada ranked higher with a total wartime production figure of 5,678 tanks manufactured!

If Italy was the best, then for Hungary and Romania the situation was grim indeed. Both nations were largely agricultural in the 1930s, with small industrial sectors and limited modern infrastructure in terms of railways, paved roads and the availability of electricity. Mass literacy and numeracy, a pre-requisite for economic growth, was still a pipe dream in both lands; in Romania's first official census in 1930, more than 38 per cent of the population over the age of seven were registered as illiterate.[1] This had a direct result on the capabilities of the Romanian military. Possibly Nazi Germany's greatest military strategist of the war, Field-Marshal Erich von Manstein, wrote in his memoirs after the conflict:

> Although the Romanian soldier – who was normally of peasant origin – was modest in his wants and usually a capable, brave fighter, the possibilities of train-ing him as an individual fighting man who could think for himself in action, let alone as a non-commissioned officer, were to a great extent limited by the low standard of general education in Romania.

In other words as long as his officers were alive and functioning, the Romanian soldier would fight well, but take away his leaders and he would fold. Much the same could be said of the *Magyars*, though they would contest that assumption vociferously!

The facts, though, were inescapable: Romania and Hungary were possessed of backward economies with little capacity to sustain a modern military machine. Hungary manufactured only 630 tanks and self-propelled guns and 450 artillery pieces during the entire war. Romania did not even reach this total. By 1938, there were only 35,800 motor vehicles in the entire king-dom, less than a third being types useful for any sort of military service, while the country's sole truck factory was limited to assembling a few thousand vehicles each year from imported components. Compare this to the incred-ible production feats of their opponents. The Soviet Union's figure for tanks

---

1 For some reason men were more likely to be illiterate than women, and more understandably, illiteracy was far higher in the countryside than in the cities.

produced was more than 105,000, for trucks it was 200,000 and for artillery – the 'god of war' – it was over 500,000. The United States dwarfed even this vast armada by turning out an almost unbelievable 2.4 million trucks, some 400,000 of which were shipped over to the Soviets and helped transform the Red Army into the motorised juggernaut it had become by 1944. US deliveries to the USSR during the war were on a truly epic scale, including 51,503 jeeps, 131,633 machine-guns, 11,155 railway freight cars, just under 5 million tonnes of food and more than 15 million pairs of army boots!

There was, though, one exception to this bleak outlook for the Axis, and it was a pretty big exception at that. It lay around a medium-sized town some 35 miles north of Romania's capital city, Bucharest. That town, the county seat of Prahova in the ancient heart of Wallachia, and home to some 40,000 people, was called Ploesti. Founded in 1596 by the renowned Romanian King Michael the Brave (*Mihai Viteazul*) it had flourished as a centre for trade, before exploding in the late nineteenth century when a discovery was made below its rich, black earth – oil, and lots of it. It is difficult to believe nowadays, in a world where the dominance of Middle Eastern oil is near universal, that in the 1930s and 1940s the relative backwater of Romania possessed one of the largest oil production and refinery complexes in the world. Investment, from the USA in particular, had opened up a total of ten separate fields – the Astra Romania, Romania Americana, Colombia Aquila and Dacia Romania being among the biggest – that in total pumped more than 600,000 metric tonnes of oil out of the ground every month. This incredible bounty was more than Germany, Italy, Hungary, Slovakia, Bulgaria, Croatia, Finland, Spain and Japan produced combined, and made Romania a truly strategic partner for a fuel-starved Third Reich. Ploesti made Romania vital to the Axis, the rest of her economy and her armed forces did not.

The armed forces – 'state of the nations'

The Kingdom of Romania

Romania's armed forces had been humbled in the First World War. The country's post-war reaction to that humiliation was neither to professionalise nor effectively modernise. Starved of money and attention, the military stumbled on for the best part of twenty years, the only noteworthy feature being a series of curious rules and regulations, such as the stipulation that only officers were allowed to wear cosmetics! Finally, in the spring of 1935, with war in Europe brewing, Romania announced a ten-year national rearmament programme. The plan was to revamp the army into a million-man force of some four armies of thirteen corps, eleven of them infantry with twenty-two first line divisions (plus an additional Guards Division), one cavalry corps of three divisions, and one mountain corps with four brigades. In reserve would be a further ten divisions – nine infantry and one cavalry. There was also a Frontier Guard Division and an assortment of various other formations including fortress and coastal defence brigades, artillery regiments, engineers and so forth. Unlike their soon-to-be allies in Italy and Hungary, the Romanians opted not to over-inflate their forces on paper by making each division smaller than the European norm. Instead they stuck with the more or less accepted continental establishment of three infantry regiments per division with accompanying arms. This meant each was about the same size as its standard German counterpart – some 17,000 men.

Impressive though this all was, the new army suffered from two major flaws: lack of heavy weapons and lack of transport. There were only fifty-two (horse drawn) artillery cannon and forty anti-tank guns per division, and these were mostly small calibre ex-First World War pieces, with little range and penetrating power. The mass of infantry were still totally reliant on moving by foot, and the mortars and machine-guns they needed were in short supply. Even the cavalry – still considered the army's cutting edge and premier force – were under strength (usually a brigade was just 6,000 strong), although they did manage to get hold of a few armoured cars and thirty-six Czech CKD AH-IV tankettes (designated the R-1 by the Romanians, they were very lightly armoured vehicles) for reconnaissance duties, supplied when Czechoslovakia was still an ally. The R-1s were split into platoons of three vehicles each, with two platoons assigned to each cavalry brigade.

The only section of the rearmament plan to meet with resounding success was the creation and establishment of the Romanian Mountain Corps. Placed in the hands of a former Imperial Austro-Hungarian officer – the Transylvanian Saxon Artur Phleps – the Romanian mountain troops soon became recognised as an elite, and were the only troops in the army to receive modern artillery, mostly Czech-manufactured Skoda pieces. Phleps himself would later go on to serve in the Waffen-SS as its highest ranking *Volksdeutsche* (foreign-born ethnic German) before being killed in late 1944 fighting the Red Army invasion of his Romanian homeland.

Apart from the impressive reforms in the mountain infantry, the most significant element of the whole programme was the creation of a wholly new force – an armoured brigade. The tank – invented by the British in the First World War – would become the dominating land weapon of the Second, and in the 1930s armies across Europe were struggling to come to terms with its emergence. Germany, France and Britain embraced the tank in different ways: France and Britain believed in the concept of small, fast-moving, light tanks acting in a reconnaissance role, effectively as 'armoured cavalry', with heavier, slow-moving tanks operating alongside the infantry as mobile artillery. Germany, on the other hand, under Heinz Guderian's influence, was treading a very different path, as it looked to develop whole formations of tanks – the 'Panzer Divisions' of legend – which would operate independently and supersede the infantry, cavalry and artillery as the premier arm on the battlefield. In Romania, the army, as in many other countries, viewed the new weapon with deep suspicion. To begin with, the tank's complexity required different skills from the officers and soldiers who manned it, not least of which were literacy and numeracy. This was a problem, as the army's rank and file was drawn overwhelmingly from the rural peasantry where only one in four could read, write or count. As for the officers, they were exclusively from the aristocracy or the emerging middle class and hence educated, but a posting to the cavalry or a smart, well-to-do infantry regiment was still viewed as the preferred option for most. Nevertheless, the new technology could not be ignored, and orders were placed in 1937 with Czechoslovak and French companies to supply several hundred tanks over the next few years. These were intended to supplement Romania's existing tank fleet – the kingdom did already possess some tanks, seventy-six to be precise – the old Renault FT17, left behind when French forces abandoned them in the Balkans at the end of the First World War. Revolutionary in their day,[1] by the 1930s they were truly obsolete. Further scavenging after the war uncovered a number of assorted armoured cars of German, French and Russian manufacture, and together this odd collection of vehicles was formed into a tank regiment in 1919. This unit constituted Romania's only armoured formation for almost two decades. Now, at last, Romania's nascent tank force would get brand new machines: 126 Czech-built Skoda S-II-a medium tanks[2] and some seventy-five French Renault R-35 – supplied via a rather circuitous route.

The Romanians had initially tried to buy a licence to produce 200 of the R-35, but as negotiations dragged on, Renault was increasingly distracted by the growing demands of the French government's own rearmament programme, and so they ended up shipping the Romanians forty-one French-built vehicles as an interim measure in August 1939 – anything to keep the customer happy while Paris was screaming at them for ever more

---

1 It was the first tank to have a fully rotating turret.
2 Designated as R-2 by the Romanians, and later renamed by the Germans as the Panzerkampfwagen 35(t), commonly PzKpfw 35(t) – t for tschechisch (Czechoslovak).

tanks, trucks and anything else they produced. The additional thirty-four
R-35 tanks were war booty, captured from their previous owners late that
same year – the Polish Army's 21st Light Tank Battalion – when tens of thousands of Polish soldiers, the national government and its gold reserves chose to
cross the border and transit through neutral Romania rather than stay in their
homeland and surrender to the invading Germans or Soviets.

Having failed to agree a licence to build the tank, Renault tried to placate
Bucharest by committing to build a factory in the country to manufacture
a fully tracked supply carrier, the Renault UE Chenillette. This was a useful
inward investment that over time could well have helped build up Romania's
heavy industry capacity, but given the timing and the storm clouds over
Europe, it never came to fruition.

As it was, with its tank park full, the new armoured brigade's order of
battle consisted of two small tank regiments, the 1st and 2nd Romanian
Armoured Regiments, motorised infantry, some limited integral artillery and
various support services, again mostly motorised. As such, the 1st Romanian
Armoured Brigade was by far the most technologically advanced military
formation in the whole army. It would go on to become the 1st Romanian
Panzer Division – the elite of Romania's forces on the Russian Front – and
would effectively be destroyed trying to save the rest of their comrades on
the Don.

In the meantime, the army was thrown into total disarray by the impact of
the Vienna Award and the loss of huge swathes of the country. Almost overnight the total military age manpower available to the country shrank from
3.5 million men to just over 2 million, and the army was almost halved in size
as 100,000 regular troops were lost as well as 300,000 reservists. This massive
downsizing forced the disbandment of multiple divisional commands as their
home recruiting areas suddenly became the 'property' of other nations, and
they themselves became 'new' nationals of Hungary, the Soviet Union and
Bulgaria. However, this was not an outcome that was always to the victors'
advantage, as testified to by a Hungarian soldier during the fighting in Russia
in August 1942:

> A senior lieutenant of machine-guns has deserted to the Russians and betrayed
> our positions to them and the locations of our store depots. During the night
> the Russians began to advance and drove off our infantry. Many soldiers and
> officers were killed. The Russians have destroyed our supply base by bomb-
> ing … in the 1st Battalion there are fifty men killed and a hundred wounded.
> The senior lieutenant who deserted was Serbian. How can we possibly trust

those who aren't Hungarian? Most of the infantrymen who ran away were Ruthenians and Romanians. There were few Hungarians. Our poor Hungarian comrades, they stayed at their posts and died.[1]

Regency Hungary

Speaking of Hungary, their armed forces were following much the same path as those of their hated next door neighbour. Bound by the restrictions on military manpower and equipment imposed at Trianon, the Hungarians ended up acting like Weimar Germany in coming up with a variety of ever-more ingenious ruses to get round them. Under national law, all able-bodied men were liable for conscription on reaching the age of twenty-one,[2] but only a fraction served in the army. Most were 'camouflaged' in police, frontier and other paramilitary formations where they could receive military training but evade the army's official 35,000 man cap. True to their martial traditions, the Hungarian *Honved* was a professional, if antiquated, force. Officers and NCOs were usually career soldiers; the officers[3] went to special military secondary schools at age ten, before attending a military academy for up to four years (this again was later reduced down to two years as whole classes of officers were killed or otherwise lost in combat). As for NCOs, each conscript intake was screened for those with potential, and they were then selected for special training. When their three years' national service was complete they were then asked to sign up for an additional twenty-six.

By the dawning of the 1930s, the *Honved* was becoming increasingly outdated; its men were organised mainly in lightly armed infantry divisions, with the cavalry the premier arm – the image of the dashing *Magyar* horseman still held sway. Budapest was finally woken out of its complacency when it looked with alarm at Romania's rearmament programme, and so decided to announce its own on 5 March 1938. The Prime Minister, Kálmán Darányi, held a meeting in the city of Győr, and in a dramatic speech, publicly cast aside the impositions of the Trianon agreement. A five-year plan was established, with a first phase that would see the expansion of the *Honved* from

---

1 This is an excerpt from the diary of Corporal Istvan Balogh, 3rd Battalion, 1st Motorised Brigade, of the soon-to-be-described 1st Hungarian Armoured Field Division. This remarkable document lay undiscovered in the Soviet archives until the incomparable historian Antony Beevor unearthed it in a bundle of papers during the research for his masterful book, *Stalingrad*.
2 This was later reduced to nineteen as the casualty lists grew and the gaps needed filling.
3 In Romania almost all were exclusively members of the aristocracy or upper middle class.

35,000 to 80,000 men. The build-up after that was designed to be rapid. The new order of battle – the Huba Plan named after the Defence Minister who oversaw it – was for a field force of three armies (*Hadseregs*) of three corps, each corps to be composed of three brigades (*Dander*) and a few supplementary battalions. An additional three corps would be separate and tasked solely to guard the border with Romania.

Again, just as with those same neighbours, the Hungarians massively lacked heavy weapons and mobility, but even more than that they lacked plain numbers. A corps in most armies of the day was composed of two divisions, with each division made up of three brigades (regiments in the German Army). So the result was that a Hungarian corps had only half the ration strength of its German, French or British equivalent – this weakness would prove fatal to Hungarian units when given vast stretches of the Don to defend in 1942–43.

As the arms race between Romania and Hungary intensified, the *Magyars* looked to build an armoured force of their own to match the new 1st Romanian Armoured Brigade. Possessing nothing more than small numbers of recently procured obsolete Italian-built Ansaldo CV33 tankettes and some Renault FT17s, they turned to those stalwarts of European arms-manufacture, Czechoslovakia and Sweden, for the heavier, modern tanks they needed. But their suppliers of choice, the Czechoslovak companies Skoda and CKD Praga, were already committed to fulfilling the orders from Romania for the R-1 and the R-2. All they were offered was a production licence from CKD Praga for the V-8-H tank, and one from Skoda for the same vehicle it was selling to Romania – the S-II redesignated as the T-22 medium tank for foreign production. Budapest settled for a licence to build the S-11 and another to produce the Swedish Landsverk Stridsvagn L-60 (Strv-L 60) light tank. Both would be manufactured by the Manfred Weiss Company, and modified from their original designs to become 'Hungarian' tanks, and form the backbone of the country's wartime armoured strength. The three-man Stridsvagn L-60 with its thin armour, single machine-gun and 20mm cannon would be renamed the Toldi I and II, while the S-II would become the Turan I, II and III. The Toldis had been delivered by September 1939, but the first Turan was not even ordered until October 1941. In the meantime, the Hungarians had to make do with their inadequate Italian tanks, and begging, borrowing and stealing old stock and unwanted war booty from their German allies.

In the skies, the Hungarians did actually possess a moderately powerful 6,000-man-strong air force, with more than 300 aircraft in thirty or so squadrons. As with their tanks, the aircraft were a mixture of foreign and Hungarian-built machines. Training and maintenance was not of the highest standard, but morale was high, with the dictator's eldest son, Reserve Lieutenant István Horthy, the 'poster boy' for the service in his dashing fighter pilot's uniform.

The land of the Roman legions in the 20th century

Having been on the winning side in the First World War, Italy had no restrictions artificially imposed on her armed forces through penalty treaties, though neither did she learn at all from the nightmare of the White War and the myriad flaws the fighting had exposed in the Italian military. Training was still routinely neglected, with no money for fuel or equipment, so conscripts did little more than close order drill and foot marching. Live firing practice, essential for any soldier, was unheard of, with not enough ready cash for the bullets. This meant that when a young soldier went into battle for the very first time – scared, sweating and nervous – in all probability that would be the first time he would pull the trigger on his rifle. This total lack of realistic training also meant that the officer and NCO cadres of the army were woefully inexperienced and unprepared for the rigours of leading men in combat. This failing was laid bare on the Don, as leadership failed and several units simply fell apart under the strain of battle. Mussolini's ascent to power actually exacerbated these problems as he duly committed Fascist Italy to a series of foreign policy adventures and invasions that her armed forces were totally unprepared for. Determined to show the world that the might of imperial Rome was reborn, *Il Duce*[1] decided it would be a good idea to commit his ramshackle military to two separate wars at the same time on two different continents. First, a large expeditionary force was landed in Spain to assist General Francisco Franco and his right-wing rebels in defeating the legitimate left-wing Republican government, while an even larger army invaded Emperor Haile Selassie's Abyssinia (modern-day Ethiopia) in a brazen attempt to expand the Italian-African empire. Both ventures were conspicuous failures. The expected victory in Abyssinia deteriorated into a bloody war as the proud and capable Ethiopians refused to simply lie down, and instead fought back. In the end, the Italians had to resort to the indiscriminate bombing and shelling of civilian targets and the mass use of poison gas. About 1,000 miles away in Spain, the inept Italians and their 50,000-strong Corps of Volunteer Troops were dealt a series of crushing blows, including an embarrassing defeat at the Battle of Guadalajara. The cost in men and treasure was huge. The Spanish campaign by itself soaked up a full 20 per cent of Italy's total national

---

1 Mussolini's self-styled description of 'leader' and the Italian equivalent of the German *Führer*, Spanish *Caudillo*, Romanian *Conducator* and Croat *Poglavnik*.

expenditure for the period from 1936 to 1939, and the country's gold reserves were more or less exhausted. Some 4,000 Italians died in Spain, with a further 3,000 killed in Abyssinia. Also, 160 tanks and 1,800 artillery pieces were lost in the fighting – dramatic losses for a country that produced only another 7,000 artillery guns during the entire Second World War. But, as ever with *Il Duce*, bombast and show took the place of reality, as the *Regio Esorcito* (Italian Army) was increased to a full seventy-three divisions,[1] fuelled by a universal conscription term of eighteen months for every male at age eighteen. The number of divisions was also inflated by the adoption in 1938 of the 'binary' system, whereby each division was reduced down to just two infantry regiments instead of the previous establishment of three. This 'reform', just as with the Hungarian Huba re-organisation, increased the size of the army on paper but severely reduced the actual combat power of the typical division. Equipment-wise, heavy weapons were still the exception and not the rule; mortars and machine-guns were relatively few and there was no integral artillery over 100mm in size (and only twelve of those in each division). What equipment there was, most was pulled by horses or man-packed, making the vast majority of the Italian Army a slow-moving, foot-borne force of fifty-nine divisions. However, there were the six elite mountain divisions[2] recruited from the Italian Alps, the Dolomites and the Apennines. These hardy troops were relatively well trained, well led and well equipped specifically for mountain warfare. That meant having 5,000 mules as the main method of transport, and just four small anti-tank guns per division.

Last came Italy's offensive might, three so-called mobile *Celere* (Swift) divisions and three armoured divisions, the latter being the *Centauro*, *Littorio* and *Ariete*, all of which, unfortunately for the men on the Don, would fight exclusively in North Africa.

The *Celere* were converted cavalry formations, reinforced with *Bersaglieri*, a bicycle and motorbike-mounted infantry regiment. Better trained and equipped than average infantry troops, the famous *Bersaglieri*, distinctive in their traditional pith helmets with black cockerel feathers, increased the overall manpower of the *Celere*, which, at 7,000, was even smaller than a standard infantry division. They also had an integral light tank battalion, mainly equipped with Ansaldo tankettes and the Carro Armato L3/35 – both little more than motorised pillboxes. The L3, for example, was armed with two Breda machine-guns and had very thin armour, and was actually based on a 1930s British vehicle. The *Celere* did eventually receive a few heavier M13/40

---

1 The British Army had just thirty-four divisions at the time.
2 The famed *Alpini*, originally five, the sixth – the *Alpi Graie* – was formed in 1941.

tanks, armed with a 47mm Bohler cannon rather than just a machine-gun. Only 13 tonnes in weight, the armour plate on the M13 had a nasty tendency of shattering into pieces when hit by an armour-piercing round, and was only half the thickness of the Soviet-built T-34, the main adversary on the Russian Front.

By 1940, the reality was that the Italian Army was in a parlous state; some 2 million men were in uniform, the majority of them barely trained, inadequately led and with massive gaps in the equipment required. The army, which would bear the brunt of the fighting on the Russian Front, had too many divisions, many of which were as much as 50 per cent under strength, with nowhere near enough heavy weaponry or transport. Up to half its artillery were small calibre 20 and 47mm pieces, barely worthy of the name and which would prove useless against almost anything except infantry and soft-skinned vehicles at close range. Even the most basic military weapons – the infantryman's rifle and the hand grenade – could not be relied on. The army was in the process of replacing the former, a First World War vintage 6.35mm rifle, with a newer, more powerful 7.35mm version, but in the meantime soldiers just had to put up with 40-year-old technology. As for the latter, the standard issue SRCM Model 35 grenade, was, as one Italian general put it during a practical demonstration on the Russian Front

… manufactured with precision and with a record of many years of use. It is equipped with safety devices that allow its safe transportation … and will not allow it to explode even if the grenade itself is flattened.

He then proceeded to pull the pin on one, activating it so it was 'live', and then threw it away from his audience as far as he could, with all expecting a loud bang as it hit the ground. The general, however, forgot that his pet German shepherd dog was standing next to him. Trained to obey his master's command, and obviously looking to enjoy the game, the dog bounded after the grenade, picked it up in his jaws and proudly brought it back to his dumbfounded owner. Expecting an explosion any second that would kill the dog, the general and several spectators, a brave sergeant grabbed the dog, prised open its mouth, pulled out the grenade and threw it away again – this time making sure he kept hold of the animal. It hit the ground and, yet again, no explosion. Everyone, and the dog, was safe, but this was not exactly a ringing endorsement for the weapon!

The Italian High Command knew all of this, but were unable, and unwilling, to face the truth that the armed forces were not capable of anything more than defence of the homeland. An internal Italian Army report compiled by its own intelligence service acknowledged this fact:

> Our army is antiquated in its training methods and concepts of war – as war moves from being static to being one of motion.

Even Mussolini had his doubts about the capability of his military, hence his private requests to Hitler for huge consignments of German war materiel, but like most dictators he was capable of staggering feats of self-delusion and saw no contradiction in sending that same military into ventures for which it was wholly unprepared. In Fascist Italy, power was all and corruption rife.

The highest profile example of this national madness came to light in 1939 when the pride of *Il Duce*'s Italy, the *Regia Aeronautica* (air force) was caught up in a serious scandal when it was revealed that its head, General Guiseppe Valle, had been lying to the government for years about the number of aircraft he actually had, so as to secure an ever-greater share of the military budget. Suspicious official investigators discovered that the true flying strength of the air force was just 30 per cent of the 3,000 modern combat aircraft that had previously been claimed. The remainder were hopelessly obsolete models, badly damaged hulks or total wrecks and write-offs. The press splashed the story all over the country and there was a national outcry. Valle was forced to resign in disgrace, but that did not mean Italy received any more aircraft, and the air force was to remain weak.

The Finns and Bulgars

In the far north, Finland's small peacetime army fielded nine divisions organised into three corps. Tanks, artillery and aircraft were rarely available, as the Finns relied on their neutrality and the adverse nature of the weather and their lake and tree-covered terrain to keep them safe. When the Winter War proved this theory wrong, the Finnish reaction was immediate. Recruitment went through the roof and some 400,000 men - a full 10 per cent of the country's entire population – were mobilised into seven corps with as many heavy weapons as they could scrounge from the battlefields of the winter and buy abroad.

Bulgaria was playing its own game, even more than the independent-minded Finns, and although it put a full 450,000 men into uniform, Tsar Boris had no illusions about what his army could and could not do; self-defence and anti-partisan warfare were the sensible limits of his military ambition.

The 'new states' – Croatia and Slovakia

Croatia and Slovakia were the 'new kids on the block' in Europe, with Croatia only coming into being a few months before Hitler invaded the Soviet Union. Both nations considered themselves under serious threat from the day of their birth, Slovakia from its land-hungry *Magyar* neighbour, and Croatia from Josip Tito's communist Partisans and Draza Mihailovic's royalist chetniks. To survive, they needed functioning militaries and powerful political support from abroad. They had already tied their political wagons to Rome and Berlin, now they needed the armed forces to match.

With low populations (around 3 million each – Croatia's was actually double that but only half were ethnic Croats) and relatively little home-grown industry, the two countries' armies were always going to be small, and infantry-based. The Slovaks had the advantage of having been part of the thoroughly professional pre-war army of Czechoslovakia, equipped with the best weapons the extensive Czech armament industry could produce, and manned by well-trained volunteers grouped around a cadre of capable officers and NCOs. Forced to give up without a fight after the Munich Agreement, the army had split on ethnic lines with the Slovak contingent and their armouries forming the basis of the independent, three-division-strong Slovak Army. This new force was modern and effective, but with almost all heavy industry in the Czech half of the country, there was a serious lack of motorised transport, artillery, anti-tank guns and, most of all, tanks. One feature that made Slovakia unique, even among Germany's beleaguered allies, was its treatment of the 130,000-strong *Volksdeutsche*, the racial German minority who were allowed to serve in closed, ethnic German-only units in the army, which eventually comprised four entire regiments, two of infantry, one of artillery and one engineer.

Zagreb's main problem was of a wholly different magnitude to Bratislava's. Croatia was a state born in war, a creation of the Germans and Italians who invaded Yugoslavia and defeated the country in just over two weeks. The imposition of the psychopathic Anté Pavelic as the Croatian *Poglavnik* and the conversion of his terrorist *Ustase* movement into the ruling government ushered in a reign of unspeakable brutality and mass murder that has effected this beautiful part of the Balkans ever since. Determined not only to beat off the Partisan and chetnik threat but also ethnically cleanse the state of its near 3 million non-Croats, Pavelic introduced conscription for his *Hrvatsko Domobranstvo* (Croatian Home Army). Five divisions were raised, along with a number of independent regiments, including no fewer than ten battalions of *Ustase* fanatics. Incredibly, by the end of 1941, Pavelic would have some 52,000 men in uniform. 'Uniform' was a broad term though, as the men were lucky to be issued with either pre-war French helmets or old Royal Yugoslav Army clothing which they then had to adapt by tearing off the badges and insignia and stitching up the holes. Many soldiers wore a hotchpotch of their own clothing and bits of uniform. Weaponry was basic: 100,000 obsolete German and Italian rifles were handed over to them, plus anything left over from the German invasion. A US Army study after the war on the use of captured materiel by the Axis allies stated:

> The 37mm Skoda anti-tank guns captured in Yugoslavia were retained by the Croatian Armed Forces along with the majority of all the captured Yugoslav guns, and these were placed at her disposal to build up her Army. A few modern 150mm Skoda guns were also later used in coastal defence.

Despite the pressing need of the civil war at home, the best equipped formation in the army did not even fight in Croatia, as Pavelic signed up to join Hitler's much-exhalted 'crusade against bolshevism'. This clarion call raised some 3,000 suitable volunteers from across Croatia and Bosnia to form the 369th Reinforced Croat-German Infantry Regiment.[1] Alone of all the Axis allies formations committed to Operation Barbarossa, the Croats were not an independent national force, but were instead designated as a unit of the German Army; their uniforms were German, as were their weapons. The Croatian former Royal Yugoslav Army officer, Colonel Viktor Pavecic, was appointed to lead the unit, and both he and most of his regiment would end up dying in Stalingrad eighteen months later.

In the air, the Croats 'inherited' several squadrons of ex-Yugoslav aircraft as well as a few out-dated Italian types. However, when Pavelic decided to also commit an Air Legion to Operation Barbarossa, a grateful Berlin gave him a squadron of modern Messerschmitt Bf 109 fighters and a squadron of Dornier Do 17 medium bombers – as it turned out exactly what the Bulgarian Air Force would also receive to help protect the vital Romanian oil wells.

The creation of the Axis panzer force

While the story of naval warfare in the Second World War was of the end of the battleship era and its replacement by the aircraft carrier, on land it was all about the ascendancy of the tank. This machine, still less than 30 years old

---

1   The term Reinforced referred to the fact that the regiment had its own integral 105mm artillery battalion.

by the outbreak of the war, became *the* dominating weapon of every single battlefield of the European conflict – though interestingly not in the Asia-Pacific sphere. Conceptually simple, every tank in history has a combination of three main properties: mobility, protection and firepower. At the beginning of the war, mobility was the key element of most tank designs, hardly surprising given the total immobility of the war in which they were born. By the end of the war, firepower had replaced mobility as the most important component of a tank's make-up, and just to complete the circle, from the 1970s onwards it was protection for the crew that had its turn as the dominant factor when casualties became politically unacceptable to governments and their populations.

All that was still to come, but the late 1930s saw a huge awakening of interest in the tank and how it could change the nature of battle, and the soon-to-be Axis allies were no exception. As it turned out, nowhere was the primacy of the tank, and of mechanised troops as a whole, as prominent as it was in the campaigns in the southern Soviet Union, to which the allied Axis armies would be committed. The side that possessed more and, crucially, knew how to use them to their best advantage, would win.

The land between the great Ukrainian and Russian rivers of the Dnieper, the Donets, the Don and the Volga is dominated by seemingly limitless steppe and endless horizons. This was, and is, ideal tank country, and it would form the backdrop to some of the largest mechanised battles of the war. On the grasslands, vast numbers of tanks, self-propelled artillery and motorised infantry would be manoeuvred across huge areas like so many giant chess pieces. The foremost exponents of armoured warfare from both sides – 'Fast Heinz' Guderian, Hermann 'Papa' Hoth, Erich von Manstein, Konstantin Rokossovsky, Georgy Zhukov and Nikolai Vatutin – would all make their mark here. In recognition of this fact, the Germans initially assigned no less than five panzer and four motorised infantry divisions to their southern thrust during Operation Barbarossa. This represented more than 30 per cent of the *Wehrmacht*'s entire motorised strength, and more than 25 per cent of her precious panzers. With distances between objectives, such as rivers and cities, measuring in the hundreds of miles, the most valuable forces an army possessed were those that could move fast on wheels and tracks, and could punch hard with big guns and plenty of them – those formations would be the ones in demand.

Unfortunately for them, this was not a description that could be applied to the bulk of the Axis allied armies in the Soviet Union, from Operation Barbarossa in 1941, through to the cataclysm of the winter of 1942–43. With all of Italy's (three) tank divisions committed in the deserts of North Africa, it was left to Romania and Hungary to try to provide a modern, effective armoured force on behalf of the Axis allies on the Eastern Front. Make no mistake, this was a life or death endeavour, and in that endeavour, the two neighbours – mistrustful, paranoid and downright hostile to each other – conspicuously failed.

Romania and her 1st Romanian Panzer Division

Romania had out-manoeuvered her detested *Magyar* enemy by committing to a military reform programme in 1935. Having very little in terms of a national heavy weapons industry, she had turned to her Czech and French allies to equip her first serious attempt at a modern armoured force, the 1st Romanian Armoured Brigade, and had then decided to further upgrade the new formation to become the 1st Romanian Panzer Division.

The division was the first unit of its kind in the Romanian Army, organised very much according to *Wehrmacht* doctrine and established with the help of German Army instructors,[1] hence why it was colloquially known by the German term 'panzer division'. Formally established on 17 April 1941, the division adopted a '2 + 2' structural model, with the Czech-built R-2 tanks concentrated in the 1st Panzer Regiment and the French-built R-35 tanks in the 2nd Panzer Regiment. Both regiments had two panzer battalions, with each battalion composed of three companies of tanks and a maintenance company. With more R-2 than R-35 tanks, the 1st Regiment's companies comprised fifteen tanks (five platoons of three), while the 2nd Regiment's companies had just nine vehicles each. The infantry element was composed of two motorised regiments – the 3rd and 4th *Vânători Moto*[2] – and there was also the 1st Motorised Artillery Regiment. Alongside these key sub-units were various other support formations, including an engineer battalion and a reconnaissance group. All were to be vehicle-borne and sustained by a regimental-sized Divisional Training Depot. Overall, the whole idea was to create nothing less than a Romanian version of already-famous German units such as the 7th 'Ghost' Panzer Division commanded by Erwin Rommel.

By Romanian standards, the 13,000-man division was going to be lavishly equipped. Its infantry would field 318 machine-guns, forty mortars (twelve were the 120mm type, the heaviest available) and even seventeen flame-throwers. The artillery regiment was not large and only possessed thirty-six pieces, but the upside was that twelve were among the largest the Romanians had – the much-prized Czech-built 105mm. There were also no integral

---

1 Primarily infanteers from the 64th Panzergrenadier Regiment, tankers from the 4th Panzer Regiment and gunners from the 4th Anti-Aircraft Regiment.

2 *Vân tori*, a traditional Romanian military term for hunter.

anti-tank and anti-aircraft sub-units; instead, each of the panzer regiments had only four 47mm Schneider model 1936 anti-tank guns and ten 13.2mm anti-aircraft machine-guns. The former were not effective, while the latter were actually quite good.

The division's *raison d'être*, though, were the two panzer regiments, and they received everything that Romania could supply. The 126 new Czech-built R-2 tanks and seventy-five Renault R-35 tanks were the mainstays, with the seventy-six ex-First World War Renault FT17s only used for training and reconnaissance as they were gradually phased out from front line service. That gave the division an approximate first line panzer strength of 200 fighting vehicles, much the same as its German equivalent. Indeed, the *Wehrmacht's* own 6th Panzer Division went into Operation Barbarossa equipped with 160 self-same PzKpfw 35(*t*) tanks, even though the Germans had declared the tank officially obsolete in January that same year.

All was not rosy though in the 1st Romanian Panzer Division garden. The unit suffered from three major flaws that would hamper its entire wartime life and greatly contribute to its downfall in that crucial winter of 1942–43.

First, transport. Just as an individual tank was meant to embody the three elements of firepower, protection and mobility, so a panzer division was intended to provide the three holy grails of armoured warfare in total: mass firepower, command and control, and operational mobility. The latter is crucial to the panzer concept of enabling the entire unit of thousands of men and machines to manoeuvre freely, and at speed, around the battlefield in order to defeat an often larger, more static enemy. In the offensive, this is about identifying an opponent's point of weakness, piercing it and then flooding through to get behind his main defences, dislocate his structure by destroying his command, control and supply systems, and thus shatter his ability and will to resist. In defence, it is about the ability to form a powerful, mobile reserve that can cover large areas of ground, can react to any enemy breakthrough and make a fast, hard-hitting counter-attack to seal off any dangerous breaches in the line. This latter role would be exactly what the Romanian tank crews were asked to do on the Don some eighteen months later. Both tasks, though, could only be accomplished by the application of the internal combustion engine, and not by boot leather – a panzer division had to have an adequate number of vehicles, and the Romanians simply did not possess sufficient quantities. A German panzer division of the same overall size and strength was equipped, in total, with some 600 tracked vehicles and almost 3,000 wheeled vehicles, mostly trucks for ferrying around troops and supplies, but also fuel bowsers, light vehicles, motorcycles, armoured cars, towing vehicles for light guns, artillery prime-movers, staff cars, ambulances, signals wagons, field kitchen units, mobile bakeries and recovery vehicles, all necessary for the multiplicity of tasks a division needed to live, move and fight. The Germans were experts in mobile warfare, but the Romanians never had the equipment to master it.

At the time, the standard equipment table for a Romanian infantry division was for just under 8,000 horses pulling more than 1,500 wagons and carts, and for only 202 motor vehicles at a ratio of eighty men to each vehicle (even an Italian alpine division intended to fight in the mountains had an establishment of 500 vehicles), but even this meagre number was a dream, as in reality a normal division was lucky to have 50 per cent of this number of trucks, cars, motorbikes and other vehicles. After all, just before the war broke out there were less than 40,000 motor vehicles in the entire country – so how could just one division, out of almost thirty in the army, be equipped to that level, even if it was the country's one and only panzer unit? The answer was it could not. So, from the very beginning a large proportion of the 1st Romanian Panzer Division was still either on foot, riding bicycles or on horseback.

Second, there was firepower, and the need for masses of it. A panzer division's punch was all about 'shock', the ability for the unit to land an overwhelming volume of high-explosive and armour-piercing fire on an opponent in a matter of minutes or hours, to paralyse and confuse him utterly. In practical, operational terms, the divisions' tanks were meant to be protected by a solid wall of anti-tank and anti-aircraft defences, and be able to call on hard-hitting mobile artillery that could overwhelm an enemy with a barrage of high-explosive shells. Yet again, the equipment needed to deliver this concept simply was not available in sufficient numbers or quality. There were too few guns available, and those they did have were usually too small. This fault also permeated down to the divisions' most important asset – the panzers.

The mainstay of the formation was the R-2 of course and, good as it was in the early 1930s, such was the frenetic pace of tank development that by 1941 it was completely outdated. Its main armament was a 37mm gun, the standard calibre for German Army panzer and anti-tank guns at the beginning of the war. But even in the French campaign in the summer of 1940, it had been proven to have insufficient hitting power. The Allied counter-attack at Arras had seen British-built Matilda tanks literally roll over German anti-tank gun screens as the 37mm shells simply bounced off their armour. A year later things were considerably worse. Operation Barbarossa would see the R-2 in combat against one of the finest examples of tank design in history, the Russian-built T-34 medium tank. Mikhail Koshkin's design was a master class in getting ahead of the competition. Everything about it worked, from the sloped armour and the V-2 diesel engine that reduced engine fires while increasing vehicle range and reliability, to the superb Christie-type suspension and wide tracks that gave the T-34 excellent cross-country and rough terrain capability.

The R-2 was poor in comparison. Its main armament was capable of firing an armour-piercing shell at some 690 metres per second, which could penetrate 31mm of armour at a range of 500 metres – fairly close, but still an acceptable range in a tank engagement. The problem was that the turret armour on the T-34 was 52mm thick at the sides, and a full 60mm at the front. Penetrating the hull was no better, with the sides and rear being 40 and 45mm thick respectively, and the front even thicker at 47mm. Even at the suicidal range of 100 metres, the 37mm gun could only penetrate 37mm of plate. Effectively the T-34 was therefore invulnerable to most of Romania's panzer fleet unless they could fire directly down on the top of the turret or shoot into the underbelly, and even then this had to be at close range.

The Romanian panzers suffered from other drawbacks, too. The tank had a one-man turret, which meant that an individual not only had to command the vehicle but also operate the gun. The 76mm main gun on the T-34 was more than powerful enough to penetrate the R-2's relatively thin armour, sending large shards of red-hot metal detaching off the interior in what tank crews call 'scabbing'. The R-2 was also prone to that most dreaded of events for tank crews – on-board fires. If a fire broke out the crew struggled to escape through the hatches, and for the driver it was an almost impossible task.

Astounding as it might seem, these disadvantages could, and were, overcome – by the Germans – and the key to that was the quality of their leaders and the control they exercised on their panzer units. The German panzer divisions were often little better equipped than the Romanians when they came up against the T-34 and the even heavier KV-1, but after overcoming their initial shock, the German commanders were able to adapt their tactics and procedures to beat the Soviet 'wonder weapons'. The same was not true for their Romanian allies. This lack of strong leadership started at the top.

Command of the 1st was initially given to Brigadier General Nicolae Stoenescu; however, he was also the Secretary General of the Ministry of National Defence at the time, so real authority was exercised by his deputy, Ioan Alec Sion. Born in the northern Wallach trading town of Pitesti, Sion was a career artillery officer who had been decorated for bravery in the First World War. Staying in uniform after the armistice, he had risen through the ranks carrying out a series of mainly staff jobs, lastly as the director of the Materials Department for the Undersecretary of State for Supplies, before being plucked from this post to become the 1st's deputy commanding officer. Without doubt

the 51-year-old Sion was a professional soldier who took his new responsi-
bilities seriously, and in Stoenescu's absence he threw himself into the task of
preparing the division for action. However, he was a gunner and a staff officer
by training and background, not a tanker nor an inspirational combat leader.
The leaders of Nazi Germany's armoured might – the *Panzerwaffe* (Tank
Force) – by contrast, were drawn from men steeped in the new doctrine and
practices of mechanised warfare and *Blitzkrieg* (Lightning war) after they had
received several years' training and practice to hone their skills and expertise.
Hence, when they met the unexpected, such as the T-34, they were able to
improvise and adapt quickly and effectively. By contrast, Sion and his cadre
of officers were only just beginning that mental journey, and were woefully
unprepared to lead the newest and most powerful formation in their country's
army. What they needed above all else was time – and as it turned out they
would have just over two months before their baptism of fire.

So, overall, the division was without doubt the right way for Romania to
go, and given time who knows how it could have developed? But as it stood
in the spring of 1941, it did not have nearly enough motorised transport,
or raw firepower, and its commanders were novices. These major problems
would never be solved in the unit's lifetime, and on the Don would prove disastrous. When the critical moment came, the Romanians needed to launch a
sophisticated, co-ordinated counter-punch to the Red Army challenge – and
they could not.

Hungary – the genesis of the 1st Armoured Field Division

Important as the 1st Panzer was for the fate of the entire Romanian war
effort in the East, no less a role was destined for its *Magyar* counterpart – the
1st Hungarian Armoured Field Division. Late as the Romanians were to the
Axis 'panzer party', their neighbours were even later, and come the Red Army
onslaught against them in January 1943, the position the Hungarian armour
was in mirrored their Axis allies almost exactly. Positioned behind the front
lines as the vital mobile reserve, the 1st Armoured Field Division would be as
ill-suited for its task as the 1st Panzer, and its subsequent failure led to a fate
for the Hungarians that was all too reminiscent of the Romanian disaster less
than two months earlier.

The genesis of the 1st Armoured Field lay, as with most nations, in the cavalry arm, and again as with most nations there was the usual struggle of the old
against the new with the transition from animals to machines; the stink of oil
and axle grease and the crash and grind of gears and motors seemed a far cry

from the dash and elan of man and horse, lance and sabre. Hungary found it especially difficult given its proud, centuries-old traditions of the courageous and colourful *Magyar* hussars; plus the huge costs of armoured formations were prohibitive for a nation shorn of so much of its land, people and wealth after Trianon. As a result, Budapest's response to the new age of mechanised warfare was slow, confused and almost resentful. However, despite all of this, the *Honved* ended up fielding three tank divisions at different times in the war: the 1st and 2nd Armoured Divisions[1] and the formation that would end up meeting its end on the Don in the new year of 1943, the 1st Armoured Field Division. Created more as an ad hoc stopgap to plug the panzer deficiency in the army's capability before the 1st and 2nd Armoured Divisions were ready, the Armoured Field was even weaker than the 1st Romanian Panzer and its destruction horribly predictable.

With the departure of the Armistice Commissioners in 1927, Hungary began to quietly rearm, and in 1934 felt confident enough to go out and procure the self-same models of tanks that were being sold all across an increasingly nervous Europe – in Budapest's case 65 Italian-built Ansaldo CV-33 tankettes and some French-built Renault FT17 tanks. You could almost hear the clink of champagne glasses in the boardrooms of Milan and Paris. Both vehicles – small, relatively slow and armed with only two machine-guns – were designed to act as support for infantry and nothing else, and come the war they were not even capable of that. This toe in the water approach changed with Prime Minister Kálmán Darányi's public rearmament announcement in 1938, and the subsequent follow-on decision by the Hungarian Ministry of Defence that the *Honved* desperately needed its own tank force. With no current indigenous tank manufacturing industry, the Hungarians again looked abroad, and like so much of Europe they beat a path to the doors of the thriving weapons industries of Czechoslovakia.

The Hungarians mirrored the Romanians and chose the Skoda SII model after a demonstration at the tank proving grounds in Pilsen, where the vehicle excelled. The Hungarians then insisted on 'magyarising' the five-man, sixteen-ton tank with a locally designed 260-horsepower V8 engine, and by replacing the original two-man turret with a larger three-man version with an integral radio – a very sensible adaptation indeed that allowed tank commanders to communicate with each other in combat and operate much more effectively as a unit. The new tank had two machine-guns: Hungarian copies of the

---

1   In a sequence only the military could engineer, the 2nd was established but was then the last to go into actual action in 1944.

Czech-built 8mm Z830, and the main gun was also replaced with a special version of the standard Hungarian-issue 40mm towed anti-tank gun. This gun was a version of the German 37mm anti-tank gun and was designated the 40mm 41M. Immensely proud of their achievement, the Hungarians christened their new wonder weapon the Turan I – after the legendary Turan tribe from whom the *Magyars* claimed their original descent – and finally in October 1941 an initial order for 190 of the type was placed (soon increased to 230): seventy from the Manfred Weiss & Cspel works, fifty from Ganz, forty from MAVAG (all in Budapest) and seventy from a factory in Győr.

With the Turan designated a medium tank, Budapest also looked to acquire a light tank for reconnaissance and scouting duties. With the Czechs unable to supply it, it was Sweden that benefited as the Hungarians agreed to a licence to build the Landsverk Stridsvagn L-60 (Strv-L 60) light tank as the Toldi – 202 of which were built. The Toldis were ready for Operation Barbarossa, while the Turans would roll off the production lines and head east to become the mainstay of the Hungarian armoured force only after 1943, when the war was already lost for Hungary.

In the meantime, Budapest had to make do with their fleet of antiquated Ansaldo tankettes, the new but light Toldi and anything they could procure from Nazi Germany, all gathered together into a makeshift formation based on their existing 1st Motorised Brigade and the German/Czech tanks they had purchased. No prizes for guessing what these latter were – none other than the PzKpfw 38(t), exactly the same tank that Romania had purchased and of which Germany now had large numbers. So, entirely by accident of circumstance, the three key armoured units on which the entire Axis war effort in Russia would rely in the winter of 1942–43 – the 1st Romanian Panzer, the 1st Hungarian Armoured Field Division and the German 22nd Panzer Division – would all employ the by then inadequate PzKpfw 38(t) as their main tank on the Don.

In summary, Nazi Germany's Axis 'big three' allies – Italy, Romania and Hungary – were not rich and powerful countries, filled by millions working in highly industrialised economies that could quickly be moved to efficient war production. The largest of them – Italy – had, at 44 million, a population that was smaller than that of Great Britain, and even when added to by Hungary and Romania it was still dwarfed by Nazi Germany's 78 million industrious workers. The Balkan countries in particular were still-young nations, seething with ancient enmities against their neighbours and ill suited to co-operation. Most of their peoples still earned a living by tilling the soil much as their ancestors had done for generations, and as farmers tend to be, they were far more interested in the vagaries of the weather and the harvest than they were the unstable politics in their far-off capitals.

National armaments industries were in their infancy, and only Hungary and Italy were able to manufacture tanks and other heavy weaponry, and even then they were few and of relatively poor quality. To equip their out-dated armed forces, they were compelled to go on the hunt abroad, restricted further by the meagreness of their national treasuries. After all, was the priority to procure the latest medium tank or to build schools to educate their populations? So when war came, the bulk of their contribution would be mainly infantry, more reminiscent of the First World War than the Second.

So as allies, these nations were not cut out to be war-winners, but there was an exception to this reality, and that was when it came to what was probably *the* key war commodity: oil. The Kingdom of Romania would produce no less than 25 million tonnes during the war – that is, 180 million barrels – and even Hungary's far smaller fields would pump 22 million barrels into the fuel tanks of the Axis military machine. But in the end, this would not be enough to tip the war in Berlin's favour.

CHAPTER 3

OPERATION BARBAROSSA
THE WORLD HOLDS ITS BREATH!

Soldiers of the Eastern Front! Weighed down for many months by grave anxieties, compelled to keep silent, I can at last speak openly to you, my soldiers. About one hundred and sixty Russian divisions are lined up along our frontier. For weeks this frontier has been violated continually – not only the frontier of Germany but also that in the far north and in Romania ... A build-up is in progress which has no equal in world history ... You are standing on the Eastern Front. In Romania, on the banks of the Prut, on the Danube, down to the shores of the Black Sea, German and Romanian troops are standing side-by-side, united under the Conductor Antonescu ... You are about to join battle, a hard and crucial battle. The destiny of Europe; the future of the German Reich; the existence of our nation now lie in your hands alone.

So were the prophetic words of Adolf Hitler, *Führer* of Nazi Germany and the man about to launch the mammoth venture that was Operation Barbarossa. Planned in 1940, the intent was to destroy communism as an ideology, and occupy the western and central Soviet Union all the way to the Ural mountains in the east, with a 'border' running on a line from Archangel in the north to Astrakhan on the Caspian Sea in the south. Once this was achieved, Himmler and his SS were to go to work exterminating and enslaving the majority of the former Soviet peoples in order to create a new German Empire in the East – the so-called *Lebensraum* (Living space) for the Aryan master race that he and Hitler fantasised about.

H-hour was set as 03.15 a.m, on 22 June 1941, for what was planned to be nothing less than the military event of the second millennium, a demonstration of sheer power and overwhelming military might, that in Hitler's own words would 'make the world hold its breath'.

For once Hitler, a man given to hyperbole, was not exaggerating. The statistics of Operation Barbarossa were truly awe-inspiring. The *Wehrmacht* invasion force totalled no less than 3.4 million men grouped in eleven separate armies, of which four were powerful *Panzergruppen* 1-4 (Panzer Groups 1-4) equipped with 3,332 tanks and other armoured vehicles. A further 600,000 wheeled vehicles (vast numbers of them captured from the French Army the previous year) and 750,000 horses would provide the rest of the transport, while 7,184 artillery guns would bombard the enemy. Overhead, the *Luftwaffe* readied *Luftflotten* 1–3 (Air fleets 1-3) equipped with 2,770 modern aircraft to support the attack.

The Soviet Union was going to be invaded with three sharp prongs, initially designated C in the north, B in the centre and A in the south.

Heeresgruppe C (Army Group C) in the north was commanded by the Bavarian Catholic commoner Field Marshal Wilhelm Ritter von Leeb.[1] His forces were ordered to advance from East Prussia; take the Baltic states of Lithuania, Latvia and Estonia; and capture Russia's second city of Leningrad before finally linking up with their Finnish allies.

Those allies had been informed of the impending invasion by Hitler and asked to participate. Determined to win back the lands they had forfeited under the Treaty of Moscow in March 1941, the Finns, under the leadership of Gustav von Mannerheim, readily agreed, although the wily old Marshal made it clear that the Finnish Army would operate independently of Army Group C and would not come under German command in any circumstances. On the eve of Operation Barbarossa, the sixteen-division strong Finnish Army was much the same as it had been since independence – an extremely well-led and well-trained infantry army, woefully lacking in modern weaponry and equipment, including tanks, aircraft, artillery, anti-tank guns and radios. They compensated for these shortfalls in part by the superb quality of the soldiers, and by their extraordinarily high motivation to right the wrongs of the 1939 Soviet invasion of their homeland.

However, despite the importance of the objectives assigned to von Leeb, the north was viewed by OKW as a relative sideshow, its terrain of rivers, lakes and vast forests making it unsuitable for the rapid armoured warfare they envisaged, and therefore unlikely to be the sector where the decisive battles would be fought. Leeb's forces, therefore, were the weakest of the three invading Army Groups comprising the Sixteenth and Eighteenth Armies and Panzer Group 4 commanded by Erich Hoepner, known as *Der Alte Reiter*

---

[1] He was elevated to the nobility with the rank of knight and the particle 'von' by winning the Knight's Cross of the Military Order of Max Joseph in the First World War.

(The Old Cavalryman) totalling twenty-six divisions in all – three of them panzer, three motorised and the rest infantry.[1]

To the south, set to strike out from German-occupied Poland, was the Prussian-born Field Marshal Fedor von Bock commanding *Heeresgruppe B* (Army Group B). Later renamed *Heeresgruppe Mitte* (Army Group Centre) – C was renamed *Heeresgruppe Nord* (Army Group North) and group A was changed to *Heeresgruppe Süd* (Army Group South) – this formation was to be the fulcrum of the entire German effort in the East throughout the war. When it succeeded, Nazi Germany succeeded, and vice versa, so its utter annihilation in the summer of 1944 during the Red Army's Operation Bagration offensive would herald the end of the state that created it.

Von Bock's group was intended as the strongest of the three composed of the Fourth and Ninth Armies and Panzer Groups 2 and 3 (under the already legendary Guderian and Hermann '*Papa*' Hoth respectively), with a staggering thirty-five infantry divisions, three security divisions, one cavalry division, five motorised divisions and no less than nine panzer divisions, plus the premier motorised regiment in the *Wehrmacht*, the *Grossdeutschland* (Greater Germany). Von Bock's objectives were the destruction of the main Red Army formations in eastern Poland, Belarus and western Russia, but, critically, he was not given the explicit aim of capturing Moscow.

Further south still, and stretching down through the border states of Romania and Bulgaria, lay Army Group A under the venerable Field Marshal Gerd von Runstedt. Already aged 64 before Operation Barbarossa, this epitome of the Prussian officer class would command the most diverse of the three Axis army groups, and the only one with significant numbers of non-German troops in its ranks. His German-only force was larger than von Leeb's entire Army Group, and was made up of the Sixth Army under von Reichenau, the Eleventh under von Schobert and the Seventeenth under Stülpnagel,[2] with Panzer Group 1 commanded by Ewald von Kleist.[3] These men commanded twenty-two infantry divisions, six mountain divisions, three security divisions,

---

1 Hoepner was to be stripped of his rank, decorations and pension rights by Hitler for withdrawing in the face of the Red Army's winter counter-offensive in front of Moscow. Later, Hoepner was part of the plot to assassinate Hitler on 20 July 1944. When it failed he was arrested, tortured, tried, convicted and hanged.

2 Another senior commander who, like Hoepner, would take part in the 20 July plot and ultimately be hanged for treason.

3 Kleist was a rare beast in the Ostheer in that he advocated treating the Soviet populations well to get them on Germany's side. In 1948, he was extradited to the Soviet Union and charged with the amazingly ridiculous offence of 'alienating the Soviet population through mildness and kindness'. He died in a Soviet prison.

four motorised divisions and five panzer divisions. In addition, von Runstedt also had the entire military commitment of Germany's main allies: fifteen Romanian divisions (their 3rd and 4th Armies), the Hungarian Mobile Army Corps (also called the Carpathian Group), the two divisions of the Slovak Army Corps and, soon to follow, a further three divisions of the so-called *Corpo di Spedizione Italiano in Russia* (Italian Expeditionary Corps in Russia – CSIR).

The Field Marshal's objectives for Operation Barbarossa were to cut off and destroy the Red Army west of the River Dnieper, capture Kiev (the capital of the Ukraine) and Kharkov (the fourth largest city in the Soviet Union), occupy the Crimea (including the enormous Black Sea naval base at Sevastopol) and then push east to the River Volga and the city of Stalingrad. Just in case they got bored, they were then to wheel south, invade the Caucasus and take the oilfields intact.

Along the vast 930-mile front, the *Wehrmacht* and its Axis allies would cross the border to face a Red Army that, on paper at least, dwarfed even their own massive resources. The Soviets mustered a truly immense 12 million men in uniform, of which 4.5 million were based in the so-called 'Frontier Areas' bordering German-occupied Poland and Axis Romania. These forward-based troops were grouped in ten armies, and were equipped with 20,000 tanks and armoured vehicles, plus more than 8,000 aircraft (the Soviets had almost 15,000 in total).

They were, however, configured very differently from their soon-to-be Nazi opponents. While the Soviets agreed with the German planners at OKW that the north of the country was of secondary importance – thus only a relatively small force of thirty Red Army divisions and eight armoured brigades would face von Leeb's men – they also believed the central zone, criss-crossed as it was with prehistoric marshes, sprawling forests and various rivers and water courses, made it unattractive for mechanised formations. As a result, the Soviets only positioned some forty-five divisions and fifteen armoured brigades to face the *Wehrmacht*'s main thrust. In Moscow's view, the major threat they faced was in the south, to the Soviet Union's bread basket and industrial heartlands of the Ukraine and the Donets Basin. As such, the Romanians, Italians, Slovaks and Hungarians would face the best the Red Army had: Colonel-General Mikhail Petrovich Kirponos's Southwestern Front of some 1 million men and 4,800 tanks, grouped in four armies with a huge sixty-four divisions and fourteen armoured brigades, all emplaced behind lines of pillboxes, field obstacles and gun positions. Seriously weakened though the Red Army was by Stalin's murderous 1930s purges of the officer corps, this was still a formidable force. Well equipped and organised, the Southwestern Front was definitely no easy proposition. As for its leader, Mikhail Kirponos had distinguished himself as a divisional commander in the war against the Finns the previous year, and as a Ukrainian, he knew the land over which he would fight.

That fight would actually be for his people's very existence, though he did not know that at the time. Just two days before Operation Barbarossa was launched, Alfred Rosenberg, the Baltic German Nazi Party ideologue and designated *Kommissar fur die Zentrale Steuerung betreffenden Fragen mit den Ostgebieten* (Commissioner for Central Control of Questions Concerned with the Eastern Territories) announced in a confidential speech to his subordinates:

> The southern Russian territories will have to be used to feed the German people. We see absolutely no reason for any obligation on our part to also feed the Russian people with the products of that land. We know this is harsh, and bare of any feelings, but it is necessary, the future will hold some very hard years in store for the Russians.

Rosenberg would be convicted of war crimes at Nuremberg and was hanged in 1946.

H-hour – 22 June 1941

Von Runstedt's attack commenced at Radymno,[1] now the official 'border' between the Nazi- and Soviet-occupied zones of Poland. At its heart was a huge railway bridge over the San River, across which endless numbers of goods trains passed, day in, day out. Those trains were a product of the Non-Aggression Pact between Nazi Germany and the Soviet Union that established a massive trade between the two states. In essence, raw materials and food went from east to west, while finished goods and hard currency went from west to east – at least in theory. Surprisingly, the Soviets had been scrupulous in keeping their end of the bargain, and more than 1.5 million tonnes of wheat, rye and oats were delivered to feed Germany's hungry workers, along with 2 million tonnes of oil, 3,700 kilograms of platinum, 140,000 tonnes of manganese and 26,000 tonnes of chromium – the latter two elements vital in the production of weapons-grade steel. On the other hand, unsurprisingly, the Nazis had been less than punctual in their own deliveries, and were some 239 million Reichsmarks in deficit on the balance of trade. Having said that,

---

1 Founded by the Polish monarch Casimir the Great in the fourteenth century.

they had still sent some 500 million Reichsmarks of manufactured goods east, including the half-completed battlecruiser *Lützow*. Now, as H-hour for Operation Barbarossa approached, it was vital for the invaders that the bridge was captured intact, and this role was assigned to Second Lieutenant Alicke of the 257th Infantry Division and the Berliners of his assault detachment.

Crawling forward as the minutes ticked by, Alicke was heard to whisper, 'Thank God for the noise of the frogs' as the men struggled not to alert the Soviet sentries on duty at the customs shed next to the bridge. Then, at 3.15 a.m. precisely, Alicke charged and led his men on a dash to seize both the shed and the bridge. The guards were stunned, and most were gunned down before they knew what was happening, but a few managed to fire back, and Alicke fell dead, his division's first fatality of the Russian campaign.

Further south the German 457th and 466th Infantry Regiments were Army Group South's spearhead, and they crossed the San River only to run headlong into cadets of the Red Army Non-commissioned Officers' Training School at Vysokoye, accompanied by the advance detachments of the Soviet 199th Reserve Division. The fighting in the fields of standing grain was hand-to-hand, and so fierce the Germans had to call in artillery strikes to make any headway.

For the Axis allies though, the morning of 22 June was an anti-climax. Hitler had actually told Romania's General Antonescu about Operation Barbarossa just ten days earlier, to which the *Conducator* had bullishly replied:

> Of course I'll be there from the start. When it's a question of action against the Slavs, you can always count on Romania.

This tough talk did not translate into immediate action though, with the 3rd and 4th Romanian Armies positioned on the western bank of the River Prut alongside von Schobert's Eleventh Army as von Runstedt's reserve. As their comrades farther north confronted the Soviet border defences, the Romanian sector was all quiet. This would not last long, and in less than two weeks the Romanians were committed as the first of the Axis allies to participate in Operation Barbarossa.

Indeed in truth, it would be the Romanians who would lead the way in 1941, with the other allied nations making relatively minor contributions. The Slovaks and Hungarians would end up fighting well, while the Italians and Croats struggled to keep up with the speed of the battles that first summer and autumn. Those battles, the retaking of Bessarabia and northern Bukovina, the advance across the Dniester River and on into the Ukraine and, in particular, the bloody siege of Odessa, would prove the Romanians' value in combat.

Italy and the CSIR

Before dawn on that fateful morning of 22 June, the Italian dictator of the last nineteen years, Benito Mussolini, was awakened at his summer residence at Riccione on the Adriatic by a phone call from Count Galeazzo Ciano – his son-in-law and Foreign Minister. Ciano read out a letter from Hitler informing Mussolini of Operation Barbarossa and listing his reasons for the invasion. Rather than being appalled at the size of the risk the Nazi leader was taking and the fact he was only now finding out about it, Mussolini responded by immediately declaring war on the Soviet Union and pledging troops to the cause. Strangely, this was not what Hitler wanted to hear, and he pointedly suggested to his fellow despot that any spare Italian troops could be far better employed fighting the British. After all, by the end of that February the Italians had lost an entire nine-division army of 130,000 men, 845 artillery pieces and almost 400 tanks in North Africa.[1] But *Il Duce* would not hear of it, he thought the *Wehrmacht* would win a swift victory, and he wanted Italy to have made a contribution so it could share in the glory. As he said to his military Chief-of-Staff, Pietro Badoglio, with the callousness of a true monster: 'I need several thousand dead to be able to take my place at the peace table.'

But his immediate reaction committed Italy to an expeditionary force in southern Russia that would eventually expand into an entire army standing shivering on the banks of the River Don.

This expeditionary force, the CSIR, was formally established on 10 July 1941 and was composed of the 60,000 men of the 9th Pasubio, 52nd Torino and 3rd Duca d'Aosta Divisions. The two former were semi-motorised infantry, while the latter was one of the new *Celere* (Swift) mobile units. Vittorio Giovannelli's Pasubio, and Roberto Lerici's Torino, both had the usual complement of two regiments of infantrymen each, along with an artillery regiment, mortar, infantry gun and anti-aircraft companies. To help compensate for lack of numbers, and to help 'stiffen their fascist sinews', each division also had a volunteer Fascist *Maglia Nera* (Blackshirt) infantry battalion plus companies of mortars and anti-tank guns from Filippo Diamanti's 3rd of January Brigade – named after the date the Fascists had taken control of the Italian parliament. The Duca d'Aosta, named after its aristocratic patron, had two cavalry regiments, the 2nd Savoia Cavalry and 3rd Novara Lancers, a regiment of horse-drawn artillery, plus its *Bersaglieri* and light tank battalion.

---

1 Operation Compass – where the British by contrast had lost just 500 men killed, 1,400 wounded and fifty-six missing.

The cavalry were still in a world of their own, even then. Never mind that the world of warfare had passed them by and now belonged to their armoured successors. In Mario Marazzani's 3rd Duca d'Aosta the old traditions still reigned supreme, with the colonel of the regiment and his officers superior to everyone else, and Count Alessandro Bettoni of the Savoia Cavalry embodied this principle totally:

> ... the colonel was treated like a divinity, and surrounded by the greatest names among the Italian – and in particular the Roman – nobility.

Bettoni, a monocle wearer and proud winner of two Olympic equestrian gold medals from before the war, was not going to let just anyone into his beloved regiment, so of the 900 or so well-born young men who volunteered each and every year as prospective cavalry officer cadets, only a mere thirty successfully won a commission in the Savoia.

The divisions' tanks, very much viewed with suspicion and sufferance by Bettoni and his fellow aristocrats, were placed into the rather grandly titled San Giorgio Armoured Battalion, and commanded by Paolo Tarnassi. Although his vehicles were disliked by the cavalrymen, Tarnassi himself was not as he was 'one of them', being the former commander of the 13th Cavallegeri di Monferrato Regiment and a veteran of the First World War, the Turkish-Italian War and the Abyssinian campaign.

All of the divisions consisted of conscripts and volunteers from northern Italy – the Torino from Turin of course, the Pasubio from Verona and Mantua, and the Duca d'Aosta from Italian Savoy.

On paper, all three divisions of the corps were reasonably modern, mobile formations, with a level of experience gained in their involvement in the successful invasion of Yugoslavia earlier that year. However, appearances were deceptive. As ever with Italian formations the lack of men, lack of transport and lack of equipment made the CSIR a far from potent force. The corps only had some 100 artillery guns, mostly light calibre weapons with a limited range, and very few anti-tank guns – again size being an issue as the ones they had were too small to destroy Soviet tanks. Manpower-wise, the Duca d'Aosta was only 7,000 strong, while the two infantry divisions had just seven battalions of riflemen each, compared with the German nine per division. Transport was very limited with the corps having 5,000 vehicles in total, of which a large number were requisitioned commercial trucks with their original company logos quickly painted over. This meant, for instance, that the Duca d'Aosta's *Bersaglieri* had one company's worth of motorcycles, and everyone else had a bicycle. The Pasubio and Torino fared even worse, and despite their official classification as 'motorised' divisions, the vast majority of their men had no alternative but to march across southern Russia in lightweight uniforms and boots that Private Alarico Rocchi of the Torino described as 'flimsier than ballerina shoes'.

Perhaps the only thing going for the CSIR was its commander, one of the few high flyers of the Italian general officer corps – the dashing and relatively youthful Giovanni Messe. Messe had been decorated for bravery in the First World War, and had seen further active service in Abyssinia, Albania and Greece. He had been expected to get the prestigious job of commanding one of Italy's three armoured divisions alongside Rommel in the desert, but instead he was hurriedly appointed to command the CSIR and lead it east into the Soviet Union when its first commander, Francesco Zingales, fell seriously ill before deployment.

Messe also had an air unit under his command – *Il Corpo Aereo Spedizione in Russia* – with fewer than 100 aircraft (51 fighters, 22 reconnaissance and light bombers and just 10 transport aircraft), although given the overall parlous state of the *Regia Aeronautica*, this was not a bad outcome for the CSIR.

Hurriedly departing in August, the CSIR soon realised that this would be a very different campaign from the invasion of Yugoslavia where most of its members had seen their first ever action. First, the distances involved were vast. Day after day went by with the men marching along dusty roads through the seemingly endless steppe and wheat fields of the Ukraine. Villages and collective farms were miles and miles away from each other and, mostly coming from the relatively advanced cities of Italy's north, the soldiers found those same villages and their inhabitants extremely backward. This view of the local inhabitants being very primitive was a common one among the invading troops, but the Italians reacted very differently to it from their German allies. Messe himself wrote:

Right from the beginning I wanted to establish our relationships with these people who did not know us, based on the principle of paying for anything we took … Nobody could ever stop any Italian soldier from showing his kindness, innate generosity, and sensitivity towards the Russian population, and to reassure prisoners captured by us of treatment and conditions worthy of civilised people, which was often in stark contrast to the Germans.

German behaviour in the East, conditioned by years of unrelenting propaganda to view the Slav population of the Soviet Union as *Untermenschen*

(Inferior beings), was steeped in blood and barbarity. A German soldier at home on leave from Russia said to his friends on an alcohol-fuelled night out:

> Do you know how we behaved to Russian civilians? We behaved like devils from hell, we left them to starve to death behind us, thousands and thousands of them … if the Russians should ever come knocking at our door and pay us back just one half of what we've done to them, then you wouldn't ever smile or sing again!

The men of the CSIR were disgusted by what they saw; one of their soldiers, Arrigo Paladini, witnessed the brutality of the fighting and then the massacre of 150 Jews by German soldiers on 31 July:

> Until now we thought this would be an easy war, instead today our eyes were opened … They preach 'civilisation' but we are becoming soiled by their barbarism. I used to admire the German soldier but from today he presents himself in a different light, that of a strong but profoundly barbaric warrior.

Initially part of von Schobert's Eleventh Army, the CSIR began its campaign by pursuing fleeing Red Army units between the Dniester and Bug rivers, then, when the Eleventh Army was switched to work with the Romanians in besieging Odessa, the Italians were assigned to Panzer Group 1 commanded by Ewald von Kleist – the most powerful and mobile military formation in the whole of southern Russia. At this point, Mussolini and Hitler decided a morale-boosting visit to the troops was in order, and the two dictators arrived to see Messe and von Runstedt on 28 August. Messe did not waste the opportunity, and confronted his supremo with the facts of the CSIR's situation; the troops were ill-equipped, and the lack of transport and fuel was severely hampering operations as the Germans were becoming increasingly exasperated at the Italians' inability to keep up with the advance. Buoyed up as ever by the spectacle of his troops standing smartly to attention in straight lines, *Il Duce* was in no mood to hear his field commander's matter-of-fact report and simply brushed it off: 'I am sure you deserve the trust which the Führer places in Italian troops' being his totally inadequate response.

A quick briefing, some food and then it was time to leave – objective achieved for the two men who had committed so many of their fellow countrymen to such a terrible venture. With the lightning visit concluded, the advance continued, becoming ever harder for the footsore Italians. Lieutenant Luciano Mela, a cavalry officer in the Savoia, wrote a description of the fighting around Kiev that September:

The Soviets only leave ruins; they even wreck trails with an easy, practical method, causing movement of our trucks to be delayed. When leaving a village without bridges to blow up, or roads to wreck, but only trails like the ones they have here, tractors follow them with ploughs making large zigzag ruts. This doesn't seem like it amounts to much, but afterwards on such a trail our trucks can't go more than eight to ten kilometres per hour.

It was late October, on the Donetz River, when von Kleist used Messe's men to assault the important eastern Ukrainian steel-manufacturing city of Stalino, and the neighbouring towns of Gorlowka and Rikovo. They performed well, and once the fighting was over the CSIR settled in with the local populace. The Torino set up medical clinics for civilians in Rikovo, and men billeted in local homes soon began to trade their rations for laundry and extra clothes as temperatures plummeted throughout November and beyond.

The arrival of that dreadful winter of 1941–42 at least brought a measure of respite to the CSIR, as they were rested where they stood in the quiet zone around Stalino. Although this was not enough to quell the anger of Luciano Mela:

> I've had it! I'm not afraid to say the person responsible for sending a division ahead in the condition in which ours finds itself is an assassin. We're without food, with broken shoes, uniforms in tatters, with only a little ammunition issued to each individual, since the rest is on trucks stranded without fuel some two hundred kilometres away.

Unfortunately for Mela and his compatriots the new year of 1942 would not bring significant improvements in their situation, in fact it would materially worsen as Mussolini compounded his original error in sending the CSIR east, by massively increasing its numbers but not its capabilities, and thereby creating the potential for future disaster.

Finland and Bulgaria

Operation Barbarossa for the Finns was a non-event, until 10 July 1941 when they finally launched their own attack on the Soviet Union. Facing stiff resistance, they advanced only slowly, with the Red Army launching a series of strong counter-attacks as they contested every inch of ground. After crawling forward, on 12 December 1941 the Finns finally reached their pre-Winter War border, and there they halted and dug in. As far as they were concerned they had achieved their goal and would remain there for the next 36 months until the Red Army launched a major offensive against them in 1944. Nevertheless, in that initial six-month period in 1941 the Finns lost 25,000 men killed and twice that number were wounded.

As for the Bulgarians, they had no intention of becoming embroiled in Hitler's war with Stalin, and instead they devoted their out-dated army of some twelve divisions to a ruthless anti-partisan war in the 50,000 square kilometres of Macedonia, Thrace and Salonika awarded to them by a grateful Hitler following the Greek conquest. Villages were burnt, civilians terrorised, atrocities committed. In one documented case, a group of Bulgar soldiers played football with the severed heads of their civilian victims in Drama, a village in north-eastern Greece.

As for Tsar Boris' air force and navy, both were small and poorly equipped; indeed, the former was even banned after the First World War by the provisions of the Neuilly Treaty. That same treaty had been repudiated in 1938, and that opened the door to at least a modicum of air power, with the purchase of some 130 Polish, Italian and German-built aircraft. The signing of the Tri-Partite Pact brought German advisers along with more than 100 captured Czechoslovak aircraft, as well as a total of ten modern German-built Messerschmitt Bf 109 fighters and eleven Dornier Do 17 medium bombers – the so-called 'flying pencils' – all supplied to help protect against Allied air attacks on the Ploesti oil wells in neighbouring Romania, rather than launch raids against the Soviets. The Bulgarian Navy, equipped with four destroyers and five torpedo boats, was based at Varna on the Black Sea from where they would fight occasional skirmishes with the Soviet Navy.

Hungary, Slovakia and Croatia

Putting aside the fact that Hungary would have far rather been attacking Romania, the *Magyars* were only ever reluctant participants in Operation Barbarossa. The Slovaks too were not hugely enthused by the thought of fighting a people with whom they felt a great deal of Slavic kinship. Indeed, after the political events of 1939 and the Hungarian seizure of Slovakian Ruthenia, the government in Bratislava were more worried about the threat from a rapacious Hungary than they were about Soviet Communism; a point not lost on the Nazi leadership, who received regular reports on public opinion, not only inside Germany but also among allied states. This work, some of the very first comprehensive 'public opinion polls', was carried out by Himmler's Office III, *Analyse der Bereiche des Lebens* (Analysis of Spheres of Life) team, a sub-section of the SS security intelligence service, the feared *Sicherheitsdienst* (SD). Under the leadership of the food economist SS-Colonel Otto Ohlendorf,[1] this unit conducted regular in-depth surveys, and distributed the findings throughout the upper echelons of the Nazi leadership as the so-called *Meldungen aus dem Reich* (Reports from the Reich) series. These reports often made for uncomfortable reading, especially when they conflicted with the official propaganda line. The July 1941 report into Slovak popular opinion on Operation Barbarossa fitted into this category:

> Wide circles in the country are of the opinion that the fight against Bolshevism by Slovaks against their own Slavic brethren has to be condemned. Much of the army is of the same view.

Himmler did not share the survey findings with the Slovak government, and even if he had the Slovak President, Josef Tiso, felt that only German support would keep any further Hungarian territorial ambitions at bay. Maintaining that support meant committing to Operation Barbarossa and not just a token force either; amazingly, the Slovaks dispatched two-thirds of their armed forces to Russia, including two of their three fighter squadrons and a reconnaissance squadron. On the ground the 42,000-strong Slovak Army Corps was established for Operation Barbarossa, composed of two of the country's three infantry divisions, plus their most up-to-date mechanised brigade, which was partially motorised and also contained their only panzers – a small number of the same Czech-built PzKpfw 38(*t*) tanks that every other Axis country seemed to possess – plus a few of the Swedish-built versions, the Strv m/41. As with all the Axis allies' forces, transport and heavy equipment were in short supply. The Slovak Army Corps only had 700 trucks in total, so the vast majority of the men would have to march, and the two infantry divisions could only muster twenty-seven horse-drawn artillery pieces each. Having said that, the Slovak divisions had a 'German' structure of three infantry regiments, so, at 15,000 men they were about the same size as their *Wehrmacht* counterparts.

As for Budapest the question was very much – 'what can we get away with sending?' To which Horthy answered, 'not a lot'. Grandly titled – the

---

1 Ohlendorf was later given command of one of the SS special extermination units – *Einsatzgruppe* D (Taskforce D) – whose area of operations was the southern Soviet Union. In this role, he would become one of the most infamous mass murderers of the war as he and his men butchered more than 90,000 innocent men, women and children, mostly Jews.

Carpathian Group – the 44,444-man force was in reality a far from grand amalgamation of the *Honved*'s existing Mobile Corps,[1] and from the VIII Corps, the 1st Mountain Brigade and 8th Frontier Brigade – ten battalions of crack troops. As for much-needed panzers, only a few were available. With the 1st Hungarian Armoured Field still being planned and no orders placed yet for the Turan tank, the Hungarians had to fall back on their 1st Motorised Brigade's sixty-five Italian-built Ansaldo tankettes and a few Toldi light tanks that were not facing the Romanians across the border in Transylvania. An armoured fist it was not!

Both the Hungarians and the Slovaks were assigned to Karl Stülpnagel's Seventeenth Army in the south, and the latter swiftly set about impressing their German allies with their courage and professionalism, even though their lack of motorised transport often meant they struggled to keep up with the German advance.

The Carpathian Group, which crossed into Ukrainian Galicia and marched on to the River Dniester was protected by its own air cover of three fighter squadrons – two of obsolete Fiat biplanes and one of MAVAG *Heja* (Hawk), a licence-built version of the Reggiane Re2000 monoplane fighter. The two brigades of VIII Corps troops then remained on occupation duties, while the rest of the group (now increasingly known as the 'Mobile Army Corps') went on alone into the Soviet Union under the leadership of Major-General Bela Miklos, a well-respected senior officer in the *Magyar* military and a personal confidant of Horthy's. In late 1944, he would end his career with a period as Hungary's acting Prime Minister. In the meantime, Miklos and his men pushed east, reaching Kamenets-Podolskiy on 10 July, Rogozna on 21 July and Holovaniv'sk on 6 August. The endless miles of rutted dirt roads swiftly wore down the Hungarian transport, and abandoned and broken-down vehicles littered their line of advance. The men fared little better, and by the time they reached the city of Nikolayev on 16 July, they were exhausted. The troops had to be kept out of the city though, as it had been taken by the Romanians and von Kleist was worried that the two sides would end up fighting each other if they were not kept apart.

As for the Slovaks, at the beginning of August, with the corps often lagging behind the swifter-moving Germans, and with 106 of their men dead and some 200 wounded or missing, it was time for a rethink, and Bratislava agreed with the OKW to pull the formation out of the line. Recognising

---

1 The 1st and 2nd supposedly Motorised Brigades with six regiments of infantry and two of artillery, and a two-regiment cavalry brigade with some horse-drawn artillery.

they could not adequately support such a large force so far from home, the Slovaks decided to reduce their numbers down to something more manageable, while at the same time increasing overall quality and combat power. The solution they came up with was to concentrate all the motorised transport, the twelve remaining panzers, and most of the heavy weapons into a 10,000-man *Schnelle division* or *Rychla Divizia* (Fast Division in German and Slovak, respectively), with the majority of the remaining men (some 12,000) sent home to carry out garrison duties. The new division was composed of the 20th and 21st Infantry Regiments, the twenty-seven gun 11th Artillery Regiment, plus a reconnaissance battalion and the sole company of serviceable tanks, all under the able command of the 49-year-old Slovak, General Jozef Turanec. Most definitely the cream of Slovakia's remaining manpower, the troops of the Fast Division were fit, motivated and well led by a cadre of ex-Czechoslovak Army officers and NCOs. At last able to keep up with the advance, Turanec led the division in the fighting for Lemberg (Ukrainian *L'viv* and Russian *Lvov*), alongside the Italians at Kiev and on to the bitter winter fighting on the River Mius.

In addition, 8,000 men from the original 1st and 2nd, who were just below the entry level for the Fast Division, were formed into a new Slovak Security Division – which, as the name suggests, was destined to be deployed behind the front lines in the rear area, fighting a vicious war against the increasingly powerful and pervasive partisans. However, the Slovaks had no artillery and no heavy weaponry except a few mortars, and their only transport was some 2,500 horses and 600 wooden farm carts.

As for the Croats of the 369th, they only set off east on 22 August, two months after Operation Barbarossa was launched. Marching on foot to join the German 100th Light Division, to which they had been assigned, they finally reached the front a few weeks later, footsore and somewhat windblown, but still capable of giving a good account of themselves during the fighting, first at Kharkov and then onwards towards the Don. The 369th was unique among the federated Axis troops, in that they were not federated; in fact the regiment was formally designated as an integral part of the *Wehrmacht*, and its members were paid and equipped as 'German soldiers'. As such, the unit was part of the Sixth Army, and this twist of fate would be their doom as they marched unknowingly towards the disaster that awaited them in Stalingrad.

The 369th were not the only Croats committed to the Russian Front that summer. Insulted by the fact that their leaders in Zagreb had offered to supply the Germans with troops, Rome made a rather pointed request for 'our loyal

Croat brothers' also to contribute to the CSIR. More from a sense of hedging his bets rather than genuine conviction, Pavelic ordered the establishment of the Croatian *Laki Prijevozni Zdrug* (Light Transport Brigade) – a 1,200-man unit that, despite its nondescript title, was in reality a light infantry battalion with a few mortars and artillery pieces. The men were all volunteers, initially intended as reinforcements for the 369th, but like it or not they were switched over to serve with the Italians. Trained at Varazdin in Croatia, the brigade became involved in local sweeps against Tito's Partisans while it waited for the CSIR to become organised. Finally, in mid-December, they went west to Italy for three months' additional training before a passing out parade in front of Italy's Chief of the General Staff, Ugo Cavallero, and their own Defence Minister, Slavko Kvaternik. Commanded by the Croatian Lieutenant-Colonel Egon Zitnik, the brigade would not go into combat until *Fall Blau* (Case Blue) in 1942.

Meanwhile, at Nikolayev the Hungarians were literally sitting outside the captured city, restlessly watching the Romanians settle in and enjoy all the comforts on offer. OKW was sensitive to the issue, and quickly sent Miklos and his men away to the north-east, where they were given responsibility to defend an ambitiously long stretch of the line on the River Dnieper between Nikopol and Dnepropetrovsk as the *Wehrmacht* fought its massive encirclement battles at Uman and Kiev to the north. Those engagements have since gone down in history as possibly the greatest of their type ever fought, together rewarding the Germans with more than one million prisoners of war and thousands of captured tanks and guns.

At the beginning of October, those same battles were finally over, and the *Ostheer* resumed the drive east, with von Bock aiming to capture Moscow in *Operation Taifun* (Operation Typhoon) and von Runstedt tasked with pushing on to the Donetz River. The Hungarian Corps took its place in the line and crossed the mighty Dnieper on 12 October, defeating a Soviet rifle division near the town of Izyum before going on to reach and then cross the Donetz towards the end of the month.

By now the Hungarians had marched 1,100 miles, suffered 3,000 casualties and lost 75 per cent of their armour and the majority of their aircraft. With winter fast approaching the new Chief of the Hungarian General Staff, Ferenc Szombathelyi, decided to halt operations and managed to get the OKW's agreement to recall the corps and air wing back to Hungary. The troops heard the news with a great deal of relief as snow was settling in a deep blanket on the Ukraine and the temperature was plummeting. The men marched off as fast as their sore feet would carry them, and by mid-November there was not a single *Magyar* soldier left in Russia. The last aircraft, pilots and ground crew joined them back in Hungary before Christmas.

Discounting the Finns, who were very much fighting on their own behalf, and the Bulgarians, who were not prepared to co-operate with Berlin at all, the total combat might contributed to Operation Barbarossa from Italy, Hungary, Slovakia and Croatia was not exactly overwhelming. All in all, it added up to fewer than 140,000 men, 250 aircraft and just 150 tanks. These numbers, meagre as they were, were not even the whole story, as the majority of those same aircraft and tanks were obsolete and of questionable fighting value, while the general lack of motorised transport and heavy weaponry severely degraded the actual effectiveness of the troops. Having said that, the Germans, never slow to criticise others, were surprisingly complimentary about some of their allies, with an *Ostheer* officer writing at the time that the Slovaks in particular were 'brave soldiers with very good discipline'.

And they were equally magnanimous about the Hungarians, although they tended to see the *Magyars* through rose-tinted glasses coloured by appreciative memories of Hungarian valour during the First World War, plus in Russia a good proportion of senior *Honved* officers were either ethnic Germans or at least spoke fluent German from their days in the Imperial Austro-Hungarian Army.

German views on the Italians, however, are mostly unprintable.

Romania – the greatest burden

Despite the sometimes valiant efforts of the *Magyars*, Croats, Slovaks and Italians, the story of the Axis allies in the Soviet Union in 1941 belongs overwhelmingly to one nation and one nation alone – the Kingdom of Romania. It would be Romania who would make by far the greatest contribution of forces to the struggle in the East in 1941, and indeed would continue to do so in 1942 and right the way through to their eventual defection from the Axis in late 1944. They would fight by land, sea and air, and would be the only Axis nation to be given separate, significant military objectives by the German High Command. However, the cost to their armed forces would be catastrophic, and would eventually culminate in the wholesale destruction of their entire field army on the Don in the winter of 1942.

The 'phoney war'

An absolute pre-requisite in the hoped-for success of Operation Barbarossa lay in the plans to achieve German supremacy in the air. The *Voenno-Vozdushnye*

Sily (Soviet Air Force – VVS) was very large, very powerful and a real threat to the *Ostheer's* ambitions. This threat was going to be neutralised by a massive wave of co-ordinated air strikes up and down the frontier in the first hours of the invasion, all aimed at destroying the VVS while it was still on the ground.

In the south, the man responsible for achieving this goal was a Romanian-born ethnic German airman – Alexander Löhr. To crush the opposing 2,600 VVS aircraft of Generals Ptukhin and Michugin, Löhr had at his disposal the 800 modern aircraft in his *Luftflotte* 4 (Air Fleet 4), of which just over half were stationed on Romanian airfields at H-hour, plus he also had the majority of the *Fortele Aeriene Regale ale Romaniei* (Romanian Royal Air Force – FARR) under his direct command.

The FARR was a reasonably sized force, with some 700 aircraft in total, quite a few of which were of the latest type. However, a major flaw in its composition was the sheer number of different aircraft types. Romania's procurement policy had been to buy aircraft from whoever was an ally at the time, so there were Polish-, German-, Italian-, Czech-, French- and British-built aircraft (twelve Hawker Hurricane fighters and thirty Bristol Blenheim light bombers), as well as Romanian-built machines. With so many different aircraft types to service and keep airworthy, maintenance was a real issue, and so Bucharest made the eminently sensible decision to concentrate the best of what it had in a single formation – the *Gruparea Aeriana de Lupta* (Combat Air Grouping) equipped with some 250 aircraft. It would be this unit which would go forward with the 3rd and 4th Armies into the Soviet Union and form the protective umbrella over the infantry.

Fifteen minutes before H-hour the reconnaissance aircraft of the Romanian's 1st Squadron were crossing the Prut River border leading the way for the main bomber strike force. Surprised Soviet personnel, awakened by the drone of aircraft engines overhead, looked up into the lightening sky but were unable to react as they were then hit by a storm of artillery fire that pounded every barracks, military installation and defensive position known to the German tactical planners. Soviet communications broke down immediately, and the first thing the VVS squadrons based in occupied Bessarabia knew about it all was when the bombs started falling. Soviet aircraft, tidily lined up in long neat rows on their airfields, were easy targets and were destroyed in their hundreds. In fact, the VVS lost more than 2,000 aircraft that first day alone, of which the Romanians claimed a surprising 115, although subsequent aerial photography only confirmed fifty-two as destroyed. Axis losses were small in comparison – thirty-five German and fourteen Romanian aircraft.

Instantly ordered to strike back at their attacker, surviving VVS bombers took off the next morning to bomb Romania, but they were expected and foolishly were flying without any fighter escort. The results were entirely predictable. The Swiss-born Romanian pilot Lieutenant Horia Agarici, flying a British-built Hawker Hurricane, was on his home airfield having an oil leak fixed by his ground crew when a formation of three Soviet Tupolev SB bombers were seen in the sky heading towards the city of Constanta, intent on attacking the port. Despite the fact his windscreen was covered in oil, Agarici took off immediately, rapidly gaining height before diving down into the enemy formation, his eight .303in Browning machine-guns ripping into the Soviet bombers. All three fell to his guns, and the crews of a follow-on wave, seeing the destruction ahead, turned for home, jettisoning their bomb loads.[1]

Just as the Romanian Air Force was in action right from the start of Operation Barbarossa, so too were the 5,000 sailors in the country's navy. The twenty-nine naval vessels of the Black Sea Division and the Danube Flotilla, based respectively at Constanta and Galati, were mostly British- and Italian-built destroyers, torpedo boats, monitors and minesweepers. A three-battalion regiment of naval marines was also stationed in the Danube Delta. The vessels were hugely outnumbered and outgunned by the 200 ships of the Soviet Black Sea Fleet commanded by Admiral Filipp Oktyabrskiy, but despite this they contained their opponents in the opening days of the campaign. On 22 and 23 June 1941, the Romanian Tulcea Tactical Group (the two monitors NMS *Basarabia* and NMS *Mihail Kogalniceanu* and four small patrol boats) beat off two Soviet attacks, sinking one patrol boat and damaging two more as well as two monitors.

Nevertheless, the Soviets were still intent on depriving the Romanians of their largest naval facility at Constanta, and having had their initial air attacks beaten off by Agarici, Oktyabrskiy decided to launch a major co-ordinated sea and air attack against the base on 26 June, accompanied by a significant seaborne assault on the delta of the all-important Danube River. Two naval taskforces were assembled for the attack; the first was led by the *Voroshilov* one of Oktyabrskiy's five cruisers, accompanied by six destroyers and several smaller craft, while his one and only battleship – the *Pariskaya Komuna* (Paris Commune) – was 100 miles offshore waiting to be called in to exploit the expected initial success. As the *Voroshilov* neared its target, VVS bombers took off from their

---

1   Agarici's mother, Viorica, was a nurse during the war and instrumental in trying to protect Romanian Jews from the Holocaust. A grateful Israel commemorated her bravery at the 'Righteous Among the Nations' at the Yad Vashem Holocaust memorial just outside Jerusalem.

airfields to strike the harbour, and eight armoured patrol boats crammed with soldiers steamed towards Chilia Veche and Periprava. Unfortunately for the Soviets, a Romanian submarine had spotted the *Voroshilov* group some hours earlier, and the defences were ready and waiting. The Romanian heavy shore batteries joined with the destroyers MNS *Marasti* and MNS *Regina Maria* in opening fire when the enemy came into range. Hits were quickly scored on two Soviet destroyers, the *Kharkov* and *Moskva*. Surprised by the level of resistance and the accuracy of the return fire, the Soviets beat a hasty retreat, and by sheer bad luck sailed straight into a minefield. The *Voroshilov* was damaged but limped on, while the already-damaged *Moskva* hit a mine and broke in two. The ship sank in minutes, taking 331 of the 400-man crew to the bottom. Overhead, the Tupolev bombers flew into a wall of anti-aircraft fire and nine were shot down. Onshore, all the attack had achieved was a few burning oil tanks and warehouses among the miles of wharves.

However, in the delta it was a different story. In a clever and well-organised raid, the attacking Soviets took Lieutenant-Colonel Ioan Albescu's 15th Marine Battalion by total surprise, and annihilated them.

To the north, on the Prut River border, all was relatively quiet. The OKW's plan for the southern assault was a two-phase operation, with von Runstedt launching his main strike from southern Poland, with the Sixth and Seventeenth Armies punching a hole in the front allowing von Kleist's panzers to stream through.

As for the seven divisions of von Schobert's Eleventh Army, they were sandwiched between two Romanian Armies to the south in Romania proper, with all three collectively called 'Army Group Antonescu'. This force would sit tight until the beginning of July before beginning their campaign in earnest. The plan was partly dictated by terrain, the Prut River in particular was considered a major obstacle, and partly from lack of faith in the Romanian's capability. This harsh assessment may have been true in strictly military terms, but it did not do justice to the contribution the Romanians were making. The cream of the kingdom's available military was lined up on the banks of the Prut with little in reserve, unlike the half-hearted Hungarians. Some 325,000 men were arrayed in two armies, the 3rd under Petre Dumitrescu, and the 4th under his fellow Lieutenant-General, Nicolae Ciuperca. Under their command were fifteen divisions[1] and eight brigades.[2] Dumitrescu and Ciuperca, competent rather than outstanding, were both 59 years old, both had fought in the First World

---

1 Twelve front-line infantry, one reserve infantry, one frontier guard, and the fledgling 1st Romanian Panzer Division.
2 Three cavalry, three mountain and two fortification.

War and were now well regarded; Dumitrescu was an ex-military attaché to Paris, while Ciuperca had been the government's Defence Minister.

They faced Lieutenant-General Pavel Grigorevich Ponedelin's 12th Army and General Yakov Timofeyevich Cherevichenko's 9th Army; sixteen divisions in total, of which no fewer than four were tank and two motorised – all organised under General Ivan Vladimirovich Tyulenev as the 'Southern Front'. All three men were experienced commanders, although Ponedelin had been imprisoned during the Purges and had only recently been released.[1] In terms of straightforward numbers, the opposing forces were not too dissimilar, with the Soviets fielding some 370,000 men, but they would soon gain the upper hand when reinforced in rapid order by a powerful new army created from the Kharkhov Military District, Lieutenant General Andrei Kirilovic Smirnov's 18th Army, with four corps including three additional tank divisions.

As it was, the week or more after Operation Barbarossa was launched was the calm before the storm for both sides. As Romanian airmen and sailors carried on fighting their Red Fleet and VVS opponents, their army brethren engaged in relatively small scale skirmishing across the border. In tit-for-tat fashion, raids were carried out, bridgeheads captured and positions occupied, only to be given up later.

Typical of this activity was an attack on a group of Red Army concrete pillboxes on Bobeica Hill, north of the town of Dorohoi, by Second Lieutenant Paul Popescu's 3rd Rosiori Cavalry Squadron from Dumitrescu's 3rd Army. Dismounting for the assault, the Romanian cavalrymen showed considerable bravery in the face of stiff Soviet resistance as they methodically grenaded each pillbox one by one, killing or capturing the Soviet defenders. The attack was a success, but it cost Popescu his life. In recognition of his bravery, he became the first Romanian of the war to be awarded the country's highest decoration – the Order of Michael the Brave – albeit posthumously.[2] To the south in the German Eleventh Army sector, it was the Romanian riflemen of the 6th, 7th and 8th Vânători regiments that took the lead by taking the small bridge at the hamlet of Sculeni, 10 miles north of Iasi. Along with soldiers of the German 198th Infantry Division, the Axis allies held off a number of Soviet counter-attacks over the next few days and nights, despite being subjected to heavy enemy artillery fire. Even further south in Ciuperca's 4th Army

---

1 Tyulenev was captured at the Battle of Uman when his army was encircled and destroyed.
2 The much-coveted order was awarded only 1,628 times during the entire war and some notable non-Romanian recipients were Erwin Rommel, and the old warhorse Gerd von Runstedt.

sector, the elite 6th Guards Regiment crossed the Prut River and established two bridgeheads at Falciu and Bogdanesti. The Soviet 5th Cavalry Division counter-attacked and was only held off by repeated bayonet charges by the guardsmen of the 9th Company. The Soviet cavalrymen were undaunted, and bravely carried on the assaults during the rest of the day and on into the evening. The 6th Guards held, but lost twenty-four killed, twenty-four wounded and eight missing. The Soviets then began to pound them with artillery and air strikes for the next few hours, before launching a further series of infantry attacks, to which the Romanians responded with counter-attacks of their own. Another fourteen guardsmen died, fifteen were wounded and sixty-three went missing during the fighting.

The Guards' sister division in the V Corps, Major-General Nicolae Dascalescu's 21st Infantry, also captured a bridge to the south at the village of Oancea, with Major Ciprian Ursuleac's 3rd Battalion storming across to seize the far bank. Machine-guns were set up and the men dug in, while a company from the 1st Battalion under First Lieutenant Lizac pushed forward and took the town of Cahul almost 5 miles to the east. Unfortunately for them, both the bridges at Falciu and Bogdanesti were destroyed by accurate Soviet artillery fire and all the forward Romanian troops were left stranded on the eastern bank of the Prut waiting for their comrades to come to their relief.

The two weeks following the launch of Operation Barbarossa was indeed a period of relative quiet in comparison to what was happening elsewhere along the almost 1,000-mile front. But even so by the end of the month, the Romanian Army had suffered almost 1,500 casualties, with more than 400 men killed, 700 wounded and another 400 missing. This was just a small taster of what was to come.

Operation Munich – retaking some of Romania's 'lost lands'

With the skirmishing over, it was time for what Romania considered the main event, her very reason for getting involved in Operation Barbarossa in the first place – throwing the Soviets out of the former Romanian territories of Bessarabia and northern Bukovina lost in 1940. For the Romanians this was almost a 'holy mission', and in terms of national pride ranked alongside the desire to 'save' northern Transylvania from the Hungarians. The operation was launched on 2 July 1941, with the twin aims of 'liberating' northern Bukovina and the regional capital of Cernauti, and Bessarabia and her main city, Chisinau (in Russian *Chernovitsy* and *Kishinev* respectively). Once this was done, the troops were to push on and reach the original 1940 frontier on the River Dniester. For most Romanians this was where they thought their part in the invasion would end. It would not. Instead, it would be more than 1,000 miles farther to the east almost on the far borders of European Russia.

The Soviets knew an offensive was coming of course, and had prepared accordingly; there would be no surprises as there had been on 22 June. There was also no doubting that Tyulenev had the men and weaponry to give von Runstedt a good fight if he could position his forces in the right place. Therefore, the dilemma the Soviet cavalryman faced was where would the German Field Marshal strike? The thinking in Moscow was that the German tanks would strike across the Prut, and push along the flat plains bordering the Black Sea, their right flank protected by the sea and the Romanian Navy, and the Soviet defences were planned accordingly. But Moscow had chosen wrong. The panzers were in southern Poland, and the main attack would come in the north.

With the majority of his men in the south, Tyulenev's nightmare would come true, with spearheads of panzers breaking through the frontlines and fanning out into the rear of his armies, causing chaos and paralysing their ability to resist. The threat then would be that the Soviets could be pinned against the sea, and the country could lose some 300,000 men and masses of badly needed equipment. Furthermore, the road would be open for the Germans all the way to the Crimea and into the very heart of the Ukraine. Ivan Vladimirovich was going to have to try to hold the front in the south against the combined Romanian-German assault, while shifting the whole fulcrum of his defence 100 miles north to his weak right flank.

For the Romanians, those units bloodied in the skirmishes of the previous days, such as the Guards and the 21st Infantry, would figure heavily in Operation Munich, as would previously uncommitted formations such as the Romanian's only Reserve Infantry Division, the 35th, and the army's 'great white hope' – the 1st Romanian Panzer. All would play leading roles in the July battles.

So it was that at 4.00 a.m. on 2 July 1941, it was finally time for Major General Ioan Sion to lead his Romanian panzer troopers into action. Assigned to the aristocratic Joachim von Kortzfleisch's German XI Corps,[1] Sion was tasked with providing the 'armoured punch' for the corp's three infantry divisions as they advanced on the city of Mogilev. The division was still not trained or equipped to the level it should have been, the problems with the lack of motor transport in particular had not been resolved but nevertheless

---

1 As a regional commander in Berlin, von Kortzfleisch was caught up in the 20 July 1944 plot against Hitler when he refused to support the plotters. He was killed in April 1945 during a gun battle with US soldiers in the Sauerland.

after a short artillery bombardment Sion's infantry pushed across the Prut
at Manoleasa with the Reconnaissance Battalion striking out towards the
village of Bratuseni, some 20 miles to the east, and the town of Edinet a
few miles to the north. The panzers were quick to follow, ferried over to
the far bank, and then driving east along the good Romanian roads. The
Soviets reacted, blocking units quickly moving up to traffic junctions and
trunk roads, hoping to stall the attack and hit the panzers before they built up
some real momentum. The leading 1st Panzer Regiment's Czech-built R-2
tanks now demonstrated one of the reasons they were the choice of so many
foreign governments, by wheeling off the roads and using their excellent
cross-country capabilities to swing out behind the road-bound Soviets and
then attack their open flanks, shells smashing into armoured cars and trucks;
infantry and anti-tank gunners machine-gunned where they stood – classic
panzer shock tactics that their German 4th Panzer Regiment instructors
would have been proud to witness.

Two days later, with the Prut far behind them, a call for help came through
to the 1st's commander, Colonel Emilian Ionescu, from the German
203rd Infantry Regiment; they were pinned down west of Bratuseni by large
numbers of Soviet tanks and taking heavy casualties. Ionescu did not hesitate,
and launched his 1st Panzer Battalion in a fierce attack on the Soviet force.
In a sharp tank-on-tank engagement, the Romanians gained the upper hand
and the Soviets retreated; the German infantrymen saluted their Romanian
saviours, thankful to have been saved from destruction. Proud of their success,
the Romanian tank crews nevertheless were not so over confident as to have
missed the simple fact that their 37mm main guns had not exactly blown their
opponent's tanks to pieces. Indeed, many of those same tanks had seemingly
survived multiple hits more or less unscathed, and had then withdrawn under
their own power. The following day on 5 July, Sion pushed his force up the
main road from Branzeni, fighting elements of the Soviet 74th and 176th
Rifle Divisions supported by a small number of tanks. Again, the sheer weight
and ferocity of the Romanian attack won the day, and by nightfall the division's reconnaissance troops were in Edinet.

That same day, men from Georghe Avramescu's elite Mountain Corps
cleared out the last of the Soviet rearguards in Cernauti, and by nightfall the
capital of northern Bukovina was back once more in Romanian hands.

Without taking anything away from the bravery and professionalism of the
Romanian-German assault over the Prut River, the situation on Tyulenev's
northern flank was making his position in Bukovina and Bessarabia increasingly untenable. Von Runstedt's panzer *Blitzkrieg* was threatening the city of

Rovno to his rear, and the lack of accurate intelligence on the ground and from air reconnaissance (the Romanians and Germans were quickly winning the war in the air with the VVS suffering terrible losses) helped to errone-ously convince the Red Army commander that he was actually confronted by a force far superior to his own. Facing the Romanians in Bukovina, and the Germans in southern Poland to the north, Tyulenev was desperate to ensure his 12th Army was not outflanked, so when the STAVKA ordered a pull-back to the 1940 border, he went even further, and requested permission to with-draw Pavel Ponedelin's men all the way to the Stalin Line on the left bank of the Dniester River.[1]

It was at this crucial moment in time that the STAVKA decided to make one of the many stupid decisions that characterised the Soviet armed forces' response during that whole disastrous campaign in the summer of 1941. Tyulenev's withdrawal order was cancelled with immediate effect, and instead he was instructed to do nothing less than advance and retake the Prut River line, throwing the Romanians back across the river as a result. Tyulenev's reac-tion was one of utter incredulity. The withdrawal was already underway (he had men and equipment spread out over many miles of roads and tracks); and to turn them all back now would create mass confusion, but an order was an order, and the radio lines hummed with the news. Crazy as the deci-sion seemed, there was logic in STAVKA's decision, as it sought to halt von Runstedt as near as it could to the invasion line, and so protect the south of the country. To help achieve this it was sending in the cavalry in the form of Andrei Smirnov's 100,000-strong 18th Army, with clear instructions that this fresh force be used to block the German advance in the north, and thus allow the 9th and 12th to go over to the offensive against the Romanians. As a plan on paper this seemed eminently achievable, but as a practical military opera-tion it was not. Armies of hundreds of thousands of men, vehicles, horses and veritable mountains of supplies could not simply be turned around – to do so was just as effective a way of dislocating them as through a *Blitzkrieg*. The Red Army's Southern Front was now in a no-man's land that the Germans and their Romanian allies would ruthlessly exploit.

In the meantime, with the only clear order being to wait for a clear order, Yakov Cherevichenko's 9th Army would distinguish itself in determined resistance to the attacks of Nicolae Ciuperca's 4th Romanians. The latter was the 'little brother' to Dumitrescu's 3rd, yet still a powerful force in its own

---

1   Created by Stalin on the day after Operation Barbarossa was launched, the STAVKA was an old Tsarist name for the Russian Supreme Command Headquarters.

right. From within its ranks, three very different divisions would now take centre stage. The first would be Brigadier General Emil Procopiescu's 35th Reserve Infantry Division manned by middle-aged soldiers past their prime and lacking in modern training and weapons. Procopiescu's men were willing, but fit only for rear area security or installation protection duties, and definitely not for front line combat against a top echelon enemy like the 9th Army. This did not stop them from being in the forefront of the action though, and on the morning the grand offensive was finally launched, the ageing reservists began to cross over the Prut into Bessarabia with none other than the *Conducator* Antonescu himself in attendance.[1] At first all went well, and along with the other divisions in Major General Vasile Atanasiu's III Corps, the 11th and 15th Infantry Divisions, the 35th Reserve expanded the bridgehead on the far bank and then set off in an advance towards Chisinau, some 40 miles to the north-east. Facing them were the Soviet 95th Rifle Division and General Belov's 5th and 9th Cavalry Divisions, who mounted several strong counterattacks against the Romanians on 5 July, only to be held off as Procopiescu's men bravely stood their ground. Two days later all seemed to be going well, and the 35th was ordered to move north towards Calarisi. In the middle of the morning, Procopiescu received a radio message from a forward reconnaissance unit saying the Soviet troops in front of him were retreating towards Chisinau in a state of some disorder. Urged on by the report, he ordered his 67th Infantry Regiment to advance as quickly as possible to take advantage of the apparent Soviet weakness.

But the reconnaissance report was false.

There was no panic among the Soviets; in fact, quite the opposite. The 95th Rifle Division was no standard Soviet infantry unit, its companies full of half-trained conscripts. Instead, it was rightfully recognised as an elite unit in the 9th Army, held back in reserve until now. Finally unleashed, it charged into the exposed flank of the advancing 67th, and in short order wrecked the 2nd and 3rd Battalions and forced the survivors to retreat. Not pausing to stop, the Soviet riflemen, and some supporting tanks, pressed on into the Bucovat Valley where the reservists of the 63rd Artillery Regiment were strung out over several miles along the road in loose marching order. The result was disaster for the Romanians. The gunners commander, Colonel Cocinschi, and his two battalion commanders, Captains Alexandru Borcescu and Valerie Negut, desperately scrambled to set up a defence

---

1 Antonescu had recorded a national radio broadcast which went out at the same time that proclaimed: 'Romania has gone into action by the side of her German ally. I, the Conducator, now give the Army the order – cross the Prut!'

line. Artillerymen jumped down from their wagons and unlimbered their obsolete 75mm field guns, grabbing shells and charges. Now, with the 95th bearing down on them, the Romanians were going to break that rule and be right in the middle of the fighting. There was no need for rangefinders as the gunners fired point blank over open sights at the attacking tanks and infantry. Cocinschi grabbed a light machine-gun and poured fire into the enemy from his 1st Battery's position, to no avail. In two hours of desperate fighting, both Borcescu and Negut were killed, Cocinschi was wounded and the regiment annihilated. The 35th's third infantry regiment, the 55th, was now cut off in the adjacent Bacului Valley, and Procopiescu, horrified by what was happening to his division, counter-attacked with his remaining 50th Infantry Regiment, while he personally went forward to try to hold together the remnants of his forward infantry and artillery units. This was a brave move, but nothing could hide the fact that the 35th was now crumbling; its artillery was destroyed and its reconnaissance troops were surrounded, and of its three infantry regiments one was annihilated, another was isolated and the last – the 50th Infantry – was now committed in a desperate attempt to avoid calamity. The 95th Rifles, fewer in number than their opponents, refused to give the Romanians any respite and drove on, and only the intervention of the Romanian Air Force staved off disaster as they flew eighty sorties and dropped more than 22 tons of bombs on the Red Army riflemen during the afternoon and early evening. That night, with no other options open to him, Antonescu had to go to his German allies and ask for help. In response, the *Wehrmacht*'s 72nd Infantry Division advanced the following day, pushing back the 95th and relieving the surviving reservists, a task they were aided in by the Romanians' own 15th Infantry Division. Pulled back from the fighting, Procopiescu could count the cost to his beloved unit; in the course of two days he had lost 180 men killed, 300 wounded and an unbelievable 2,300 missing presumed captured. Some 20 per cent of his entire unit's personnel were gone, along with all of his integral artillery and two precious batteries of the attached 55th Motorised Heavy Artillery – irreplaceable weaponry for the equipment-starved Romanians. Determined not to admit total defeat, Antonescu insisted that the 35th take part a few days later in the final attack on Chisinau, but once the city had fallen it was pulled out of the line once more and quietly disbanded, its men sent home to fill the ranks of other reserve formations. In a last epitaph, the whole episode was glossed over with the posthumous award of Order of Michael the Brave medals to Borcescu and Negut for their part in the fighting at Bucovat.

The divisions of the neighbouring V Romanian Corps, the Guards and the 21st Infantry, had, of course, already been bloodied in the Prut River bridgeheads; however, these skirmishes were nothing compared with the trials these two units would now undergo as they were drawn into what became known as the 'Battle of Tiganca' – all focused on a rather insignificant little village and a small hill that overlooked the area.

Nicolae Sova's guardsmen were already on the eastern bank of the Prut, as were some of Nicolae Dascalescu's infanteers (all border men from the southern towns of Galati and Barlad). The key now was to break out of those small bridgeheads at Falciu and Bogdanesti and head east to Tighina on the Dniester. Heavy rain earlier in the week had swollen the river and flooded the water meadows, and strong Red Army forces had pushed forward to try to prevent that exact same breakout. The Guards made an attempt to push more men across on 4 August only to see the attempt foiled when their artillery cover ceased as the guns ran out of ammunition. The 21st then intervened to help out its sister division and prepared to attack, only to see the promised air cover fail to materialise at the appointed time, and when it did arrive the Romanian bombers proceeded to hit their own troops. A request for an artillery strike then went unanswered and the infantry of both divisions ended up charging the trenches on Epureni and Cania Hill and taking them all at the point of the bayonet. With no external support losses were predictably heavy, with the 21st losing twenty-six men killed and 200 wounded, whilst thirty-two guardsmen died, seven went missing and 170 were wounded. Events then took a turn for the worse over the next two days as the rain came again and brought with it well-planned and well-executed Soviet counter-attacks that at one point caused two battalions of the 21st Infantry's 11th Dorobanti Regiment to flee in near panic. Just as Procopiescu had done with his 35th Division, so Dascalescu had to do the same with his men and physically go and stop them from running all the way back to the river. The Romanian front was now in a precarious state and the Soviets piled on the pressure, vigorously attacking the remnants of the 11th Regiment, whose commanding officer, Colonel Bardan, was left holding his ground with just eight officers and sixty-eight men. The Guards fared no better, with Soviet troops managing to get between two battalions of their 6th Regiment, surprising its own command post at first light. Clerks, cooks and pioneers all grabbed their weapons and the Soviets were beaten off, but not before the regimental commander, Lieutenant Colonel Gheorghe Iliescu, became Romania's highest ranking fatality of the war to date. By the end of the day, the two divisions had lost another 1,600 men killed, wounded or missing. The Guards alone had sustained almost 1,000 casualties, and the leaderless 6th Regiment was pulled back into reserve. Ciuperca was livid, and the debacle cost Lieutenant General Gheorghe Leventi his position as Corps commander.

However, the V Corps' steadfastness under pressure had bought the Romanians breathing space, and they used it by launching their own attack on the morning of 9 July. Both divisions advanced, capturing a series of high features until Colonel Bardan's 11th finally took both Tiganca Hill and the village at its base. The fighting was frantic, with the Romanians losing another regimental commander (this time it was the 21st's turn when Colonel Gheorghe Nicolescu from the divisions 12th Regiment was killed), and the forward companies were taking so many casualties that men were being seconded from supporting and logistics units and sent forward to reinforce the line battalions. So tough was the fighting that Ciuperca gave serious consideration to pulling the whole corps back across the Prut to regroup. While the Romanians dithered the Soviets acted, throwing three rifle divisions with supporting tank units straight at the exhausted men of V Corps. The battle raged for 16 hours on 12 July, with every available man who could hold a rifle sent into the Romanian line. Overhead the two air forces fought dogfights to cover each side's bombers, the VVS hitting Romanian troop positions along the front, and the Romanians doing the same to the Soviets, dropping almost 40 tonnes of bombs and causing dreadful casualties among the rifle divisions as they tried to concentrate to continue their attacks. The Guards on Cania Hill were surrounded, and the 21st was down to just four out of nine battered battalions of infantrymen, but they held, and by nightfall that day the Soviets had withdrawn. Over the next few days they launched a few desultory attacks, but nothing major; the battle was lost, and on 15 July the Romanians began a general advance out of the Tiganca bridgehead to the east. The cost had been terrible – almost 9,000 men lost, with the 21st Infantry especially hard hit.[1] The ferocity of the battle can be gauged by the fact that a total of seventeen Michael the Brave medals were awarded, six posthumously, including to two fighter pilots; First-Lieutenant Ioan Lascu and Second Lieutenant Vasile Claru, and two young Guards officers, First Lieutenants Mihail Adabei and Victor Comsa. General Dascalescu

---

1 Dascalescu, the commander of the 21st, ended up leading the 4th Army in 1944, survived the war and then disappeared into obscurity. However, several years later a Romanian Army platoon was carrying out some training in a farmer's field when an old peasant sitting on the wall offered the young platoon commander some advice on how best to instruct his men. Surprised by the peasant's obvious knowledge and grasp of military affairs, the young officer asked how the man knew so much, and was shocked to find that he was talking to Dascalescu. In appreciation of his distinguished service the entire platoon lined up and saluted the old man.

received his own medal from Antonescu, although it was cold comfort to him given the near destruction of his cherished division.

In the north, Sion's 1st Romanian Panzer Division had defeated the 74th and 176th Rifle Divisions, before reaching Mogilev and the 1940 frontier on 7 July. It was then ordered south to help the 4th Army break out, capture Chisinau and block the Soviet retreat.

The attack began on 13 July, with the Romanian panzers pushing down the Orhei-Chisinau road and running headlong into the Soviet 47th Tank Division on 14 July. Despite heavy casualties, the Romanians won the day, and by nightfall they were only 5 miles from the Bessarabian capital. As for the Soviets, they began to retreat east to avoid being cut off, the 95th Rifle Division in particular giving ground slowly and grudgingly.

Chisinau finally fell to the 1st Panzer on 16 July, some two weeks after the launch of Operation Munich. Colonel Constantin Nistor led his motorised infantry in from the west, while Colonel Gheorghe Petrea arrived from the north-east. They entered the city at about 8.30 a.m. and began to clear it of the remaining Soviets, Captain Victor Gabrinschi's 3rd Panzer Company taking the lead when they destroyed a cavalry squadron and horse-drawn artillery battery near the orthodox cathedral. Not to be outdone, the 2nd Panzer Battalion obliterated the last Soviet redoubt on Rascanu Hill, and by noon the Romanian flag was being raised on the Holy Trinity Church by Second Lieutenant Stefan Marinescu – Chisinau had been liberated.

The next day, the 1st Panzer left the city and followed what is now the main M21 motorway east, crossing the Dniester and fighting a sharp engagement at the village of Chirca against Soviet rearguards. The STAVKA had now finally relented and ordered Yakov Cherevichenko's 9th Army to fall back into the Soviet Union proper to avoid the danger of encirclement, but the order came too late for the courageous 95th Rifle Division, who were caught off guard by the 1st Romanian, with many of their headquarters staff forced to surrender when their column was intercepted by the rapidly advancing panzers. It was a sad last act for a division, and an army, that had acquitted itself well over the previous month.

By the end of July, Cernauti and Chisinau had been taken, the 1940 border reached and, with Romanian troops standing on both banks of the Dniester, Operation Munich was declared a success for the Romanians. Army Group Antonescu was disbanded, and Bucharest could count the cost of a month's hard fighting and look at the lessons learned.

The most important of these was that this war was going to be a very bloody affair indeed. The Romanians had suffered around 23,000 casualties in less than a month, almost 10 per cent of the entire force committed to the offensive. The Soviets lost slightly fewer at some 18,000, including almost 9,000 killed or captured. Overall, Bucharest's army and air force had both performed well, especially elite units like the Guards and 1st Romanian Panzer. But there were worrying signs. The lack of motor transport had drastically slowed the advance, and the shortage of heavy weapons was a real issue, with Ciuperca's 4th Army held fast for days on the Prut as it did not have the heavy artillery needed to break through; only the intervention of Sion's panzers allowed it to break out from the bridgeheads. As for those same panzers, the Romanian tank crews had fought hard, learning most of the lessons from their German instructors and applying them on the battlefield. They had sought out weak spots, by-passed resistance when they met it and swept out to hit their opponents in the flanks and rear, although co-ordination between panzers and infantry was still not good enough. However, the real worry for Sion was with his French-built R-35 tanks. These made up some 40 per cent of his armoured strength and had simply proved too slow to even keep up with the infantry, let alone the faster Czechoslovak-built R-2.

On into Russia

Romania had now reached a crossroads in its involvement in the war, and consequently its whole future. It had declared war on the Soviet Union but had so far only taken part in an operation that could easily be justified as 'liberation' of lands that were rightfully Romanian. If they so wished, there was now an opportunity to dig in and tell the world their war was effectively over. This was what the Finns would do some five months later. In this scenario, the Romanian army and air force would remain intact, and the rearmament programme could continue to build up military strength for the future. At that moment, with an uncanny sense of timing, a letter from Hitler arrived for Antonescu. In it he heaped praise on the success of Operation Munich:

> I congratulate you wholeheartedly on this great success, for me personally as great a pleasure as it is a satisfaction. To regain Bessarabia will be the most natural reward for your efforts and those of your gallant armies.

Hitler went on to state that in his opinion the war would 'decide the fate of Europe for centuries', and he asked Antonescu to send his armies into the Ukraine proper, offering the *Conducator* a big incentive. Romania would be granted nothing less than a new province to be christened 'Transniestra'. It was to encompass all the land from the Dniester to the Bug River, from Kherson on the Black Sea and north to Vinnitsa. This huge swathe of territory would be Romania's reward for her part in the defeat of the Soviet Union. In a decision that would prove horribly fateful both for himself and his country, Antonescu wrote back to Hitler four days later:

> I am serving not only the Romanian nation and the Romanian populations across the Dniester, but also the commandment of civilisation and the need to consciously fight for the building of Europe's new fate.

Basically, Antonescu's answer was yes, he would stand with Nazi Germany 'till the end'.

Romania was now totally committed to a path that would inexorably lead to the River Don and utter destruction, and that path would begin 100 miles to the south-east of Chisinau with the slaughter at Odessa.

Odessa – the 4th Army's Pyrrhic victory

Nicolae Ciuperca's 160,000-man 4th Army now had the dubious honour of becoming the main point of effort for the country's Russian war, and was ordered (under the General Staff's Operational Directive No.31) to advance into the Ukraine, defeat the Soviets in front of the Bug River and capture the important port and naval base of Odessa in a lightning strike. This mammoth task was allocated to the 1st Romanian Panzer Division,[1] which also had first call on any reinforcements it would need from the 3rd Army – and it would need plenty. In fact by the end of the siege, the bulk of the 3rd Army would be committed alongside their 4th Army comrades as they struggled to take the city.

The defending Soviet 9th Army may have been in retreat, but the STAVKA was not going to abandon Odessa lightly. The fortifications around the city had been organised along the lines of the great Soviet naval redoubt at Sevastopol and were truly daunting. There were three lines of defence, one behind the other, with interlocking trenches, concrete and earth pillboxes and gun emplacements everywhere. The first line was 50 miles long and situated

---

1 Sion's men were split into two, with the R-35 tanks of 2nd Panzer Regiment assigned to Vasile Atanasiu's III Corps in effect as 'mobile artillery', while the main part of the division was put in V Corps as a 'manoeuvre unit' under Aurelian Son – Gheorghe Leventi's replacement as Corps commander.

20 miles from the city, and if the attackers breached it they would then hit the main 20-mile-long defensive line that was still some 5 miles out from the city limits. All the way they would be subjected to heavy and accurate artillery fire from the 240 well-positioned guns, which were ranged to cover every part of the battleground. After that, the last line of defence was in Odessa itself where the Soviets prepared for house-to-house fighting, supported by the guns of the Black Sea Fleet standing offshore. Manning the defences were some 34,500 men of General Safronov's Coastal Army, including the 4th Army's old adversaries, the 95th Rifle and 9th Cavalry Divisions, as well as a fresh regiment of superbly trained NKVD troops.[1]

The defenders could also be resupplied by sea, as the Romanians had insufficient naval strength in the Black Sea to challenge the Soviet fleet in a battle, and instead were limited to submarine patrols and a few desultory attacks using motor gunboats. Nevertheless, confidence was high among the Romanians as they advanced east during the first week of August, with the 1st Romanian Panzer Division in particular showing its ability with a classic outflanking move on the town of Katargy – 200 Soviets were killed as they were encircled by Sion's force of R-2 tanks. Halting only to refuel and rearm, the panzers charged on and hit Odessa's first defence line on 10 August. Overwhelmed by the mass of armour the Soviets gave way at Buzhalyk, their trenches were overrun and the defenders put to flight. Just as they had been trained by their German instructors, the Romanian tank crews did not stop, but drove hard towards the city, reaching the second, main line of fortifications near Blagodatnaya that same evening, a mere 6 miles from the shores of the Black Sea. The 1st Panzer's advance had taken the Soviets totally by surprise and there was a real danger that the city might fall if the Romanian infantry could reinforce the panzers and pour through the gap they had punched in the defences. The race was now on as to which side could react fastest, and with very little motorised transport, it was a race that 4th Army lost. The Soviets rushed reinforcements forward and managed to seal the breach. When the panzers resumed the attack the following day they met stiff resistance and the assault stopped in its tracks – the chance

---

1 The *Narodnyy Komissariat Vnutrennikh Del* (People's Commissariat for Internal Affairs – NKVD) was the Soviet Union's secret police and the direct descendant of Lenin's Cheka and OGPU. Responsible for public repression, executions, the *Gulag* (slave labour camps) and foreign espionage, it also guarded the Soviet Union's frontier with hand-picked units, which at the beginning of Operation Barbarossa consisted of fifteen complete rifle divisions. By 1945, this field force would expand to fifty-three divisions and twenty-eight brigades.

to take Odessa by storm had gone and the Romanians would now face two months of heavy fighting to take the city.

With all hope of a quick victory lost at Blagodatnaya, Ciuperca settled into a siege, pulled his tanks out of the line and threw a cordon of infantry and artillery round the city. When it was surrounded on the landward side, he launched an offensive on 16 August with simultaneous attacks from the I, III and V Corps. Even with air support from Romanian and German aircraft, the attack made precious little headway against strong Soviet resistance and in exasperation Ciuperca threw the 1st Panzer Division back into the battle to try to achieve a breach. The result was disaster. Without artillery support the tanks advanced on the town of Karpova along with the 3rd Dorobanti Regiment from the 11th Infantry Division. Recruited from the lowland Slatani region west of Bucharest, the 3rd had no experience of working with armour and so did not focus on eliminating the Soviet anti-tank guns. Left unmolested the Soviet gunners wreaked havoc among the unprotected Romanian panzers, knocking out no less than thirty-two, and leaving the division with just twenty-one operational tanks at the end of the day. Much of the armour lying smouldering at Karpova would later be recovered, repaired and put back into action, but nevertheless it was a calamity and the worst loss of Romanian armour in a single day until the Don over a year later. As a result Sion lost his command, when, in a fit of pique, Antonescu replaced him with Carol Schmidt, although after calming down the *Conducator* reinstated the general in early October.

At Odessa, the offensive continued, with the Soviet defenders vigorously counter-attacking all along the line, forcing the Romanians to commit the IV Corps as casualties mounted – on 24 August the 3rd Infantry Division lost almost 800 men, with 25 per cent of them killed. Within a few days, the attack petered out having achieved little more than the capture of the city's water reservoirs. Ciuperca was left to count the cost to his army, and it was high. Out of the original 160,000 men, the 4th Army had now lost 27,000, with almost 5,500 dead, and yet Odessa's main fortifications still remained in place. In a vain effort by Bucharest to boost morale, Antonescu was rewarded for liberating Bukovina and Bessarabia with promotion to the rank of Marshal, only the third man ever to achieve the distinction in Romanian history. Hitler also responded and awarded the new Marshal with the coveted Knight's Cross of the Iron Cross, Nazi Germany's highest decoration.

Meanwhile at the front, with doubts creeping into his mind as to the whole venture, Ciuperca began the thankless task of planning a fresh offensive. Planned to start on 28 August, the emphasis was on firepower – the IV Corps

attack alone was to be supported by no less than five heavy artillery battalions. At 8.00 a.m. that day, a furious barrage was hurled at Soviet lines for
a full 30 minutes before the assault troops went into action. Thousands of
Romanian infantrymen stormed forward and were met by a wall of artillery, mortar and machine-gun fire. The Romanian preparation simply was
not thorough enough against well-prepared defences, and the attack stalled.
That first day, the 21st Infantry Division managed to advance only some
800 metres. The next day was no better, with Soviet counter-attacks stopping
any forward movement.

On 30 August, the Romanians tried again and this time, on average,
advanced just 200 metres. This was reminiscent of the worst episodes on the
Western Front in the First World War, with a similar number of casualties.

In a last bid to break the deadlock, Ciuperca told Antonescu that his units
were in a very poor state after a month of hard fighting, and he proposed
the total re-organisation of no less than six of his divisions (the 3rd, 6th, 7th,
14th, 21st and the Guards) into concentrated assault units backed up by all
the artillery that could be assembled. This force would then launch an all-
out attack on the city. The *Conducator*, incredibly sensitive to any implied
criticism of his handling of the war, rejected Ciuperca's plan out of hand and
sacked him in disgrace. Instead, the Marshal imposed his own operational
solution, while instructing his Chief of the General Staff, Alexandru Ioanitiu,
to request fighter and Stuka dive-bomber support – as well as five assault
pioneer battalions – from his German liaison officer, General Artur Hauffe.[1]
Ciuperca was replaced by Iosif Iacobici, who was given command of a 4th
Army that by now totalled 200,000 men, and was further reinforced by four
regiments of German infantry, plus artillery and assault pioneers under René
von Courbier. They now faced a Red Army garrison that had also been reinforced with more than 15,000 men transported from the Crimea to replace
losses and continue the defence.

On 12 September, with the trees turning autumnal gold, Odessa and its
defenders were hit by the full might of the combined Romanian/German
artillery barrage and the third offensive against them in just four weeks.
Antonescu himself flew to the front to observe the assault, but he was not
joined by Ioanitiu. Romania's Chief of the General Staff, the second most

---

1   Hauffe's career and life ended disastrously in July 1944 when the Red Army encircled
    his XIII and C Corps at the Brody Salient in the Ukraine, due in large part to his
    own incompetence. He actually 'disappeared' during the final critical days, forcing his
    deputy, Wolfgang Lange, to try to salvage the situation. Captured by Soviet troops on
    22 July, Hauffe died later the same day when he stepped on a land mine.

senior officer in the armed forces behind the *Conducator*, Ioanitiu had landed at Baden in the Ukraine and promptly walked into a spinning aircraft propeller. He was killed instantly.

For the 4th, despite the presence of the *Conducator*, things did not go well. Yet again, waves of brave Romanian infantrymen stormed forward into the sights of the Soviet artillery and vicious local counter-attacks, and the results were the same. Antonescu's plan achieved nothing except long casualty lists, as the attack failed.

Then it was the Soviets' turn. Just after midnight on 23 September, the STAVKA decided to surprise the frustrated Romanians and landed the 2,000 men of the 3rd Marine Brigade on the shore behind them in a bold amphibious assault. As the Romanians scrambled to react, the Soviet 157th Rifle Division from inside the garrison also launched a frontal attack on the men of the 13th Infantry Division, which took 1,300 casualties in the subsequent fighting. The Romanians panicked and fell back in disarray, and it was only the intervention of *Luftwaffe* Stukas that stabilised the line. That was the end of the much-vaunted Antonescu offensive on Odessa. The major breakthrough would come only when von Manstein succeeded in reaching the Crimea a few days later on 29 September, forcing STAVKA finally to evacuate Odessa.[1] A covering attack was launched to conceal the preparations, and at the same time a withdrawal was started that would eventually save 86,000 of the Soviet garrison, as well as most of the heavy equipment still left in the city.

When Iacobici launched the Romanians' next offensive on 12 October, their Soviet enemy was already leaving. This time, no less than seventeen Romanian divisions were committed to the assault, and at last they began to make ground as the Soviets pulled back towards their embarkation point in the main port. Four days later it was all over. At 4.00 p.m., on 16 October, the tanks of the Eftimiu Detachment were positioned on Odessa's empty quayside as the last Soviet troopships sailed away over the horizon.[2] The battle for Odessa had finally ended after two months of relentless combat.

---

1 General Erich von Manstein had been commander of a panzer corps in the north on the Leningrad front, and had then been promoted to command the Eleventh Army. The previous commander, von Schobert, was killed when his personal Fiesler *Storch* (Stork), a two-seat light aircraft, accidentally landed in a minefield. His pilot also died.
2 The Eftimiu Detachment was formed after the Karpova disaster from the most battle-worthy sub-units of the 1st Romanian Panzer, and equipped with the surviving twenty R-2 tanks, a motorised infantry battalion, two battalions of artillery and an anti-tank gun company. The unit was named after its commander, Lieutenant-Colonel Ion Eftimiu, who went on to become Chief of Staff of the Cavalry Corps before ending the war as a Brigadier General in command of the 6th Cavalry Division.

For Romania, Odessa was a watershed. Overshadowed in the popular imagination by the cataclysmic encirclement battles of Uman and Kiev happening at the same time to the north, nevertheless Odessa was important as it was the only time in the Russo-German War that a significant military objective was assigned to, and taken by, an Axis ally. They had besieged and captured one of the Soviet Union's most important naval bases, inflicting more than 40,000 casualties on a skilled and well-trained enemy; destroyed a large number of artillery and anti-tank guns; and also shot down over 150 aircraft of the VVS. However, the cost had been brutal. One-third of Romania's entire field army in Russia became casualties at Odessa; 17,729 men were killed, 11,471 were missing and 63,345 wounded. Equipment losses were equally gargantuan. The 1st Panzer Division alone lost a whole battalion of tanks, almost 100 precious artillery pieces and some 1,200 machine-guns. Also, the Romanian Combat Air Grouping was decimated.

More than that, the 4th Army as a viable, effective combat formation was crippled and deprived of the leadership cadre that is absolutely necessary to fighting a war. At the beginning of August, there were 4,821 officers in the 4th Army. By 16 October, more than half of them were dead or wounded. They included Gheorghe Ionescu, commander of the 6th Artillery Regiment, killed by machine-gun fire whilst co-ordinating his gun line; Dumitru Orasanu, battle-group commander, killed in an airstrike; Caton Sorescu, commander of the 8th Vânători Regiment, died of wounds received while leading his men in an attack; and Alexandru Toparlan, commander of the 23rd Infantry Regiment, killed while leading a counter-attack. All four men were brigadiers. They were joined by others including Raul Halunga, Colonel of the 10th Vânători Regiment, lost to artillery fire, Colonel Mihail Nasta, second-in-command of the 21st Infantry Division, killed leading an assault with the 12th Dorobanti's, and by Lieutenant Commander Alexandru Popisteanu, 7th Fighter Group commander, shot down in combat over the city. It was not just senior officers; the army's divisions lost large numbers of junior commanders at platoon, company and battalion level. Men such as Second Lieutenant Marius Dumitrescu, killed along with most of his platoon as they made a bayonet charge at Karpova railway station. Dumitrescu had graduated at the top of his class at the Infantry Officers School a few months previously. Of that same class, one in four was killed or wounded at Odessa.

Partly in recognition of the extraordinary bravery involved in the siege, and undeniably also partly in an attempt to deflect from the horror of the losses, a large number of medals were awarded. All the officers mentioned above, and many more besides, were posthumously awarded the Order of

Michael the Brave, and victory parades were held in Chisinau and Bucharest. The Bucharest parade of 8 November was specifically held to celebrate the capture of Odessa. The German representative was Field Marshal Wilhelm Keitel, who congratulated Antonescu on the victory, but then rather spoiled it all by criticising the standard of the troops' foot drill! But this shower of medals and parades could not hide the damage the Odessa battle had done to the Romanians.

However, not all the casualties were as fatal as they at first appeared. More than a year later, in the chaotic aftermath of the Don fighting, Michele Lubescu, a Romanian engineer sergeant posted as 'missing believed killed' at Odessa, was arrested behind German lines by one Georgi Fiodorovich, a Cossack officer serving with the *Wehrmacht*. Lubescu's story was nothing if not bizarre. Recognised for his bravery at Odessa, he had decided he was finished with the war and, after falling in love with a local girl, had deserted. His unit, used to losing men all the time, had simply thought him killed by artillery, mines or partisans, and had listed him as such. Lubescu was now 'free' so to speak, but still needed to eat, so had hit on an ingenious plan. Gathering up a few other ex-4th Army deserters he had posed as nothing more than a simple sergeant leading a detachment of men back to their unit, and had begged food off rear area units. This plan worked well enough until the Don disaster, when it snowballed from being a matter of survival into a very profitable enterprise. With so many fleeing soldiers wandering around behind the lines, Lubescu had persuaded more like-minded souls to join him, so soon his little group was swelled with more Romanians, some Italians, Hungarians and even Germans, all fleeing the Soviet winter offensives. Travelling from depot to depot, Lubescu would report to the senior officer available, stating he had orders to gather up these individuals and take them to collection points for sorting and return to their original units. He had even obtained some 4th Army headed notepaper so he could forge written orders to that effect. Covered with official-looking stamps, no one had bothered to check the authenticity of the documents and had handed over to the enterprising sergeant everything he had asked for – usually a lot more rations than needed for the seventy men he actually had – and sent him on his way. The result was he and his men ate well, many of them for the first time in weeks, and Lubescu would then sell on the surplus food to hungry locals to make a handsome profit. But his luck had now run out. Taken to the German field police, his men were sent back to their respective armies, and Lubescu himself was handed over to the Romanian authorities for trial, with the following order posted:

Sergeant Lubescu is awaiting the verdict of the Romanian war court in Mariupol. He is also charged with usurping the rank of a commanding officer of a detachment.

One can only admire his audacity in the face of a war he and his country were increasingly having doubts about. All across Romania as the growing casualty lists from Odessa were announced, questions were beginning to be asked as to why they were still fighting the Soviets now that their occupied lands had been liberated. King Michael himself wrote:

Strategically Odessa was possibly an important point on the war map, but not on our war map, on the German one.

The young monarch was already uncertain about the war having visited Cernauti in July and seen the appalling lack of medical facilities for wounded soldiers. His revulsion was then reinforced when invited to stand next to a coldly insensitive Antonescu on a Bessarabian hill and watch as lines of advancing Romanian infantry were hideously cut down by Soviet artillery fire during a divisional attack. Now, after Odessa, he increasingly began to look for a way out of the war for his country.

Time for a Rethink

However, as the *Ostheer* swept eastwards after Operation Barbarossa, it seemed the Axis allies had indeed chosen the right side as stunning victory followed stunning victory, with millions of Soviets troops being taken prisoner – surely it was only a matter of time before the war was won and they could share in the triumph? But all was not as it appeared.

The storm clouds were gathering even before the battle of Odessa decimated the largest Axis allied contingent at the front. Casualties among all the nations' badly equipped and often poorly trained and poorly led contingents were mounting, and even the masses of Red Army men trudging into the misery and near-extinction of German captivity could not cover up the glaring deficiencies so apparent in the Romanian, Hungarian, Italian and Slovak formations. With no final victory in sight, the Axis countries began to pause for thought, and their commitment to the cause in the East dwindled.

Before the worst winter in 150 years hit the *Ostheer* in front of Moscow, the Hungarians had already brought their Mobile Corps and air wing back home, and the Slovaks had done the same to well over half of their original force. After Odessa, the Romanians followed suit to an extent and withdrew the remnants of their Combat Air Grouping and several divisions to rest and refit. One such was Nicolae Sova's proud Guards Division – it never returned to the front – and another was the 1st Romanian Panzer Division – which did go back. As it entrained for the long journey to the west, the only Axis allied armour then left on the whole Russian Front were the twelve PzKpfw 38(*t*) tanks of the Slovak Fast Division and a small number of tankettes and armoured cars.

As for the 1st Romanian Panzer Division itself, Operation Barbarossa had been the proverbial baptism of fire. Hurriedly created, with very little time for training, and with serious shortfalls in equipment and weaponry, the division had performed remarkably well. Since leaving Romania's Mechanised Training Centre in the ancient Saxon-Wallach city of Targoviste in the middle of June, it had driven more than 2,000 miles, mainly on dirt roads and tracks, the length and breadth of Romania and the southern Soviet Union. It had crossed two major rivers (one under fire) and a large number of smaller tributaries, acting as the spearhead for both the 3rd and 4th Armies. The unit's thrust south from Bukovina into Bessarabia during Operation Munich was a decisive and well-executed attack that had disrupted the defence of the otherwise excellent Soviet 9th Army, and paved the way for the liberation of Chisinau. Advancing forward into the Ukraine it had used classic *Blitzkrieg* tactics to good effect and had almost succeeded in taking Odessa by storm. But these victories had their price. Equipment-wise, the division lost 260 vehicles and a disastrous 111 tanks – almost the entire pre-Barbarossa complement. The division had not entered the war with sufficient tanks or motor transport as it was, but now the situation was far, far worse. It had also lost 1,300 men, including no fewer than 136 experienced, German-trained officers and NCOs. In Bucharest's eyes, what was needed was a complete re-organisation and refit that would end up keeping the division in Romania for nearly ten months.

The process commenced with a change of leadership at the very top. Having been reinstated in October for his second period in charge, Sion now suffered the humiliation of being demoted to second-in-command, as the tall and taciturn Radu Gherghe was brought in above him to lead the division. Ever the professional, Sion continued in this role until August when he was given command of the 15th Infantry Division in Dumitrescu's 3rd Army. As for Gherghe, he was an experienced combat leader, having taken the 18th Infantry Division through the Bessarabian and Odessa campaigns. Capable rather than spectacular, Gherghe would lead the 1st Romanian Panzer Division all the way through to the Don and beyond.

Before they went their separate ways, the two generals reviewed the division's performance during Operation Barbarossa, and they concluded above all else that the 1st Panzer Division needed dramatic improvements in two major areas: the first and most important of these was overall mobility. There simply were not enough trucks, tractors, motorcycles, in fact, not enough of every kind of motor vehicle. That had to change, and if it meant starving other divisions of their supposed allocations then so be it. Second, was the hitting power of the division: tanks. The French-built R-35 had proved to be too slow and unmanoeuverable for modern mechanised warfare, and it also lacked firepower, so the R-35-equipped 2nd Panzer Regiment was retired and became the division's training and replacement unit based in the homeland. From now on, the 1st would only have one panzer regiment in the line. While this made sense, it also significantly reduced the overall number of tanks in the unit; additionally, the only tank type the Romanians had in any number to man the now-single armoured regiment was the R-2. Already outdated at the launch of Operation Barbarossa, the R-2 was just about adequate, although the shock appearance of the formidable Soviet-built T-34 and the even heavier KV-series had highlighted the dreadful weaknesses in its armour protection and lack of firepower. The outbreak of war had accelerated design and weapons technology, and as a result, tanks were becoming larger and heavier with better firepower and thicker armour.

In 1939, the standard battle tank of most armies weighed around 8 or 9 tons and mounted a 37mm main gun. By the beginning of 1942, the average tank weighed 20 tons and was armed with a 75mm gun. However, by 1943, the average weight was 43 tons, with a mean gun calibre of 88mm.

It should be remembered as well that the Germans also had their won R-2s – the PzKpfw 35(*t*), the 6th Panzer Division alone went into Operation Barbarossa with 160 of the type in its inventory, and by October when the Romanian R-2 tanks were battling at Odessa, the 6th's divisional commander, General Wilhelm Ritter von Thoma, wrote of them:

The average distance driven by my PzKpfw 35(*t*)s is 12,500 kilometres. The situation regarding repairs to the PzKpfw 35(*t*) tanks is well-known, and that is that repairs can only be made by cannibalising other panzers because there are no longer any spare parts. This means that after the retrieval of the panzers that are scattered all over the surrounding terrain, a maximum of ten can actually be repaired out of the forty-one reported as requiring repair. In short, the vast majority of my PzKpfw 35(*t*)s can no longer be rebuilt or maintained as all the components are worn out. To be practical, perhaps the armoured hulls are still useable.[1]

The 6th Panzer Division would be sent to France to refit after the 1941 campaign, but then hurriedly recalled east to help spearhead the doomed relief attempt on Stalingrad.

The German response to this verdict was to accept the inevitable and retire their remaining PzKpfw 35(*t*)s, but this was not an option that was open to the Romanians, who had to fight on with what tanks they had available.

Gherghe and Sion did manage to convince Antonescu to ask Berlin to provide some armoured cars and slightly more advanced Czech-built PzKpfw 38(*t*)s from their war stocks, as well as the much more modern German-built PzKpfw III, and even the heavier PzKpfw IV, to supplement their obsolete R-2 tanks. The PzKpfw III mounted a 5cm gun, while the PzKpfw IV mounted the T-34 killing 7.5cm. However for the *Ostheer*, with almost 3,000 panzers lying rusting in the mud and snow of Russia, the requirements of the Romanians were low down the German priority list as the *Wehrmacht* desperately tried to rebuild its own panzer army almost from scratch. The word came back from Berlin – Romania will have to wait.

Like it or not, the obsolete and thinly armoured R-2, mounting the ineffective 37mm cannon, would still be the 1st Panzer Division's main tank for 1942.

Wilhelm von Appell's 22nd Panzer Division

As 1941 drew to a close, ahead of the Romanians on that long, long list of military priorities for the Third Reich was the creation of more panzer units. Among these was Wilhelm von Appell's newly formed 22nd Panzer Division – a unit which would, by complete accident, play a huge part in the future of the Axis on the Russian Front, and especially in that of the Romanian 1st Panzer Division.

Established in September 1941, the 22nd Panzer Division drew its officers from the Franconians of the 2nd Panzer Division, while its ranks were filled with Rhinelanders and Austrians. Allocated a forming-up area in occupied France, the division fared badly in the supply of new equipment with much

1 Von Thoma was a member of the *Reichswehr* (pre-war German Army) and a pioneer of tank warfare. He had a distinguished career in the *Panzerwaffe* (Tank Force) until he was captured by the Allies in North Africa on 4 November 1942 while commanding the famed *Deutsches Afrika Korps* (German Africa Corps).

of its allocation being vehicles captured from the French Army back in 1940.
Worse than this, though, were its panzers, as the unit was to have the dubious
distinction of being the last German panzer formation to be equipped with the
Czech-built PzKpfw 38(*t*). This was done despite the type's poor performance
in Operation Barbarossa, where a total of 772 were deployed (more than one in
five of the entire invasion strength). This after-action report from the Thuringian
1st Panzer Division stands as testimony to the shortcomings of the type:

> ... our companies opened fire at about eighty yards, but it was ineffective ...
> very soon we were facing each other at fifty to a hundred yards. A fantastic
> exchange of fire took place without any visible German success. The Russian
> tanks continued to advance, and all our armour-piercing shells simply bounced
> off them.

Needless to say, this did not bode well for the three PzKpfw 38(*t*) equipped
battalions of von Appell's 204th Panzer Regiment, nor its two regiments of
Panzergrenadiers, the 129th and the 140th, made up of two battalions each.
To give it some support, the division had several batteries of the legendary,
and very deadly, 88mm *Flugzeugabwehrkanone* (FlaK) in an anti-aircraft battalion. This gun, originally designed to fire at high-flying aircraft, soon became
an incredibly versatile weapon for German forces. Powerful and accurate, it
could destroy most enemy tanks at a range of over a mile.

Four months later, with the snows melting in the French countryside, the
division was still not ready for action, its latest operational assessment report
noting significant weaknesses in training, with not a single divisional-level
exercise having been held. Normally, in the German military this would
have meant the 22nd would be going nowhere, but January 1942 was not
what anyone would describe as a normal situation for the German Army.
Many of the men who had conquered Poland, parts of Scandinavia, the
Low Countries and France, then won the summer battles in Russia, were
now dead or lying in hospital. So at the end of February, the 22nd Panzer
Division was loaded onto railway wagons in France for the journey to the
East, and the forthcoming battles.

CHAPTER 4

THE DEATH OF THE OSTHEER
WINTER 1941–42

The winter of 1941–42 was to be a catastrophe for the *Ostheer* and Nazi Germany. It was a disaster of such magnitude that neither ever recovered. General Heinz Guderian, known as 'Fast Heinz' and father of the *Panzerwaffe*, stated at the time:

> Only he who saw the endless expanse of Russian snow during this winter of our misery, and felt the icy wind that blew across it, can truly judge the events that now occurred.

Believing that the Soviet Union would be defeated before any snow began to fall, the OKW had only ordered enough winter clothing for 20 per cent of the invasion force; they believed the campaign would be won by then, and only a limited number of men would be needed for mopping up and occupation duties. When this fantastical mirage dissolved, the *Wehrmacht* was left freezing in the open countryside on the outskirts of Moscow. More than 100,000 men were crippled with frostbite, with some 14,000 losing major limbs.

Guderian even reported that men died of the cold as they relieved themselves in the snow, their anuses freezing solid in the act of defecating.

Capitalising on this, the STAVKA threw every man available into massive counter-offensives that not only saved Moscow from capture, but almost caused the collapse of the entire invasion. With defeat staring him in the face, and against the urgings of his generals, Hitler ordered his men not to retreat but to stand fast in the snow – an order that without doubt saved the Germans from complete destruction, but in so doing created a dangerous precedent as he now considered himself a true military genius and his professional generals as inferior to his 'National Socialist zeal and inspiration'. To their eternal shame, some of those self-same generals agreed with him and would spend the next three years and more bowing to a military will that was at best amateurish and at worst downright murderously simplistic.

Filled with contempt for what he now saw as the failings of the army's senior command, Hitler sacked all three of his *Heeresgruppe Ost* (Army Group East) commanders von Leeb, von Bock and von Runstedt, although von Bock returned to take over *Heeresgruppe Sud* (Army Group South) when von Runstedt's successor, Walther von Reichenau, died of a sudden heart attack. Almost overnight, 100 years of military intellect was cast aside, and the cleansing was not confined to the Olympian heights of command either, it carried on down to officers like Hoepner and right on through to divisional level and even below. Along with the endless graves and sick troops in hospital beds, this was another serious blow to the future of the *Ostheer*.

The winter fighting was a true turning point for the Germans, and one that went on to affect the Axis allies. Hitler had always been involved in military decision making of course, but from the beginning of 1942 this meddling began to metamorphose into a level of micro-manaagement that became a handicap of enormous proportions for the Germans and the Axis, and would go on to play a major part in the eventual destruction of the *Ostheer*.

The year 1941 was, more than anything else, a year of lessons; for the Red Army, it was an *annus horribilis* that demonstrated to Stalin the need to take political interference out of most military decision making and rely on his professional officer corps, whereas Hitler took the exact opposite stance. Hitler, so long the consummate politician and orator, now saw himself increasingly as a military supremo instead, and politics took a back seat as his public appearances and speeches became fewer and fewer.[1]

Albert Speer and the arms race

Away from the power politics in the Reich Chancellory and the various military headquarters, the situation for the *Ostheer* improved marginally, as the spring thaw set in at the front. The snow melted and was then replaced by 'Rasputitsa', the almost quicksand-like Russian mud, which brought with it a desperately needed two-month lull in major operations for the exhausted Axis forces.

Far to the north, even the bloody fighting in the Demyansk Pocket came to a halt.

---

1   From 1933 onwards, when he was Chancellor, he made hundreds of public speeches per year. But in 1940, he made just seven.

The respite could not have come soon enough for the Germans, who had suffered so badly over the winter. The figures made grim reading for Hitler and his newly appointed Armaments Minister – the man responsible for replacing all the lost equipment – the architect Albert Speer. Nazi Germany was only ever geared up for a series of short, sharp campaigns and not a protracted war, and now that was exactly what Hitler was being told he had to expect. In short, the vast force that had been launched into the Soviet Union the previous summer was effectively gone. It had lost almost 80 per cent of its tracked vehicles, 50 per cent of its horse-drawn and wheeled vehicles and 40 per cent of its anti-tank guns. Even worse, the vital *Panzerwaffe* had been reduced from some 3,500 to just 160 fully operational panzers. It was not just the lack of weapons, either; even if they had been available, the Germans had nothing to fire, as ammunition supplies were down to just 33 per cent of the June 1941 level. In contrast, all of the Soviet factories dismantled in 1941 and shipped eastwards beyond the Urals were now in full production and supplying 250 million tonnes of munitions – more than four times the pre-Barbarossa amount.

All of this was a serious problem for Germany and its allies, but it was overshadowed by the one problem that was larger than all the rest combined – the desperate lack of manpower. By the end of February, some 400,000 Germans had been killed on the Russian Front since Barbarossa's launch, along with 836,000 wounded or sick and 46,000 missing, presumed dead. Almost 500,000 more had been taken prisoner and interned in Soviet forced labour camps. A German General Staff assessment of their 160 divisions in Russia after that first winter found that just eight were classed as being capable of any offensive action.

Even a country the size of Germany was not large enough to make up for losses on this scale. Soviet casualties had exceeded an astonishing 4.3 million men – in effect their entire pre-Operation Barbarossa field army in the west was lost – but the Soviet Union was a staggering forty-six times larger than Nazi Germany in terms of land, with a population of 190 million, and as 1941 came to a close Moscow could still conscript 9 million young men without running out of manpower. Such was the depth of available humanity that the Red Army was actually growing in size as 1942 dawned.

What to do in 1942

For the first time in the war, the all-conquering *Wehrmacht* had been stopped. Despite the victories at Kiev, Vyazma, Uman and elsewhere, the Soviet Union had not collapsed, and the OKW now had to prepare for a second year of campaigning in the East. The aim would be simple – attack, defeat the Red Army and finish the job. The issue was where, and with what?

The one person who would make these momentous decisions for his country sat brooding in the *Berghof*, his mountain-top villa at Berchtesgaden in the Bavarian Alps. The STAVKA, and most of Germany's senior officer corps for that matter, assumed Hitler would repeat Operation Typhoon and head straight for Moscow, the Soviet capital and epicentre of political power, as well as a massive transport hub and military-industrial complex. Take the Kremlin and the Soviet Union would crumble was the argument. It was not one that found favour with Hitler. Unlike his generals, he was not a product of the professional army staff system and instead had always relied on his 'unconventional genius' to guide his judgement. It was a 'genius' (many would say 'obsession' was a better description) that would increasingly become the greatest military asset that Stalin and the Allies possessed, and in the spring of 1942 Hitler's main bête noir was oil.

Then, as now, armies, air forces and navies consumed petroleum products in truly prodigious quantities. Ever since the advent of the Industrial Revolution, oil had been important for the military, but the increasingly mechanised nature of war meant that consumption by the combatants had increased tenfold in the two decades from 1918 to 1942. For the Allies, access to crude oil was not a serious problem. Both the US and the Soviet Union had vast reserves, and Britain had the Middle East. But the Axis was not in the same position. Germany had no large-scale oil deposits of its own, and so had no option but to find alternative sources before its carefully hoarded strategic reserves were exhausted. One such source was 'synthetic oil', usually produced from coal (a fuel Germany did have in abundance) at great expense and effort in only a few plants across the country. Germany, of course, had access to Romania's Ploesti oil fields, which supplied fuel directly to the *Ostheer*. However, Speer – rapidly proving himself an organiser of some brilliance as he completely overhauled Germany's war production – was candid with Hitler that as it stood, German oil reserves were running dangerously low, and would not be able to supply the country's needs beyond the next year. The architect-turned-industrial supremo had the figures to prove that even Romania could not supply what was needed, so Hitler's attention was drawn to the numerous oil wells, refineries and pumping stations at Grozny, Maikop and Baku in the Soviet Caucasus – modern-day Chechnya and Azerbaijan. These oil fields fed the mighty industrial production of southern Russia in the Volga valley and the Don basin, and to capture them would provide the *Wehrmacht* with all the fuel it would ever need, while at the same time depriving the Soviets.[1] What could the capture of Moscow offer in comparison to this black, shining prize? No, Hitler had no intention of becoming another Napoleon, sitting in a burning Kremlin realising he had accomplished nothing.

So, the die was cast and Hitler's mind made up; Nazi Germany's critical summer offensive of 1942 would be aimed at capturing the oil wells of the Caucasus. It was a bold decision that would totally wrong-foot the STAVKA and ultimately stretch the *Wehrmacht* way beyond its depleted capacity. The offensive – code-named *Fall Blau* (Case Blue) – would be confused in its objectives and under-resourced in its execution from the very start. Initially successful, hundreds of thousands of German and Axis troops would end up advancing into a vast openess, in a sector of the front where no decisive outcome was possible. Even as German and Austrian *Gebirgsjaeger* (Mountain Troops) conquered Mount Elbrus (Europe's highest peak in the Caucasus Mountains) and German armoured cars were positioned just 40 miles from the warm waters of the Caspian, the German Sixth Army would march on across the seemingly endless steppe to meet its destiny at Stalingrad. In the meantime, the Soviets would be pouring tonnes of concrete into the Caucasus well-heads to deny them to the Germans. The offensive would fail, and the *Ostheer*'s weaknesses would become obvious, with the Axis allies having to fill the gaps and commit no less than four entire armies to the venture – more than 750,000 men and the finest of their countries' military services. Far weaker than their German counterparts in terms of manpower, equipment, training and leadership, these armies nevertheless represented a monumental effort on behalf of their home nations, and to them would fall the task of guarding the flanks of Friedrich Paulus' Sixth Army fighting in Stalingrad. Positioned on the banks of the River Don north and south of the burning city, the situation was a disaster waiting to happen, and then, with Axis supply lines stretched to the limit, the Soviets would launch a series of well-planned, well-executed offensives that would encircle the Sixth Army, and in so doing annihilate the Axis forces of Italy, Hungary, Romania and Croatia. Hungary and Romania in particular would not recover militarily for the remainder of the war.

---

1 In 1942, total *Wehrmacht* oil consumption would be 7,305,000 tonnes. Maikop alone produced 2.5 million tonnes annually, while the Azeri fields around Baku produced an astonishing 24 million tonnes in 1942.

CHAPTER 5

HITLER'S CASE BLUE

The reasons for *Fall Blau* (Case Blue) were detailed on 5 April 1942 in 'Führer Directive No. 41':

> The winter battle in Russia is drawing to its close. The enemy has suffered very heavy losses in men and matériel. In his anxiety to exploit what seemed like initial successes he has spent, during this winter, the bulk of his reserves earmarked for later operations ... Therefore the aim of Case Blue is to destroy what manpower the Soviets have left for resistance and to deprive them as far as possible of their vital military-economic potential [author's note: i.e. oil].

The pitiful 'manpower the Soviets have left for resistance' in the southern Soviet Union totalled no less than twenty armies,[1] led by some of the best of the steadily rejuvenating Red Army – men such as Nikolai Vatutin and the half-Polish Konstantin Rokossovsky, both experts in armoured warfare, and Andrei Yeremenko, a master of planning. These commanders had learnt the hard lessons of 1941, as well as relearned Russia's traditionally most successful tactic against an invader – trade space for time, let your enemy over-extend himself and then strike back hard.

As for the Axis, Hitler's selection of objectives meant that it would be Army Group South which would be the *Ostheer*'s main point of effort in 1942. With von Runstedt sacked and his successor von Reichenau dead, Hitler was forced to recall Fedor von Bock to command the Army Group, a decision the dictator was uncomfortable with, knowing as he did the Field Marshal's critical

---

1 Eighty-three infantry and twenty cavalry divisions, plus an additional twelve infantry and nineteen armoured brigades; note, a Soviet Army approximately equated in size to a German Corps.

view of the way the Operation Barbarossa campaign had been mismanaged by Berlin:

> All along, I demanded of Army High Command the authority to strike down the enemy when he was wobbling. We could have finished the enemy last summer. We could have destroyed him completely. Last August, the road to Moscow was open; we could have entered the Bolshevik capital in triumph and in summery weather. The high military leadership of the Fatherland made a terrible mistake when it forced my Army Group to adopt a position of defence last August. Now all of us are paying for that mistake. (From von Bock's personal diary.)

Part-Russian on his mother's side, Moritz Albrecht Franz Friedrich Fedor von Bock was the archetypal straight-backed and aloof Prussian aristocrat. Nicknamed 'The Dier' on account of his belief that the greatest honour any soldier could perform for his country was to die in battle, the 62-year-old von Bock was an excellent operational tactician, but no strategic mastermind. His most often repeated line was:

> The ideal soldier fulfils his duty to the utmost, obeys without even thinking, thinks only when ordered to do so, and has as his only desire to die the honourable death of a soldier killed in action.

Aptly enough, he would become the only one of Hitler's Field Marshals to be killed by enemy fire when his car was strafed by an RAF fighter-bomber just a week before the war ended. His wife Mally and their only daughter were also in the car and died alongside him.

As it was, the Army Group von Bock took over had not suffered as badly in combat as his former Army Group Centre command, which was now under Hans von Kluge's leadership. Plus, with the decision made to strike at the Caucasus, it was Army Group South that became the main beneficiary of fresh reinforcements and new equipment. Tens of thousands of replacements poured in, along with fleets of trucks, trainloads of munitions and, best of all, hundreds of new tanks straight off the production lines. So strong did his command become that von Bock split it into two newly established 'mini-Army Groups': B in the north, commanded by the bespectacled aristocrat General Maximilian Maria Joseph Karl Gabriel Lamoral Reichsfreiherr von Weichs zu Glon (or von Weichs for short), which comprised the German troops of Friedrich Paulus' Sixth Army, Hans von Salmuth's Second Army;[1] and Hermann 'Papa' Hoth's excellent Fourth Panzer Army (the renamed Panzer Group 3). Army Group A in the south was led by the clear-thinking and sound-planning Bavarian Field Marshal Wilhelm List, and comprised the wholly German Eleventh and Seventeenth Armies, and the First Panzer Army (originally Panzer Group 1), commanded by Ewald von Kleist, an experienced panzer commander though not in Guderian's class. While in Erich von Manstein, as head of the Eleventh Army, Field Marshall List probably had Nazi Germany's greatest wartime general. He also had a new senior Romanian subordinate, with Constantin Constantinescu-Claps replacing Iacobici at 4th Army, as the latter went home to head the Romanian General Staff.

Army Group South – the men and the kit

By June, von Bock had under his command 1 million men, some 1,500 tanks and more than 1,600 aircraft – by far the most powerful force Nazi Germany possessed anywhere. But a force with some major flaws.

Despite the popular image of the *Wehrmacht* being primarily a panzer force, in reality its backbone throughout the war was its infantry – the famous *Landsers*. These men, the German equivalent of the British 'Tommy', French 'Poilu' and Russian 'Ivan', recruited from small nondescript towns and villages into their local division, given superb, in-depth training, equipped with tried and tested weapons, and commanded by professional, long-serving officers and NCOs, were the foundation upon which all the victories of 1940 and 1941 had been built. For Case Blue to work, Germany needed them in prime condition. The recruiters had been busy and those self-same infantry divisions had been brought back up to strength after the winter fighting, but many of the new boys had received barely two months' training in contrast to the six to nine of their predecessors. Just as bad, technical specialists were in desperately short supply, especially radio signallers, drivers of all kinds and artillery gunners. Because of continued fighting on the frontline, a bare third of the Army Group's divisions had been able to come out of the line to the designated rehabilitation area around Dnepropetrovsk to integrate the new men and carry out much-needed follow-on training.[2] Army Group Centre's chosen areas were near Orsha, Minsk,

---

1 The balding von Salmuth would go on to command the Fifteenth Army in France on D-Day; he was portrayed in the 1962 film *The Longest Day* by the well-known German actor Ernst Schröder playing cards in his chateau headquarters as the Allies landed.

2 Dnepropetrovsk had been selected as it had been a vast pre-war Red Army training area, and so had the necessary facilities that included barracks, ranges and vehicle depots.

Gomel and Bryansk, while Army Group North, as the *Ostheer's* poor relation, was allowed so little reconstitution, no recuperation area was even designated. Only the handful of divisions earmarked for the spearhead had received new troop transports,[1] light vehicles and prime movers, and that had been possible only by stripping almost every infantry division in Army Groups Centre and North of anything motorised, as well as requisitioning vehicles from as far away as the Atlantic coastal defence units in distant France. Notwithstanding this intense scavenging, the Army Group's eyes and ears, its specially trained reconnaissance battalions, were now overwhelmingly mounted on bicycles instead of motorbikes, armoured cars and trucks, and there were not even enough horses available despite occupied Europe's stables, fields and paddocks being emptied. The mass of follow-on formations would not have even this level of mobility and so would be strictly foot-borne and, therefore, slow and cumbersome.

As for the *Luftwaffe*, Hitler's order of the previous December, allocating the army additional resources at the expense of the navy and air force, was beginning to make a real impact. Spread thin across Russia, occupied Europe, North Africa, the Mediterranean and Home Defence, the Germans struggled to concentrate overwhelming air power anywhere, a situation not made easier by the growing lack of high-octane aviation fuel so especially important for fighter groups.

Worrying in the extreme though all this was, von Bock's biggest headache was with the supposed jewel in his crown: his mighty panzer divisions.

Where are the panzers?

The old Panzer Groups of Operation Barbarossa were vast armadas of hard-hitting armoured mobility. Designed to exploit breakthroughs with rapier-like speed, the panzers would evade direct combat if possible, aiming instead to get behind a more ponderous enemy and shatter his ability to resist by crushing his logistics and command and control. This was the essence of panzer warfare, and wherever it had been allowed to operate as such, it had triumphed. However, Hitler and many of his senior generals had never been entirely comfortable with the whole idea, preferring instead the First World War surety of mass infantry armies supported by thundering artillery. Indeed, in its own Directive No.41 in support of Case Blue, the OKW demonstrated its inability and unwillingness to grasp the fundamentals of modern tank warfare by issuing the following instructions:

---

1   A staggering 75,000 lorries had been lost in the winter fighting to the mud, snow, ice and enemy action, but only a meagre 7,500 new vehicles had been sent East as replacements; even the defeated French Army's vast vehicle parks were now empty.

It must not happen that, by advancing too quickly and too far, armoured and
motorised formations lose connection with the infantry following them; or
that they themselves lose the opportunity of supporting the hard-pressed, for-
ward-fighting infantry...

This mystifying ignorance on OKW's behalf of what their own military had
more or less created had been reinforced by the unexpected arrival of the
superb Soviet T-34 and KV-1 tanks the previous summer. The Soviet tanks,
excellent as they were, had not defeated the invasion for Stalin, but they had
fed the suspicions of the 'panzer doubters' back in Berlin and led in no small
way to a disastrous watering down of the one arm that had the potential to
win the war for Germany. For Hoth's and von Kleist's armies, that meant
diluting them down from being 'panzer-heavy' to almost 'panzer-light'.
Von Kleist, for example, went into the summer campaign leading a mighty
fifteen divisions, of which only three were panzer formations alongside
a single motorised division; the rest were standard infantry units – seven
German and four Romanian. By contrast, and seemingly for no reason, Hoth
had only four divisions in total (one panzer, one motorised and two infantry). Originally envisaged as having in excess of 200 panzers each, when Case
Blue commenced, von Bock's armoured fists had an average of just 126, with
the motorised units an additional 50 each. The majority of the panzers were
PzKpfw III and PzKpfw IVs, with only 133 of the latter mounting the latest
long-barrelled 7.5cm gun capable of defeating a T-34. Plus, despite an OKW
decision to retire them as obsolete, there was still a good number of PzKpfw
38(*t*) tanks, mainly in the newly established 22nd Panzer Division.

The other scarcity was even more vital than tanks: fuel. Proving the point
of the offensive, the Germans were unable to supply enough to allow their
panzers unlimited freedom of movement. Famous British military theorist
and writer of the time Basil Liddell-Hart said of Case Blue:

Shortage of fuel was the decisive handicap in the advance ... the panzer divisions were sometimes at a standstill for days on end awaiting fresh supplies.

In fact, from the outset, petrol was effectively rationed, and as the situation
worsened, Berlin desperately waited to hear that the Caucasus oilfields had
finally been reached.

It was these undeniable facts that worried the German planners of Case
Blue to no end – what to do, what to do?

First, they needed a plan to defeat the Red Army, and in principle that part was fairly simple: Hoth and von Salmuth would head east from Kursk to the city of Voronezh on the River Don and form the hard northern shoulder of the offensive. Paulus would then attack from Kharkov to reach the adjoining Volga River at the sprawling industrial city of Stalingrad – although the plan *did not* stipulate that the city was to be captured. Von Kleist would then swing into action and head south to the Caucasus, and on the way, Army Group South would annihilate the Soviet armies between the Don and Donetz rivers in a series of huge pincer movements.

In practice, it was anything but simple; the distances that had to be covered were epic – hundreds upon hundreds of miles of open, grassy steppe stretching away to the snow-capped fastnesses of the Caucasus Mountains and the warm, blue waters of the Caspian Sea. One of the *Landsers* wrote in his diary of the vast tinder-dry emptiness of it all:

> On this endless steppe there are no forests to give protection from aircraft and, above all, no water for the men and horses.

The Soviets outnumbered the Germans three to one, had as many aircraft and twice as many tanks and were getting stronger as their own – and US – factories produced equipment for them at quite prodigious rates, the quality of which was also improving. A veteran German *Fallschirmjäger* (Paratrooper), Wolfgang Langer, said of the captured Russian-manufactured 8cm mortars his company now used:

> … it had a weaker barrel thickness than our 8cm equivalent, but was longer and could shoot four to five hundred metres farther than our own pieces. We had Russian ammunition for these mortars, but the shells were no good: misfires and drop shorts were common so we used German ammunition … These Russian weapons were especially suited for hitting point targets. They always achieved a bullseye after the third or fourth shot.

The military delusions that were to hamper Nazi Germany so sorely in the latter years of the war had not clouded Berlin's judgement quite yet, and the Reich Chancellory and Bendlerstrasse[1] both knew that even six reasonably refreshed German armies were not enough to deliver the plan. Berlin needed an answer, and that answer was 'more men' – hundreds of thousands more – and Hitler thought he knew where to get them: his Axis allies.

---

1 Headquarters of the German Army General Staff in Berlin.

Passing round the begging bowl to the Axis

Even as the Soviet counter-offensives of the winter had begun to run out of steam, that caricature of empty-headed obedience and Prussian arrogance, Wilhelm Keitel, had been dispatched to Bucharest and Budapest on a begging mission. His goal was nothing less than a staggering fifty-two divisions from Germany's allies. The Romanians were expected to deliver the lion's share, twenty-seven in total, to increase the strength of their 3rd and 4th Armies at the front, and with some gentle persuasion, the Germans thought they could be relied on to do the right thing. As for the hitherto reluctant Horthy, Keitel was not beneath using some unsubtle arm-twisting to get what he wanted from Budapest; namely, another thirteen divisions.

But it was not just anybody that the monocled Keitel sought. He had certain men in particular in mind, and first among them was the Romanian military's primary formation: the 1st Romanian Panzer Division.

The 1st Romanian Panzer in 1942

Spring and early summer 1942 were a time of frenetic activity for the Romanian tank crews as they strove to learn the lessons of Operation Barbarossa, rebuild their division and replace their manpower and equipment losses. New recruits were drafted in to fill the ranks, but it was a tough task to train them in the many and varied technical roles the division demanded; just as the Germans were struggling with a lack of drivers, engineers, radio operators and gunners, so were their Romanian comrades. Suitably qualified officers and NCOs were also in short supply, with every division at the front desparate for replacements. Gherghe and his leadership team ploughed on though, playing on the elite nature of the unit as the kingdom's only armoured formation, and this approach succeeded in bringing in enough men to take the unit back to an all-up strength of 13,000.

With the 2nd Panzer Regiment relegated to a training and replacement role, Emilian Ionescu's two battalions of tanks were left as the division's only armoured strike force. Each battalion had three companies of R-2 tanks, many of them recovered from the battlefield and reconditioned. Plus an additional twenty-six new R-2s had arrived, sent directly from the Czech factory. In theory, this was intended to compensate for the massive losses of 1941, although serious consideration was also given to utilising the enormous stocks of captured Soviet armour. Many of these tanks, and especially the much-prized T-34, ended up filling the gaps in German panzer divisions and rear-area security units all the way to the Balkans and farther west. As it was, the government, keen as all governments throughout history to put the best possible spin on the numbers, classified almost anything with tracks as armoured fighting vehicles (AFVs) and therefore part of the 1st Romanian Panzer. This included large numbers of woefully obsolete tankettes and even gun tractors, alongside large numbers of useless hulks and totally unserviceable wrecks. The end result was to artificially inflate Romania's supposed armoured strength by mid-1942 to almost 800, a very respectable number indeed given that Germany was struggling to reach 3,000 at the same time. The reality, as ever, was far, far different. Ready to head east, Ionescu actually only had 109 R-2s and 2 ex–Red Army tanks. His fellow colonels, Constantin Nistor of the 3rd and Gheorghe Popescu of the 4th *Vânători* motorised infantry regiments respectively, mustered two battalions each, with the majority of men being truck-borne infantry and equipped, for once, with a reasonable number of automatic weapons – some 340 machine-guns, of which 61 were heavy calibre.[1] The division's heavy weapons were in the 1st Motorised Artillery Regiment, which comprised thirty-six pieces - twenty-four light 100mm field howitzers and twelve excellent 105mm field guns. The latter was the standard field gun of the *Ostheer*, with an effective range of more than 7 miles, and some 10,000 were produced during the war. Additional firepower was provided by Colonel Otto Benedict's 'Motorised Special Weapons Group' – a Romanian invention bringing together a Heavy Weapons Battalion (which included twenty anti-aircraft pieces and fifty-two 47mm anti-tank guns) – and Constantin Husărescu's Recce Battalion with its two motorcycle companies. A motorised pioneer battalion, some traffic police, service companies and all the other various specialist troops for an armoured unit made up the balance.

Overall, the division was in reasonable shape given the circumstances. Romanian industry had not taken a leap forward and suddenly flooded the gates with modern tanks, heavy weapons and fleets of motorised transport, but the 1st Panzer did still have some 1,400 vehicles at a time when the standard allocation for a Romanian field division was just 202 (and the actual average was 50 per cent of that). The major weaknesses now were in the overall numbers and quality of artillery and anti-tank guns and, crucially, tanks. It was a subject that Gherghe and his fellow Romanian commanders would raise with their German allies again and again as they advanced east in the heat of the July sunshine.

---

1   In German panzer and panzergrenadier divisions, by this stage of the war, at least one battalion of infantry was carried in armoured half-tracks, but the Romanian forces had only eight of the ubiquitous SdKfz 251.

Hungary

When Antonescu agreed to the renewed commitment of the reinforced 3rd and 4th Armies to the offensive and the re-introduction of the 1st Panzer, Miklos Horthy was put in an impossible position.

The *Honved* had lost a lot of hard-to-replace equipment the previous summer, and Hungarian industry was struggling to fill the gaps. The army was also being slowly restructured, a large part of which was the redesignation of twenty-six infantry brigades as new 'light' divisions. This had the effect of doubling its size on paper but did little to increase its overall numbers or effectiveness. Each light division did indeed have its manpower increased from around 6,500 up to 10,000, though this was achievable only with the addition of raw recruits and over-age reservists, and these men were then handed barely half the automatic weapons of a standard German infantry division and only about a third of its artillery (a paltry twenty-four outdated Skoda and Rheinmetall artillery pieces). Motor vehicles were almost non-existent, as were anti-tank weapons, the latter being made up of a few anti-tank rifles that were totally useless against the T-34. Horthy knew all this and had absolutely no military ambition beyond defending Northern Transylvania against his Romanian neighbours, but he feared Hitler would force him to hand the much-prized province back to Bucharest for services rendered unless Hungary entered the fight. As a result, on 22 January 1942, he reluctantly signed the order to send one of his country's three armies to Russia: the Budapest-headquartered 2nd Army.

Weak though the *Honved* was, the 2nd Army was the very best it could produce. Nine of the new light divisions were organised into three Corps: III Corps with the 6th, 7th and 9th Divisions; IV Corps with the 10th, 12th and 13th; and VII Corps with the 19th, 20th and 23rd. These troops made up the bulk of the army, but its real combat power came in the form of Hungary's new panzer division: Lajos Veress' 1st Hungarian Armoured Field Division.[1] The experience of the Mobile Army Corps in the Soviet Union's wide-open

---

1 Veress was a Szekely, an ethnic minority closely related to the *Magyars*. In 1944, he would command the 2nd Army before being imprisoned by the Germans on suspicion of being involved in trying to surrender his forces to the Soviets. He survived, only to be sentenced to death by the communist People's Tribunal in the spring of 1947 on charges of conspiracy. The sentence was commuted to life imprisonment, and nine years later, the Hungarian Revolution allowed him to escape prison and flee the country. A staunch critic of communist repression in his homeland, Veress served as Chairman of the World Federation of Hungarian Freedom Fighters from 1958 until his death in London in 1976 at the age of 87.

spaces during Operation Barbarossa proved to the Hungarian General Staff that a greater effort was needed in the field of armoured warfare, and a spur was added by Hitler's demands on his allies to supply more troops for the forthcoming summer offensive. With the 2nd Armoured Division based at home waiting for the long-expected Turan tanks to arrive, the Hungarians scrabbled for a response and ended up assembling a makeshift formation based on their existing 1st Motorised Brigade and the German/Czech tanks that had been procured before the war. Officially established on 4 March 1942, the *1st Panceloshádsztalynak* (1st Hungarian Armoured Field Division) was only ever intended to bridge the gap before the Turan-equipped 1st and 2nd Armoured Divisions took their places in the line. As it turned out, the 1st Armoured Field became very much the Hungarian version of the 1st Romanian Panzer Division, and the new unit ended up suffering from the same flaws as its loathed 'sister' formation, and just like its Romanian equivalent, it would also fail to save the day on the Don and would instead be destroyed.

First and foremost among its faults was the curse of all the Axis allies: lack of transport. Mobility was as sadly lacking in the ad hoc division as it was across the *Honved*, with horses rather than motor vehicles being in relative abundance. Command and control from Colonel General Lajos Veress down was not of the highest calibre, with the cadre of officers and NCOs from the 1st Motorised Brigade being career soldiers but not mobile warfare experts, whilst most of the rank and file they led were barely trained. In fact, the majority of men were conscripts who had received a mere eight weeks' basic training. This was just about enough time to master the necessities of military life but nowhere near enough to become ingrained with the doctrine, skills and specialities that a modern panzer division demanded. As for Lajos von Dalnoki Veress, the 53-year-old aristocrat had begun the war leading a brigade of cavalry in the invasion of Yugoslavia before being appointed as the commander-to-be of the 2nd Armoured Division as it waited for its tanks in Hungary. Transferred over in something of a hurry to take charge of the newly formed 1st Armoured Field, he was a hardworking, respectable officer, but not in the class of Rommel or Guderian, and he proved unable to completely grasp mechanised warfare and turn his command into a truly effective elite force. For example, one issue with which the new division had to contend, as indeed did the whole *Honved*, was the dubious loyalty of some of its men, having absorbed a good number of ethnic Romanians, Slovaks and even Ukrainians from its re-acquired territories. Veress did not inspire a *corps d'esprit*, coupled with innovative programmes of integration, that would mould his multi-ethnic companies into deadly units bound together by shared experience and faith in their leaders. Instead, he simply adopted the same solution as every other *Honved* formation, which was to weed out those considered a potential threat and place them in unarmed Labour Service Companies tasked with carrying out construction and maintenance work in the rear areas.

Last, and definitely not the least, of its problems was the division's size – or rather lack of it. All of the formation's sub-units were far smaller than their counterparts in German panzer units, or even in the Romanian 1st Panzer Division; true, there were battalions of engineers, signallers and support troops, but only three motorised infantry and two artillery battalions equipped with 105mm guns (i.e., 50 per cent of what other units had). Mortars and machine-guns were in short supply, and the divisions entire anti-tank capability was a single company armed with just four 50mm guns and a small number of 20mm anti-tank rifles that were barely effective against armoured cars, let alone against modern Soviet tanks. As for the all-important armoured capability – the 30th Tank Regiment – its commanding officer, Colonel Endre Zádor, had just six companies of tanks in two battalions equipped with seventy-two of the Czech-built PzKpfw 38(t) and twenty-two German-built Pzkpfw I.[1] The latter was an obsolete machine-gun carrier, while the former was armed with the 37mm gun that had proven to be hopelessly inadequate against the T-34 and KV-1 during ealier combat. This mediocre force was supplemented by twenty-two Toldi light tanks and some more Hungarian-manufactured vehicles – fourteen 39M Csaba armoured scout cars and twelve 40M Nimrod anti-aircraft tanks in the reconnaissance and anti-aircraft battalions. The 39M Csaba was lightly armoured and mounted an 8mm machine-gun and a 20mm cannon. The 40M Nimrod was a Hungarian copy of the Landsverk L-62 built by the same Ganz works in Budapest that was now responsible for producing some of the long-awaited Turan tanks. Armed with 40mm Bofors cannon, the 135 Nimrods produced were effective but never battle winners.

In total, the entire division could muster some 100 armoured fighting vehicles, which meant the 1st Hungarian was half the size of its German panzer equivalent and two-thirds the size of the 1st Romanian Panzer Division. Given inevitable losses, repairs and breakdowns, a figure of 50 per cent operationally effective at any one time was about the norm for all

---

1 Zádor would survive the fighting, commanding the newly established 2nd Hungarian Armoured Division from 1944 until the end of war, including in the tough tank battles around Székesfehérvár in Hungary in early 1945.

mobile formations. With such a low starting point, Veress' division was going to find it very hard indeed to take on the role of a credible armoured force at the front.

Nevertheless, just as with the 1st Romanian Panzer, the 1st Hungarian Armoured Field was the very zenith of the *Magyar* war effort in the East. Almost 15,000 men strong, the division had first call on the *Honved's* slender resources of transport and artillery, which enabled it to fully motorise an entire infantry regiment, plus the reconnaissance and anti-aircraft battalions. As for heavy weapons, the force was under-equipped, with nothing newer than its old 105mm guns and barely twenty mortars.[1] As for panzers, with the Turan still not ready (although an order for seventy more was placed in anticipation), Veress would rely on the ex-German, Czech-built tanks that were the mainstay of the division's armoured force. True, the PzKpfw 38(*t*) was more heavily protected than the Romanian-built R-2, but it still only mounted a 37mm gun. In a twist of fate, the 40M Nimrod mounted the heaviest-calibre main armament in the division, but its 40mm Bofors gun was designed as an anti-aircraft weapon rather than to penetrate Soviet tank armour.

Overall, the 2nd Army was an impressive accomplishment. With a complement of 209,000 men, it made up over half of Hungary's total mobilised manpower of 350,000. Given relative population sizes, the corresponding force from Great Britain would have been no fewer than 1 million men. However, nothing could dispel the sense of foreboding among its ranks as they departed for war. One of the troopers described those feelings in his diary as they headed for the Soviet Union:

> In the name of God we are leaving for the blood-soaked land of Russia, and we ask him to return us safe and sound and bring us final victory! Mother of God guarding over Hungary, pray for us and defend us from all sins and disasters! Saint Stephen, raise your miraculous right hand over us and plead for your orphan people. Amen.
>
> At 6.40 a.m. people fall silent, and amid the sad sounds of bugles we pull out [author's note: from Budapest central railway station]. We are going off with sadness and confidence in future victory.
>
> We pass through Slovakia, then Poland. Everywhere people are cultivating their land but the traces of war can be seen on their faces. They stand like a wall

---

1 Even though the same calibre as the standard field-guns in service with the *Ostheer* and Romanians, the Hungarian 105mm was far less potent, being slower to load and with far less range; also, the shells had less explosive power.

alongside the track, begging for bread. Children call to us all the time; 'A small piece of bread!' but if someone throws a hunk they begin to fight over it. (From the diary of Corporal Istvan Balogh.)

Balogh was a combat soldier, one of what is termed a unit's 'bayonet strength'. He and his type, however, only constituted some 50 per cent of the overall manpower in the 2nd, while the rest were service troops – important posts, of course, but of limited value during the crisis that would engulf them less than a year later.

As it was, the best of Hungary's war effort was entrusted to the 58-year-old Gustáv Vitéz Jány, one of his country's most experienced and respected generals, responsible for many years for training the army's officer corps as Commandant of the prestigious Ludovica Academy, Hungary's equivalent to Britain's Sandhurst and West Point in the USA. He was also a member of the 7 per cent of Hungary's pre-war population that were German in ethnic origin. Traditionally, Hungary drew much of its officer class from this group, but in the nationalist atmosphere of the 1920s and 1930s, many of these men thought it prudent to 'Magyarise' their names to ease future promotion. Gustav Hautzinger was one such individual, and overnight he became Gustáv Jány.

Axis air power

It was not just boots on the ground and tanks and artillery that made up the Axis fighting forces in the East that summer; it was also air power. In 1941, all of the Axis countries had contributed at least something to the air armadas of Operation Barbarossa with a miscellany of aircraft types – German, Czech, Italian, Polish and even British-built types – but attrition, mostly through accidents and poor maintenance rather than aerial fighting, had forced almost all of them to be withdrawn over the winter. Now, with the skies clearing and German industry increasing production, the allies were asked to step up once again and were supplied with at least some modern German and Italian aircraft.

Romania headed the list, unsurprisingly, with the 100-plus aircraft of the 1st Romanian Air Corps – Messerschmitt Bf-109E and Heinkel He-112 fighters, Junkers Ju-88, Heinkel He-111 and Italian Savoia-Marchetti SM-79 medium bombers and even a number of the legendary Junkers Ju-87 Stuka dive-bombers.

The Slovaks also received twenty ex-*Luftwaffe* Bf-109E fighters recently retired from service in North Africa that now became their air force in Russia.

The Hungarians were once again Romania's poor relations, so while the air brigade they sent east in June totalled some 100 aircraft, it was made up mainly of inferior Italian types such as the Reggiane Re2000 fighter and Caproni Ca135 bomber, alongside a few Heinkel He-111s. Horthy tried to arrange licensed production of the Messerschmitt Bf-109 and the twin-engined Me-210, but as ever, German insistence on pre-payment slowed the deal, and aircraft did not start rolling off the production lines until mid-1943.

The *Regia Aeronautica* (Italian Air Force) had suffered appalling losses in 1941 over North Africa as the RAF's excellent Desert Air Force shot their aircraft from the sky. Aircraft production in Italy could not produce sufficient replacement machines, and from the beginning of 1942, Italian air power was in rapid decline. Spare parts were difficult to locate and fuel even harder to obtain as Rome's crumbling war economy stumbled blindly on. The result was that Italian air power in Russia diminished from almost 100 aircraft operational in 1941 to barely sixty ready for the 1942 offensive.

Bulgaria still resolutely refused to send troops or aircraft into the Soviet Union and was instead tasked with protecting the strategically important Ploesti oilfields. To achieve this task against Operation Tidal Wave, (the US-led air offensive against Axis oilfields), the Germans supplied Bulgaria with 100 captured French-built Dewoitine D-520 fighter aircraft and forty-eight Messerschmitt Bf-109G. The results were less than spectacular; in the first major attack on 1 August 1943, only three US Air Force (USAAF) B-24 Liberator bombers were shot down by Bulgarian fighters out of a total of fifty-four aircraft lost in the raid.

The air contribution by the Axis allies in 1942 was approximately the same in number to 1941 but higher in quality, with the majority of the 300 or so aircraft being far more modern German types. These also had the advantage of common servicing and maintenance with those in service with the *Luftwaffe*.

Italy

Rather oddly, the one major ally Hitler was loath to approach was in fact his oldest: Fascist Italy. Believing – rightly, as it happened – that Italy's military strength was seriously depleted, Hitler would have preferred Mussolini to concentrate all his efforts on containing the British in the Mediterranean. But such was the need in Russia that he was forced to change his mind, and he despatched the head of the *Luftwaffe*, Reichsmarshall Hermann Goering, to plead the case. Not that Goering was a man much given to pleading.

A glutton and cocaine addict, as well as a voracious art thief and avid hunter, Ciano wrote of his arrival in Rome:

> As usual he is bloated and overbearing ... at the station he wore a great sable coat, something between what motorists wore in 1906 and what a high-grade prostitute wears to the opera.

Between Goering's trip and a return invitation to *Il Duce* to Salzburg, the deal was done. Italy would back Case Blue. The question was: with what?

By the beginning of 1942, the Italian army and navy, just like its air force, were reeling from a succession of hammer blows. Losses at Taranto and Cape Matapan had crippled the fleet, and while the British struggled to handle Rommel in the desert, they positively relished facing his Axis ally, launching lightning campaigns that filled the Eighth Army's prisoner-of-war cages to overflowing with bedraggled and bewildered Italian soldiers. Between December 1940 and the final Axis surrender in Tunisia in May 1943, the Italians lost a catastrophic twenty-seven divisions in North Africa. Rome tried to fill the gaps by raising twenty new divisions, but Mussolini seemed incapable of either seeing the huge deficiencies in his country's ability to arm, train and equip such a force or, and even more importantly, the strategic imperative of concentrating his limited military power on one decisive front. That front was clearly North Africa, but *Il Duce* refused to accept reality and spread his troops all over the place, from Italy to southern France, Corsica, Croatia and the Greek islands. By the time Italy changed sides in autumn of 1943, it still had more than 1.5 million men under arms in eighty-three divisions, with thirty-two in central and southern Italy, Sardinia and Corsica; thirty-one in the Balkans and the Greek islands; and twenty in northern Italy and southern France.

By June 1942 in Russia, Giovanni Messe's three-division CSIR had already been at the front for ten months, and the entire corps was in a parlous state. The men's uniforms were in rags, much of their equipment had been lost, and their boots and gun barrels were worn thin. Morale was fragile, and as far as Messe was concerned, it was time to go home. Instead, having seceded to Berlin's entreaties, the bombastic Fascist dictator decreed that, instead, significant reinforcements would be sent to create a new force – the grandly titled *Armata Italiana in Russia* (Italian Army in Russia – ARMIR), also known as the Italian 8th Army. Messe complained in person to Mussolini that the planned establishment of the ARMIR was a mistake, citing:

Our meagre, antiquated armaments, the absolute lack of suitable armoured vehicles, the insufficient number of trucks, the grave problems of transport and supply, made more difficult by the lack of understanding and unyielding selfishness of the Germans, will create problems for the army that are really insoluble.

The dictator sacked his less than enthusiastic general with a response that was the epitome of murderous buffoonery:

Dear Messe, at the table of peace the two hundred thousand men of the ARMIR will weigh a lot more than the sixty thousand of the CSIR. The decision has been made.

Thus the Torino, Pasubio and Duca d'Aosta divisions would now be joined by a further four infantry divisions (the 2nd Sforzesca, the 3rd Ravenna, the 5th Cosseria and the 156th Vicenza) and three elite mountain divisions from the famed *Alpini* (the 2nd Tridentina, the 3rd Julia and the 4th Cuneense). The new army was organised into three corps: the XXXV, comprising the original CSIR divisions; the II Corps, with the northern Italian Sforzesca, Ravenna and Cosseria; and, finally, the treasured *Alpini* Corps, with the Vicenza in reserve. In addition, in line with normal practice, three Fascist Blackshirt volunteer legions were also assigned to the 8th, as was the Croat Light Transport Brigade, the latter now having completed final training. As a 'just in case' measure, the OKW placed the Italians with the Seventeenth Army, commanded by Richard Ruoff, to try to ensure that it didn't get in too much trouble.

This huge infusion of fresh troops equalled Hungary's commitment in manpower terms, with the 8th Army numbering around 220,000 men, and exceeded it in equipment, with some 1,000 artillery pieces and 420 mortars providing the heavy weaponry, as well as 17,000 vehicles and 25,000 horses (plus 12,000 mules for the *Alpini*) for transport. As with the CSIR, on paper the 8th Army was impressive enough, but it was an edifice built on sand. The old flaws were still there for anyone with eyes to see – the largest anti-tank guns they had were the barely adequate 47mm type, meaning the men would be forced to rely on little more than hand-grenades to attack Soviet tanks, and those grenades were still faulty, either exploding early or not exploding at all. Most of the mortars were the 45mm Brixia type with poor range, and each infantry division had only twelve 100mm howitzers; the rest were the much smaller 75mm type (the *Alpini* did not even have the howitzers but were equipped with light mountain guns carried on mules). The new troops brought no armour with them, although, almost in embarrassment, the Germans did reinforce Paolo Tarnassi's battalion with twelve modern PzKpfw IV tanks mounting the 7.5cm gun and a small number of captured Soviet tanks.

With Messe recalled home, *Il Duce* cast around for a more malleable commander for his Russian folly and settled on Italo Gariboldi, whose own son, coincidentally, was a serving officer in the Tridentina's 5th *Alpini* Regiment. Already 63 years old when he was handed command, Gariboldi had had a steady, if less than stellar, career, finally ending up as Italy's Governor General of Libya during the desert fighting. Personally brave, like so many of Italy's senior officers, he was far too slow-witted to make sense of modern, mechanised warfare, and his appointment confirmed the general view of the ARMIR as an infantry force better suited to the First World War.

At last, though, OKW had something approaching the force its planners said Case Blue needed. Standing alongside the 1 million Germans in von Bock's force were now about 700,000 Romanians, Hungarians, Italians, Slovaks and Croats. Crucially, almost every single tank the Axis allies possessed (except Italy which still had three armoured divisions in North Africa) took its place in the line – some 300 mostly outdated and under-gunned armoured vehicles. This would be their ultimate test.

Hitler's plan, with the help of Goering and Keitel, had worked. The Axis allies had all answered the call and effectively wagered their military futures on the success of Case Blue. But Hitler was uneasy. A bombastic charlatan he may have been, but even he was apprehensive at the thought of relying too much on his allies. His solution was to 'corset-bone' the Axis troops – that is, to intersperse allied formations with reliable German units. This way, help was always close at hand. This proposal, and the lack of trust it implied, was totally unacceptable to Rome, Bucharest and Budapest, and in a completely uncharacteristic move Hitler acquiesced. On 15 April, Hitler sent out an order decreeing that national units should fight under their own army commands. It also stated:

> As the Don front becomes increasingly longer in the course of this operation it will be manned primarily by formations of our Allies … These are to be employed in their own sectors as far as possible, with the Hungarians being farthest north, then the Italians, and then, farthest south, the Romanians.

Another step had been taken towards disaster.

The 'League of Nations' army

Back in the Reich, the sacked Army Group South commander, Gerd von Runstedt, was filled with foreboding. On the night of 30 May, he had witnessed the RAF's first ever 'Thousand-Bomber Raid' on Germany, with the ancient city of Cologne as the target. During the raid, 1,455 tons of bombs were dropped, destroying over 16,000 buildings, including seven banks, nine hospitals, seventeen churches, four hotels and two cinemas – the Flak barracks was the only military installation damaged – and killing just under 500 people. The RAF lost forty-three aircraft, with Flying Officer Leslie Thomas Manser awarded a posthumous Victoria Cross for sacrificing himself to save his crew. As von Runstedt unpacked his bags, he thought about his ex-command, which he described as an 'absolute League of Nations army'. An Italian observer in the town of Dnepropetrovsk described it thus:

> ... the khaki uniforms of General Antonescu's Romanians with their large moustaches rivalled the blue of the air force, the red of the Cossacks, the grey-green of the Italian and German infantry, the yellow of the party leaders and the green and brown of the gendarmerie. The Italian *Carabineri* (Italian paramilitary police) had on their marvellous three-cornered hats ... the rectangular pointed hats worn by the French soldiers and the light caps of the seamen from the Black Sea were no match for them. The troops of the Croatian Legion, with their little shields on their right sleeves, were few compared to those of other armies, but they also contributed something with their Balkan personality, as did the French, Slovak, Dutch and Hungarian contingents.[1]

Von Runstedt, on the other hand, was not concerned with the multiplicity of uniforms on show, but rather with the men who wore them, and he was not impressed. In his own words, the Romanian officers and NCOs were 'beyond description', the Italians 'terrible people' and the Hungarians 'only wanted to get home quickly'. Not exactly a ringing endorsement.

The Crimea and the 22nd Panzer Division

In preparation for Case Blue, the OKW ordered the capture of the Crimea – a beautiful, sun-drenched land of vines and famous Russian red champagne,

---

1 The French were almost certainly members of the anti-communist collaborationist Grenadier Regiment 638, while the Dutch were members of the Waffen-SS *Wiking* (Viking) Division – see *Hitler's Gauls* and *Hitler's Vikings* by the author for more details.

inhabited for hundreds of years by descendants of Genghis Khan's Golden Horde and also home of the Soviet Black Sea Fleet and the heavily defended naval fortress of Sevastopol. In preparation for the assault, a new panzer formation arrived at the railway sidings, fresh from its training grounds – Wilhelm von Appell's 22nd Panzer Division, whose fate was to be intimately tied to the Axis allies and the Romanians in particular. Arriving on 20 March 1942, the newly activated unit was given no time to acclimatise and get used to its surroundings but instead was ordered straight into a counter-attack against a Soviet penetration over the 11-mile-long isthmus of Parpach (the land bridge between the Crimea and the Kerch Peninsula). With no preparation or reconnaissance, and with visibility down to yards due to thick early morning mist, the tank crews of the *Ostheer*'s newest panzer unit and their accompanying grenadiers stumbled blindly forward into the path of the Soviet attack. The result was near disaster, with the inexperienced Germans suffering very high infantry and tank losses – more than 30 per cent of their combat strength became casualties – as they were fired at on open ground near the 11-yard-wide and 16-foot-deep anti-tank ditch dug across the isthmus. Withdrawn to recover, the division was attached to Constantinescu-Claps' 4th Romanian and von Manstein's Eleventh Army to prepare for the May offensive aimed at seizing Kerch. The attack was von Manstein's brainchild, and it was to be a masterclass.

Fighting alongside a mixed force of Germans and Romanians, this time the 22nd was held back while the infantry made the initial breach through which the panzers then attacked. Charging north, von Appell's men then drove and destroyed the Soviet 47th and 51st Armies trapped against the shores of the Sea of Azov. Within days, it was all over, and close to 200,000 Soviets were prisoners of war, along with 260 tanks and 1,100 guns – a number of which the Romanians commandeered.

In July 1942, Constantinescu-Claps' men moved on, with the Eleventh Army, to reduce the heavily defended Sevastopol naval fortress. An important victory for the Romanians, although not achieved with the same price in blood as at Odessa, they still suffered 20,000 casualties they could ill afford. As for their German counterparts, some 25,000 were killed, causing a significant delay to the start date for Case Blue and reducing the already low ammunition stocks as the siege absorbed a massive 50,000 tonnes of munitions in a single month. According to the pilot of a German Stuka dive-bomber,

> ... the Soviet defenders were bombed and bombed again; one explosion next to another ... the whole peninsula was fire and smoke – yet in the end thousands of prisoners was taken, even there. One can only stand amazed at such resilience – it is

unbelievable in the truest sense of the word … The whole country had to be literally ploughed over by bombs before they yielded a short distance.

As for the 22nd Panzer Division, the Crimea operation helped it prove its ability, but it also left the division a long distance from the rehabilitation and equipment centres near Dnepropetrovsk. As the *Ostheer* phased out the remaining PzKpfw 38(*t*) tanks from all its other armoured units, the 22nd was forgotten. In fact, at the end of the fighting, it had ninety-five tanks operational, of which no fewer than sixty-three were the PzKpfw 38(*t*). Even by August, when the division had been sent north to support Italian forces, it had received only ten more modern PzKpfw IV medium tanks and had just 50 per cent of its total complement of armoured vehicles. These weaknesses would prove pivotal in determining the fate of the Axis allies in the coming winter.

Case Blue is launched

On the morning of 28 June 1942, German artillery split the air with a short, furious bombardment that officially started the major summer offensive on the Russian Front. Von Weichs' Army Group B (accompanied by Jány's Hungarians, Gariboldi's Italians and Dumitrescu's Romanians) took the lead, striking east towards the city of Voronezh on the Don River. Taken by surprise, the Soviets still put up strong resistance, and only began to fall back in earnest when Paulus' Sixth Army joined in two days later.

STAVKA was astonished by the attack and refused to believe it was the *Ostheer*'s main assault. Red Army reserves were kept out of the fight in the north, waiting for the expected thrust towards Moscow by von Kluge's Army Group Centre. It was only on 13 July, when the assault detachments of the German 73rd, 125th and 298th Infantry Divisions confronted enemy forces on the outskirts of the city of Rostov-on-Don, that realisation dawned – this was it – there would be no attack on Moscow that year.

Backed up by heavy artillery, the experienced German infantry soon began to punch holes in the Russian lines through which the armoured and motorised formations could advance. Through one such gap charged panzergrenadiers of the SS-*Wiking* (Viking) Division,[1] along with their Slovak allies and the 13th and 22nd Panzer Divisions. Fighting hard, they entered Rostov on 23 July and advanced towards the river. The *Wiking*'s panzer battalion overran

---

1 A mainly German division that also counted hundreds of Scandinavian volunteers among its ranks.

the city's airfield, while the panzergrenadiers did the dangerous work of street and house clearing. The fighting in the city was hard, especially around the headquarters of the NKVD, whose excellent troops were in Rostov in strength. The Soviets had turned the city centre into a deadly assault course, with strongpoints, mines, boobytraps, hidden bunkers and firing points. It took several days of savage hand-to-hand fighting to take the city and then a daring raid by men from the Brandenburg Regiment secured the vital road bridge over the Don to allow the advance onwards to Bataysk.[1] It cost a large number of the Brandenburgers their lives, but the way to the Caucasus was now open.

This was the oportunity for List and his Army Group A (along with Constantinescu-Claps' 4th Romanian and the *Alpini* who were earmarked for the Caucasus Mountains) to release the panzers. The tanks would now spearhead the advance, racing east and southeast, confident of getting behind the Red Army formations and repeating the mammoth encirclement battles of the previous summer.

It did not happen, though. The Soviets had learned their lesson. Trading space for time, the majority of the Soviet divisions avoided the trap. Von Bock, in one of his last acts before Hitler sacked him once more for his lack of success, told the Nazi dictator that the Soviets were 'gradually getting smart'. Franz Halder, as Chief of the German General Staff, agreed with von Bock, only for Hitler to cut him short:

> Nonsense. The Russians are in full flight, they're finished, they are reeling from the blows we have dealt them during the past few months.

The Italian 8th Army

This would have been surprising news for Gariboldi's men. Hampered by lack of transport, the Italians and their Croat allies were stubbornly marching forward over the parched landscape. Day followed day as the miles of marching infantrymen headed east through the choking dust of Ukraine's dirt roads.

With the Red Army retreating in front of von Weichs' armour, big battles were off the agenda, but there were plenty of skirmishes as the advancing troops came up against Soviet units left behind by the pace of the offensive.

---

1 The Brandenburgers were the *Wehrmacht*'s elite Special Forces unit, selected and trained to carry out only the most difficult and dangerous missions, usually behind enemy lines. They had already earned an enviable reputation during the campaigns in the West, capturing key installations.

One such skirmish occurred on 16 April, in between the small Ukrainian towns of Harcjusk and Pervomajska. The Croat Light Transport Brigade, attached to Marrazini's Duca D'Aosta, was moving forward and ran into a company of Russians. It lost five men killed in a short, fierce firefight – its first ever battle casualties. Over the next two months, the brigade fought through endless small villages and towns – Stokovo, Greko-Timofejevka, Veseli-Nikitovo – places that were memorable only to their inhabitants and the men who fought and died defending or capturing them.

The footsore Croats were still advancing when, on 13 July, they were joined by a Blackshirt battlegroup and ordered to launch a full-scale assault on the fluctuating Soviet lines ahead. The attack was a success, with the Croats punching through and rapidly advancing some 30 kilometres behind the Soviet front. Battles followed around Vladimirovka, Krasna Poljana and Fjodorovka. Within two weeks, the brigade had crossed the Don River at Lubanskoje and proceeded to dig in.

The Magyar 2nd

As for Jány and his Hungarians, they advanced through Kursk and then turned south-east to the town of Stary Oskol on the Oskol River. Corporal Balogh and the 1st Hungarian Armoured Field were behind the German lead units and saw the aftermath of the fighting, from both the previous year's campaign and Case Blue, as they pushed up towards the front:

> We pass by the sites of the great battles of 1941. Everywhere destroyed Russian tanks can be seen. We look at them and fear the idea of this Red hell moving against Hungary ... we are firmly confident that we shall smash the Red threat to Europe.
>
> Remarkable sights are seen from our window. It is frightful to think how many people sacrificed themselves, how many of our heroic German comrades gave their lives here.

But as the realities of the struggle began to dawn on the young junior NCO, his diary entries became less self-assured:

> 1 July. Artillery fire can be heard. We are likely to enter battle soon. Everywhere the remains of burnt-out German vehicles can be seen. Are the Germans starting to lose their military luck? ... The graves of German and Hungarian soldiers can be seen ... Everywhere there are corpses, field guns, vehicles and scattered weapons.

Advancing from the Oskol, the leading Hungarian units finally reached the western bank of the Don on 7 July, an achievement that the Red Army immediately challenged by launching a counter-attack to re-establish bridgeheads on the western bank. This was a favourite tactic used by the Red Army to great effect throughout the war. The concept was simple: bridgeheads provided the Soviets with safe areas on the enemy side where troops and equipment could be ferried over, landed and marshalled, ready to attack.

The Magyars' bridgehead battles

As it was, the *Magyars* had not yet arrived at the Don in force, so the Soviets found it relatively easy to get back across the river and dig in around the villages of Uryv, Karotyak and Stutye. Jány knew the Stutye penetration was easily contained but recognised the danger that Uryv and Karotyak posed and resolved to destroy them as quickly as possible, alloting the task to Deszo Laszlo's 7th Light Division and a battlegroup from the 1st Armoured Field. The attack was to begin on 18 July, with Uryv the priority.

Endre Zádor commanded the panzer troops, mustering all three battalions of the 1st Motorised Infantry Regiment, a cyclist battalion and his 30th Panzer Regiment's complete 1st Battalion – some forty PzKpfw 38(*t*) tanks and the eleven German-supplied PzKpfw IV. No fewer than four artillery battalions would provide support, and additionally the 51st Armoured Anti-Aircraft would deploy its twenty or so 40M Nimrod and 38M Toldi light tanks.

As well as dug-in infantry, the Soviets had moved armour across the Don into the bridgehead, including T-34s and lend-lease US-built M 3 light tanks. This would be no easy operation, but neither was this a token effort by the Hungarians. By this stage of Case Blue, the whole of Army Group A's eight spearhead divisions in the south could muster just 500 serviceable panzers, and 50 per cent of the army was immobilised by a lack of fuel. This made the Uryv assault very important indeed.

After an initial artillery barrage, the Hungarians advanced, sensibly using Captain Lászlo Makláry's PzKpfw IV tanks to lead the attack – they had the thickest armour and mounted the most effective gun. The Soviet tanks did not stand off, and soon a full tank-on-tank battle was raging, one that the Soviets were not losing. Using all the skills their German instructors had passed on to them, the Hungarian tank crews were getting the upper hand as Soviet tank after tank was hit by accurate gunnery and set on fire. Desperate to turn the tide, a company of Soviet T-34s tried to flank the Hungarians by using a forest as cover. Unfortunately for them, they were spotted by Captain József Henkey-Hönig, commander of the 3rd Anti-Aircraft Company, who tried to alert friendly panzers to the threat. However, his radio was Hungarian, while those of his panzer comrades were German, so in the confusion of battle the signal could not be sent; the incompatible equipment meant potential disaster loomed. Henkey-Hönig in his Toldi light tank did not hesitate and ordered his six 40M Nimrod anti-aircraft tanks to follow him into the attack. The crews in the lightly armoured Nimrods poured fire from their 40mm Bofors cannons into the Russians, and after one lucky hit on a T-34 that caused it to burst into flames, the Soviet tanks retreated back to the treeline, firing as they went. At last, the panzers noticed what was happening on their flank, and Lieutenant Colonel János Törcsváry (commander of the 1st Battalion) led a counter-attack to clear the forest of the tanks and also some anti-tank guns the Soviets had moved forward in support. Six Soviet T-34s lay burning in minutes, and by the end of the day, a total of twenty-one had been destroyed, with a further four captured intact and incorporated into the 1st Armoured Field as much-needed reinforcements

With their armour wiped out, the Soviet infantry stood no chance, and the Hungarian troops methodically worked from trench to trench until the bridgehead was captured. The men of the 7th Light Division consolidated the newly won positions, but the exhausted troops were then hit by a counter-attack launched once their own panzers had withdrawn to a nighttime position. All the gains of the day were lost, and attempts to repeat the initial success proved fruitless.

The Soviets hurriedly pushed fresh troops into Uryv, while Jány built up a force to eliminate them once and for all. It was a race against time. But it was not just to their front that the Hungarians had to look; the enemy was all around them, as Istvan Balogh knew well:

At night we were again attacked by partisans. One of our men was wounded.
At seven o'clock we set off to sweep the district. We killed five Russian soldiers.
Two more were taken for interrogation and shot afterwards.

The young *Magyar* NCO had come a regrettably long way from the hope and idealism of Budapest's railway station just two months earlier.

Next, the Hungarians attempted to storm Karotyak in the first week of August, the 1st Armoured Field in the forefront again as infantrymen from Ulaszlo Solymossy's 12th Light managed to reach the Don and seemed on the verge of victory. Alas, for the men of the 12th, Soviet counter-attacks at Uryv drew off the supporting Hungarian panzers and left them without armour protection. The defenders now turned attackers, and the Hungarians were lucky to hold off the counter-attacking Soviets, who almost reached the *Magyar* artillery lines.

As the Hungarians prepared for a second assault on Uryv, they were constantly under attack. Corporal Balogh noted:

> Bombers were flying constantly overhead and one of our panzer colonels was killed. The 2nd Company of the 1st Battalion suffered considerable losses with four or five officers killed. Thanks be to God that the night passed quietly ... One prisoner-of-war was shot.

And the next day:

> A continual artillery bombardment from 3 to 6 a.m., the shells whistled over our heads. At home they must be preparing for holidays, but here death can find us at any moment. Stalin Organs [the dreaded Katyusha multiple rocket-launchers] start speaking. Our hearts stopped beating. The village caught fire immediately and everyone ran away. The Russians destroyed an anti-tank gun. The fire has died down, but there is a mass of smoke. There are wounded. Those still at home cannot imagine what a struggle we have to have with ourselves to survive this battle.

On 10 August 1942, the day after this miserable entry, the 1st Armoured Field attacked the Uryv bridgehead again, this time accompanied by the 13th Light Division; however, the end result was the same as before. Initial success was swiftly followed by disappointment as the Soviets hit the attackers with massive air and artillery bombardments, causing dreadful casualties.

Balogh took part in the assault and recorded his disappointment at the failure:

> We are back in our former position, because Russian troops have broken through again. We reached Uryv. A very hard battle. Now we have retreated. After that an infantry regiment started a real panic, but they were halted and brought back. An artillery bombardment, Russian shells hit the 6th Regiment's ammunition vehicles and they exploded one after another.

After that, Balogh's entries are a litany of despair as the fighting carried on remorselessly. Casualties mounted, and he protested against poor food, lack of air support and the sheer weight of firepower the Red Army was able to bring to bear:

16 August. A sad Sunday ... the ground is covered with corpses. We don't have a chance to carry the wounded away.

17 August. We've been bombed by Russian aircraft. Our own Hungarian aircraft circled high in the sky. Either they could not find us to help, or else they were afraid. Our aircraft don't support us, God help us and make this battle short. We are to attack one more time. Everyone is bombing us, we advanced twice but both times had to retreat, many wounded and killed.

20 August. The Day of St Stefan. At five fifteen the advance started. Our tanks fired at the Russians ... There are just two NCO's left in the company – me and a corporal who is the company commander's assistant ... We have been attacked again by bombers. Artillery and tanks are shelling us. It is like hell ... The Russians are frighteningly brave. They are fighting to the last. They don't want to surrender.

Air accident

On the same day as this last entry, István Horthy, eldest son of Hungary's Regent Miklos Horthy, died at the Alexeyevka airbase when his Hejja crashed due to a mechanical failure. A year earlier, Bruno Mussolini, one of the Italian dictator's sons, had been killed in an aviation accident when the new Piaggio bomber he was testing for the *Regia Aeronautica* crashed near Pisa.

This was yet more grim news for an increasingly despondent Corporal Balogh:

21 August. We were bombed throughout the night. Oh God how little human life is worth! The Russians, having been pushed back across the Don, are attacking again. We counted the losses in our company: twenty dead, ninety-four wounded, and three missing [author's note: more than half the company's total strength] ... Morale is very low. All my friends are wounded.

22 August. We have been reinforced with a new draft ... These infantrymen should have gone home, but instead they have been transferred to us ... We spent the whole day redistributing the weapons of those who have been killed or wounded ... If we have to go on our nerves will break.

The last cavalry charge

It was not just the Hungarians who were feeling the heat. On 20 August, the Soviets attacked the Italian 8th Army and their Croat allies positioned alongside the *Magyars* on the Don.

The Italians resisted hard for a full three days, giving the lie to the often-repeated theory that they always gave up when under pressure. The Croats were also involved in heavy fighting and managed to hold their lines, killing and capturing 120 Soviets for the loss of twenty of their own, eight of them dead. For their steadfastness the brigade was awarded the *Sul Campo*, the Italian Army Croat Legion Badge for bravery, by the commander of the XXXV Corps, Francesco Zingales.

The *Alpini* of the 2nd Division Tridentina, marching north after being told they were joining the Italian infantry on the Don rather than going to serve in the mountains of the Caucasus, were put on suddenly available trucks and shipped to support Carlo Pellegrini's beleaguered 2nd Mountain Infantry Division Sforzesca. Arriving at the front, the *Alpini* immediately began to engage the Soviets, one small patrol undergoing an experience that was typical of the chaotic madness of the Russian Front. The alpine troopers were moving through a wood when they were surrounded by a much larger force of Soviets accompanied by a political commissar. Realising the hopelessness of their situation, the Italians reluctantly threw down their weapons and raised their hands in surrender. Congratulating his own patrol commander, the commissar then boarded a concealed staff car and drove off. As soon as he was gone, the victorious Russians gave the surprised Italians their weapons back, handed their own over to the amazed *Alpini*, formed into an orderly line and gave themselves up as prisoners.

Plus, it was only in Russia that you would ever see squadrons of sabre-wielding Italian cavalrymen, led by white-gloved officers, charging lines of enemy infantry armed with machine-guns and artillery. Such was the picture on 24 August near the small village of Izbushenski in Ukraine.

The night before, the entire Savoia Regiment had been out in the field, trying to maintain the links between the spread-out Italian units fending off repeated Soviet attacks. Confronted by one such Red Army force near Izbushenski, the splendidly idiosyncratic Alessandro Bettoni decided that with dusk turning to night the best option was to draw the regiment into a defensive square, eat a good meal and prepare to fight in the morning.

That meal was as totally out of place and time as the men who sat down to eat their food. The officers, as they always did, sat at folding tables spread

The beginning of the Axis: Hitler and Mussolini bask in the adulation of the Roman crowds.

The Hungarian dictator and his family, from left to right: eldest son Istvan, Admiral Miklos, wife Magdolna, younger son Miklos Jnr and daughter Paulette. Istvan would die on the Russian front and Miklos Jnr would be kidnapped as a hostage by the Austrian Waffen-SS commando Otto Skorzeny.

The young Romanian king, Michael, and the country's real ruler, the *Conducator* Marshall Ion Antonescu.

General Nicolae Ciuperca – the Romanian Fourth Army commander sacked by Antonescu for his failure to take the Soviet port city of Odessa.

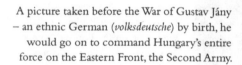

A picture taken before the War of Gustav Jány – an ethnic German (*volksdeutsche*) by birth, he would go on to command Hungary's entire force on the Eastern Front, the Second Army.

General Jozef Turanec – an experienced and able commander, Turanec would lead the excellent Slovak Fast Division during Barbarossa.

The venerable Renault FT tank (this one is in the Army Museum in Brussels). Cutting edge when it first appeared, it was hopelessly outdated by the advent of the Second World War; nevertheless, it formed the core of the infant Romanian armoured force.

The Renault FT was superseded in the Romanian arsenal by the Czech-made Panzer 35 (this model is in the Military Museum in Belgrade), which, renamed the R-2, became the mainstay of Romania's panzer force for most of the war.

The Axis allies possessed little, if any, modern anti-tank capability. For example, these 47mm guns being paraded through the streets of Budapest would prove to be hopelessly inadequate on the Eastern Front.

The staple tank of the Red Army for most of the war – the rightly famed T-34. With its 76mm main gun, innovative sloping armour and superb Christie suspension, the T-34 was arguably the finest tank of the war and was light years ahead of anything the Axis allies possessed.

Forward! Panzers of the 1st Romanian Panzer Division cross the River Prut into Bessarabia at the launch of Barbarossa.

A Slovak artillery battalion advances into the Soviet Union. Like the majority of the invaders, the Slovaks relied on horses for their transport.

Hungarian panzers enter the disputed Polish/ Ukrainian city of Kolomea in 1941.

General Messe (with cane) watches some of his motorcycle-mounted *bersaglieri* negotiate the muddy and rutted roads of the Ukraine, summer 1941.

One of the Finns' few modern anti-tank guns, a German PAK40. The gunners themselves wear a mix of uniforms.

One of Italy's elite – the famed *bersaglieri* – poses for the camera with his cockerel feathers adorning his helmet.

Members of the Slovak Fast Division advance warily through a cornfield in southern Russia, summer 1941. The soldier in the foreground has armed himself with a captured Soviet PPSH submachine-gun, while his comrade holds a German stick grenade – the famous 'potato masher' – aloft.

Italian troops advance towards the Don in the summer of 1942, with their trusty mules carrying the load.

Back in Bucharest the victorious panzers of the 1st Romanian parade to the cheers of the crowds.

At the front Romanian infantry are dug in under the scorching Russian sun.

Romanian infantry take cover from Soviet artillery fire during the final assault on Odessa in October 1941.

This was how the Axis wanted to portray the fight in the Soviet Union, all comrades together. From left to right: a Romanian, an Italian and a German.

The head of Nazi Germany's military mission to Romania, General Artur Hauffe, presents medals to Romanian infantrymen in 1942. Hauffe would be killed in 1944 when he stepped on a landmine.

Inadequately equipped though they were, the Axis allies still fought hard. Here two Hungarian soldiers pose beside a destroyed Soviet KV-1 behemoth.

The Hungarian regent's eldest son, Istvan, prepares to board his own Hejja fighter. He would later die in an accident in the self-same plane.

The German colonel, Walther Wenck, Chief of Staff for the LVII Panzer Corps, was ordered north to take over as Dumitrescu's new head of operations for the Romanian Third Army following the Soviet Uranus offensive. Here he is pictured following his promotion to general.

General Ferdinand Heim. Heim commanded the ill-starred XXXXVIII Panzer Corps, which comprised the German 22nd Panzer Division and Radu Gherghe's 1st Romanian Panzer. His corps would conspicuously fail to stop Uranus and his arrest would be ordered by an enraged Hitler.

The mainstay of the 22nd Panzer Division and almost every Axis allied armoured force throughout the war, the Czech-made Panzer 38. The Bulgars, Romanians and Hungarians would be issued several hundred of these tanks, despite their increasing obsolescence.

Infantrymen of the Romanian Fourth Army wait in the snow to go into battle against the southern prong of the Red Army's Uranus offensive.

During the Don offensives troops of the Hungarian Second Army struggle through atrocious weather in a desperate attempt to avoid capture or death at the hands of the advancing Soviets.

A seemingly endless line of Romanian POWs captured during the Soviets' Uranus offensive file dejectedly past their Red Army captors.

Hundreds of Hungarian dead, from the fighting near Voronezh, litter the Russian steppe.

Thousands of Axis troops went into the bag during the Red Army's Little Saturn operation. For these Italian POWs marching east into captivity the future was bleak indeed.

The Knight's Cross-wearing Romanian General Radu Korne (left), who distinguished himself during the Don fighting, stands with two German officers in September 1943.

The Ploesti oil industry (this is the Columbia Aquila field), so vital to the Nazi war effort, burns after the 1943 raid by American B-24 bombers.

Following the Don calamity, Hungary went into overdrive to try and produce a new range of armoured vehicles to equip her forces. This is the long-awaited Turan 1, which was obsolete by the time it finally came into service in late 1943.

Still armed with German MP40 schmeisser submachine-guns, these Bulgar paratroopers parade through Sofia to mark the liberation of Germany's most lukewarm Axis ally.

In Italy the ex-dictator Mussolini was caught by communist partisans, with his mistress, Clara Petacci, and over a dozen compatriots, and shot. Their bodies were then taken to Milan and they were hung by their feet as a spectacle for the mob.

The ex-commander of the Hungarian Second Army, Gustav Jány, on trial in Budapest in 1947. Like so many post-war communist so-called 'judicial' events, the decision was never in doubt and Jány was convicted and executed.

Romania's King Michael then and now. After struggling bravely to save his country from communist oppression after the war, he was forced to abdicate in 1947 and sent into exile abroad. He was not allowed to return to his homeland for a visit until forty-five years later, in 1992.

with immaculate starched white linen tablecloths. Almost to a man wealthy aristocrats (Bettoni himself was a count, of course), they saw no contradiction between the strangeness of the setting and dining off the elegant regimental silver while being served by white-jacketed orderlies.

Rising very early the next morning, it became clear to Bettoni that he faced a much larger enemy than had been visible the previous nightfall. His men had now identified a full three battalions of the Soviet 812th Infantry Regiment, an excellent formation filled with hardy Siberians, encamped a few hundred metres away over the steppes and supported by numbers of machine-guns and infantry cannon.

Bettoni knew he was outgunned and outnumbered – in total, he had four full squadrons of 156 men each, plus another squadron equipped with machine-guns as the Savoia's only concession to the twentieth century – but over a breakfast served in a similar manner to the meal on the previous evening, the Colonel announced to his brother officers that the Savoia's moment of glory had come: they would charge the Red Army lines. The decision was met with universal approval, and then, as was the tradition for a Savoia charge, the officers proceeded to don their white gloves in anticipation, their grooms bringing their magnificent chargers – almost all were mighty stallions – to their waiting masters. Swinging themselves up into their highly polished saddles, the officers fanned out to join their squadrons, taking their positions out to the front of their men, sabres drawn from their scabbards and held at the at-ease position, resting against their right shoulders.

With the dawn light beginning to flood the steppe, the 2nd Squadron was the first to move, its serried ranks of horsemen filing out from the defensive square, forming up into lines and then moving forward across the flat land at a walk. The horses brushed past bright yellow sunflowers, calm and composed, men and animals alike falling back on endless hours of training in just these manoeuvres. Now, here, in the middle of nowhere, when it had seemed that this method of fighting a battle had long been consigned to history, the Savoia would relive the old ways one last time. The walk became a trot; then a canter, stirrups and mouth-bits jingling; and then, finally, with a loud cry of 'SAVOIA!' from the squadron commander, the 2nd entered its charge, the sabres sweeping down to the point position. One of the officers, a captain, later recalled those heady few minutes:

> In the ranks the enthusiasm was unstoppable, especially when in the early stages
> of the gallop we were joined by Major Manusardi followed by his orderly. The
> major, formerly commander of the 2nd, and ever faithful to his calling as a

soldier, had leapt into his saddle to be part of such a big moment with his old troopers. The enemy was drawn up in two lines: 'Sabres ... To hand ... Charge!' It was the cry we had awaited for so long, the cry that we had dreamed of since childhood. Now at last it had come amidst the roar of battle, the explosions, and the howling of the machine-guns ...

Those same machine-guns scythed down men and horses, sending them sprawling and screaming in the grass and dust, but the distance to cover was short, and in moments the captain and his men crashed into the Siberians left flank, causing havoc, their sabres cutting down onto the enemy. Riding clear of the fight, the cavalrymen expertly turned and charged the same flank again, this time from behind, the troopers liberally throwing grenades among the dazed Soviet troops.

Bettoni, viewing the attack through his field binoculars, judged the enemy to be badly shaken, and decided to follow up with a dismounted assault from his 4th Squadron straight into the centre of the Soviet infantry. A sensible military decision, the order to leave their precious horses and go forward on foot was met with dismay by the officers and men of the 4th who had just witnessed the glory of the charge by the 2nd. Nevertheless, they advanced, firing their carbines and hitting the Soviets hard. In response the 812th began to fall back in confusion, but there was no respite as Bettoni now took the opportunity offered to him of catching retreating infantry on foot, and flung his 3rd Squadron into them with a full-blooded charge. The Siberians broke and the rout was complete.

After the battle, 150 men of the 812th lay dead, and a further 500 were rounded up as prisoners by the jubilant Savoia. The Siberian unit had, for all intents and purposes, ceased to exist. As for the Italians, thirty-two men and seventy horses had been killed making this small piece of history, in what was arguably the last ever full-scale cavalry charge in the war. There was one further dramatic occurrence when the horse carrying the regimental pennant trotted back to the Italian lines, riderless and blinded in one eye, but with the all-important pennant still intact.

For the survivors the plaudits awaited; no fewer than fifty-six of them were awarded medals for bravery. A senior *Ostheer* officer remarked to Bettoni:

You were magnificent. We in the Wehrmacht no longer know how to do these things.

The Magyars continue to suffer

The Italian front stabilised over the following few days, and along the Don that situation was repeated, although not everyone was optimistic about what the future might hold, including Istvan Balogh:

> 29 August. Yesterday my rank of corporal was confirmed. I am not very excited. I'd much rather go home.
>
> 1 September. Bad news came. Our divisional commander has been replaced by a German panzer officer [author's note: Baron Herman Lang replaced Lajos Veress] … Little chance of returning home. Let the war come to an end soon or else we will all be killed. Half of us have already died.
>
> 3 September. My friend died in hospital. He was badly wounded, but if he had received better treatment he might have been saved … Our rations consist of looted corn and potatoes.
>
> 6 September. We're preparing for a new battle. All of our armoured division and a few German regiments are advancing … We were given the best meal possible – chocolate slabs, preserves, lard, sugar and goulash.

This new offensive Balogh talks about was yet another attempt to wipe out the Uryv bridgehead, this time with four light infantry divisions and the 1st Armoured Field, plus the German 168th Infantry Division (this division was later to be a part of Corps Kramer along with the 1st Hungarian Armoured Field), all operating under German command and supported by no less than thirty-five artillery batteries. The end result would be depressingly familiar to Balogh and his comrades; stubborn Soviet resistance, high casualties and eventual *Magyar* failure:

> 9 September. At five a.m. the advance begins … Hungarian and German tanks are moving forwards and taking death to the Russians … Wounded are continually being carried to the rear. The Russians are holding hard.
>
> 11–13 September. We are advancing … Many of our men are wounded. We entered a village – Storozhevoe – many German and Hungarian bodies. The village is smoking. The Russians are resisting strongly … The Russians have retreated into a wood. The battle is not over yet … Our shells bounce off their tanks.

On 14 September, the offensive was called off. Casualties were heavy on both sides; the Hungarians had lost 1,200 killed and another 7,000 wounded or missing. Balogh wrote that day, 'If anybody dies here nobody weeps over him.'

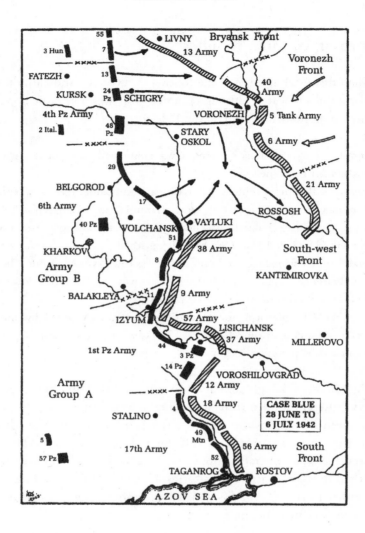

Three days later, his diary was taken from his dead body by a Russian soldier. His war in Russia had lasted just three months.

With the Red Army still holding out on the Don, the *Magyar* tanks were withdrawn into reserve along with their cavalry comrades, while the infantry resigned themselves to digging the trenches they would sit in over the coming winter months. It was the same for the Italians and the Romanians. The spotlight was definitely off them as the eyes of the world focused on the grim struggle that was reaching a climax to the south, in the city on the banks of the mighty Volga River – Stalingrad.

CHAPTER 6

STALINGRAD

Lieutenant Reiner, a German officer from Hermann Hoth's Fourth Panzer Army fighting in Stalingrad, wrote:

> Stalingrad is no longer a town. By day it is an enormous cloud of burning, blinding smoke, a vast furnace lit by the reflection of the flames … Animals flee from this hell. The hardest stone cannot bear it for long. Only men endure.

What had started out as a 'by-product' of Hitler's summer offensive to secure Soviet oil had become an all-consuming obsession for the Nazi leader. The Sixth Army was fighting a never-ending battle in the city, to which the most power-ful field formation in the *Ostheer* was totally unsuited, consisting as it did of no fewer than twenty-one divisions, including three motorised infantry and three panzer divisions; Martin Lattman's Dresdeners of the 14th; the Westphalians of the 16th under Hans Valentin Hube;[1] and the 24th, formerly the elite East Prussian 1st Cavalry Division, astonishingly the only cavalry division of the *Wehrmacht* to be converted to a panzer division during 1941 and 1942.

The result was that the Sixth Army was being decimated in a city the Germans did not even want a few months before. Hundreds of men were dying every day; battalions that had been built up over the spring with pre-cious replacements were now burnt out, forced to amalgamate to keep up the struggle. As always, casualties were highest among the junior leaders – corpo-rals, sergeants, lieutenants and captains – and new arrivals, the latter dying in large numbers owing to lack of experience, their more experienced comrades

---

1 A brilliant panzer commander and the only one-armed general in the *Panzerwaffe*, he died in an aircrash the day after receiving Diamonds to his Knight's Cross on 20 April 1944, Hitler's birthday.

not even bothering to learn their names so unlikely was their survival. It was the time of the Red Army sniper, with men like Vassili Zaitsev and Anatoly Chekov each killing well over 100 of their enemy.[1] Chekov was a quiet, intro-verted youngster, not at ease in the spotlight and totally matter-of-fact about his job. He recounted how he always went for a head shot:

> When I shoot, the head immediately jerks backwards, or to one side, and he drops what he was carrying and falls down.

Yet Hitler himself said of the city still wreathed in the fog of war:

> We've got it really, except for a few enemy positions still holding out. Now people say why don't they finish the job more quickly? Well, I prefer to do the job with quite small groups. Time is of no consequence at all.

This statement would have been a great surprise to the Croats of the 369th Infantry Regiment who were being worn down alongside their German comrades in the ruined city and knew they were no closer to vic-tory. The reality was that the Red Army was still resisting fiercely and that the Germans had to pour more men and equipment into the battle, with no end in sight. Von Weichs, now very much feeling the same pressure that had assailed his predecessor von Bock, was being forced to remove German troops from the northern and southern flanks of the advance to feed them into rein-forcing Paulus in Stalingrad, and he asked the Axis allies to fill the gaps.

The Axis allies begin to cover the flanks

The Hungarian 2nd Army was von Weichs' northern most allied force, dug in on the banks of the Don near the city of Voronezh and just to the south of von Salmuth's German Second Army. Jány's *Magyars* were exhausted after their failed bridgehead battles at Uryv and Karotyak, and as autumn became winter, their morale fell along with the air temperature. The Germans began to complain that the *Magyars* were becoming reluctant to fight unless they had no choice, preferring to leave their Red Army foes to their own devices. This was a harsh judgement on units strung out across the lines, frequently harried by Soviet raids, with ammunition stocks low and with few, if any, reserves in

---

1 Zaitsev, a Siberian former shepherd, was immortalised in the Hollywood movie *Enemy at the Gates*, where he was played by the British actor Jude Law.

support. High Command in Budapest tried to restore the situation by adding a fresh reconnaissance battalion from the newly organised 'Mobile Troops' arm to every light division, but this did not solve the anti-tank problem and simply meant more troops to feed for the already-creaking supply system.

As in Hitler's pre–Case Blue directive, on Jány's right and also positioned unhappily on the banks of the Don were Gariboldi's 8th Army and then Petre Dumitrescu's 3rd Romanians, tired and weary after literally marching hundreds of kilometres in the baking sun while fighting continuous skirmishes. Both the Italians and Romanians had ten divisions each and were allocated a ridiculously long front of more than 100 miles, which was way beyond their capabilities or strength.

The Romanians were positioned with the town Lugovsky on their left, down to Sukhoy Donetsk on their right, with their headquarters at Cernashevskaya. Dumitrescu placed four corps with eight divisions forward in the line and two divisions in reserve – the 7th Cavalry and the 15th Infantry Division under a new commander, Ioan Sion, once of the 1st Panzer of course. This disposition made sense but condemned the eight front line units to even longer sectors of, on average, 13 miles in length. Just as in the Hungarian sector, the Romanians had Red Army bridgeheads to contend with, theirs being at Serafimovich and Kletskaya. Dumitrescu, just like Jány, recognised the threat they posed and was determined to destroy them, but in a grave error of judgement, von Weichs vetoed the operations, perhaps fearing a repetition of the Hungarian failures and a weakening of the already depleted front.

Things were even worse south of Stalingrad, where Constantinescu-Claps' 4th Army had to stretch more than 200 miles from Straya Otrada to Sarpa. From his command post in Kotelnikovsky, Constantinescu-Claps viewed his front with real concern. His seven divisions (organised into two corps) were all under-strength after the taking of the Crimea and the other summer battles; his strongest unit was the 18th Infantry, at just over 70 per cent of its establishment, and his worst was the battered 1st Infantry, which was more or less combat-ineffective with numbers reduced by 75 per cent. With infantry strength so low, all he could afford to put in reserve were three battalions of pioneers, some lightly armed reconnaissance troops and a regiment of cavalry – what would become known, albeit briefly, as the 'Korne Detachment', named after its dashing commander, Radu Korne. The Romanian army commander was so concerned that he managed to persuade the reluctant Germans to supplement his forces with two of their own divisions to bolster his combat force.

Along fronts stretching hundreds and hundreds of miles, the story was the same. Von Weichs was placing the fate of Army Group B in the hands of four armies of Romanians, Italians and Hungarians who could barely position one armed man every fifty metres – the disaster to come was beginning to take shape. However, Berlin may have been negligent, but it was not completely mad, and it had realised the issues involved and the risks being taken. There seemed only one viable solution – mobile, hard-hitting, panzer reserves – and OKW thought these were available.

The 1st Romanian Panzer and XXXXVIII Panzer Corps

During August, with the summer sun still beating down, Radu Gherghe and his men had enjoyed about as much time as they were going to get at home among the taverns, eateries and lush countryside of Targoviste. New orders came through from Bucharest – destination Russia – and the troopers, some reluctantly, began to load their vehicles and equipment onto railway flat-bed wagons for the long journey east. As the men waved goodbye to their wives, sweethearts and even their old commander, Ioan Sion (sent to command the Moldovans of the 15th Infantry at the front), they could reflect on a division that was now at the very height of its wartime prowess. Almost back up to a full complement of 13,000 men, the unit had been retrained and re-equipped and was well rested as it set off for southern Russia. In less than four months, it would be annihilated.

Assigned to the 4th Army south of Stalingrad on arrival at the front, it was linked with the Germans and Austrians of the 22nd Panzer Division, fresh from their action on the Kerch peninsula in the Crimea. Together, both formations now composed the newly established XXXXVIII Panzer Corps.

A typical panzer corps was an extremely powerful unit – a fast-moving force with a massive armoured punch that was more than a match for any of the Red Army's new tank armies just coming into being – and it was envisaged that the XXXXVIII Panzer Corps would easily fulfil this role. But just to be sure, the Sixth Army's 14th Panzer Division was also assigned to the corps. This was good news for Ferdinand Heim, who had previously been Chief-of-Staff of the Sixth Army and now commanded the XXXXVIII. The 14th Panzer Division (previously commanded by Heim himself) was a veteran outfit; formed in 1940 from the 4th Infantry Division, it had fought with distinction since the beginning of Operation Barbarossa. From 1 November 1942, the division was commanded by Hans Freiherr von Falkenstein, but he was soon replaced on 19 November by Johannes Baessler.[1] The only problem was that the 14th Panzer Division was an integral part of Sixth Army and had been fighting in Stalingrad for weeks, losing the majority of its armoured vehicles and combat strength in fierce house-to-house fighting. It was not withdrawn from the city into reserve but instead was earmarked to join Heim's new corps if the situation arose.[2]

In comparison, to the 14th the 22nd Panzer Division was still a relatively inexperienced unit and was desperately in need of further extensive training to learn and fully absorb the lessons of the Crimea and Kerch. It also had a new commander at the helm, Wilhelm von Appell having been replaced by the 46-year-old aristocratic infantry general Hellmut von Chevallerie, who in turn gave way to the 47-year-old Bavarian cavalryman Eberhard Rodt. A First World War veteran, Rodt[3] had won the Knight's Cross in France during 1940, when he was a reconnaissance commander, but had limited experience of panzer operations and was unable to improve materially the status of his new command in the brief time he had before the Red Army onslaught.

Then, with the fighting in Stalingrad consuming more and more German manpower, the fateful decision was made to transfer Heim's XXXXVIII Panzer Corps north to a position to the rear of the 3rd Romanian Army and use it as the strategic reserve along the length of Army Group B's vulnerable northern flank on the Don. For any panzer corps, this was a tall order, but for the XXXXVIII it was very risky indeed.

Rodt had arrived to find his men not concentrated in one area ready to intervene where necessary along the Don, but instead spread out behind the Romanian frontline divisions, trying in vain to bolster the shaky defences. Worse still, the division's Engineer Battalion had been detached and sent to the *Rattenkrieg* (Rat's War) house-to-house fighting in Stalingrad, while one of its two infantry regiments – Colonel Michalik's 140th Panzer Grenadier

---

1 Baessler would be seriously wounded during the Uranus offensive and then sent to recover in the West, where later he was given command of the defences of the southern French port of Toulon. He would die there defending the port from Allied forces.

2 As it turned out, it was never fully released, even though the situation most definitely did arise, and under Martin Lattmann's leadership it would fight to extinction in the ruins of Stalingrad. In Soviet captivity, Lattmann would become one of the members of the National Committee for a Free Germany and would live out his days after the war as a senior police general in communist East Germany.

3 Who would later go on to great success leading the 15th Panzer Grenadier Division in the Sicilian, Italian and D-Day campaigns.

– had been sent north to Second Army to act as a cadre for the newly forming 27th Panzer Division. Rodt then asked about the fuel situation for his
panzers and received the unwelcome reply that there was none available. No
training had been possible for weeks; his men did not even have enough fuel
to turn their engines over regularly as required by normal maintenance procedures and instead had been forced to park their panzers in dug-outs to
try to protect them from the ravages of the Russian winter. The cold was so
intense that even this was not enough, so the Germans did what the German
military of the time did so very well: they improvised. Collecting straw from
the local peasantry, the crews packed it in bundles around their precious panzers, hoping to keep the searing cold and freezing snow away, while crossing
their fingers they would not be needed for any major action. As they waited,
they did not notice the rustling of tiny animals amongst the straw, a noise that
would change the course of the war.

Radu Gherghe's Romanians, for once, were in moderately better shape than
their German counterparts. The supply of Ploesti oil ensured their panzers'
fuel tanks did not run dry, and they maintained a regular running and maintenance programme to keep their vehicles in prime, operational condition.
German support, so often criticised as inadequate by its Axis allies, also came to
Gherghe's aid, with the arrival of something his Italian and Hungarian neighbours would have given much to receive. On the morning of 17 October,
eleven PzKpfw III and the same number of PzKpfw IV tanks arrived, along
with nine 7.5cm PaK40 and another nine 5.0cm PaK38 anti-tank guns.
At last, the Romanians had something substantial to counter the heavy Soviet
armour, and the anti-tank guns alone gave Gherghe more capability than
was possessed by either the entire Hungarian 2nd or Italian 8th Armies. The
smaller PaK38 fired an armour-piercing shell at 835 metres per second, while
the newer and more powerful PaK40 had a muzzle velocity of some 1,000
metres per second – that meant the weapon had the ability to penetrate more
than 100mm of armour. As for the crews of the PzKpfw IVs, they could sit
safe behind 80mm of rolled steel frontal armour while firing their long-barrelled 7.5cm main gun, which could penetrate 77mm of plate armour up to
a range of almost 2,700 yards. With the hull armour on the T-34 being 60mm
thick, this made the PzKpfw IV and PaK40 excellent Soviet tank killers. The
PzKpfw III were issued to the 8th Company of the 2nd Panzer Battalion,
the PzKpfw IV tanks became the 1st Battalion's 4th Company and both
types were given Romanian designations: T-3 and T-4, respectively. Taking
these new vehicles and weapons into service also meant changing tactics and
operating procedures, but it was a full month before the battalions could get

out and train together, and that delay was time the Romanians would come to rue.

Fate, or rather the STAVKA, had decreed that the twenty-two new PzKpfw III and PzKpfw IV tanks would soon be used with the Romanian R-2 and Czech-built PzKpfw 38(*t*) tanks and face hundreds of Soviet tanks in a true David and Goliath struggle.

So on paper, XXXXVIII Panzer Corps looked to be a strong military force – 14th and 22nd Panzer Divisions and the 1st Romanian, packed with armoured power – but this was a mirage, a fantasy that would eventually condemn hundreds of thousands of Axis soldiers to injury, capture or death.

Having said that, it is difficult to accurately grade the corps against its contemporaries, as there were huge variations in panzer establishments and strengths; the standard for a division was usually a single regiment of two battalions of armour, but six panzer divisions had just one battalion with three companies of tanks, while seven were more than double that size at two battalions of four companies and another seven were even larger at three battalions of three companies. Putting this to one side, and also discounting the 14th Panzer Division, the corps should have had close to 300 modern panzers in its ranks, four regiments of motorised infantry, two of artillery, two of anti-aircraft and numerous anti-tank guns. This simply was not the case, and the *Oberkommando des Heeres* (Army High Command – OKH) was aware, but was Hitler? The dominating feature of Nazi military activity during the latter half of the war was that Hitler increasingly took decisions divorced from the reality on the ground, and this moment was a significant step on that journey – the XXXXVIII Panzer Corps barely had enough tanks to fill one division, let alone two, and the majority were obsolete, lightweight, under-gunned Czech-built vehicles. Hitler should have been aware of this; instead, his assigned adjutant from the *Luftwaffe* later claimed that 'Hitler was misinformed about the quality of this panzer corps.'

Whether or not Hitler knew the poor state of XXXXVIII Panzer Corps, that did not change the reality of its weakness or the importance of the role it was to perform. That role was to be positioned behind the Sixth Army, ready to intervene to the north or south as required, and how crucial this was is impossible to overstate.

The 1st Hungarian Armoured Field

Although they would have doubtless hated to admit it, the Hungarians of the 2nd Army would end up following much the same path as their loathed neighbours to the south. With the *Ostheer*'s strength stretched thin and unable to provide them with a strong reserve, they would come to rely almost totally on their own elite forces – the 1st Hungarian Armoured Field headquartered behind the front in the village of Nikolayevka – to fulfil the role.

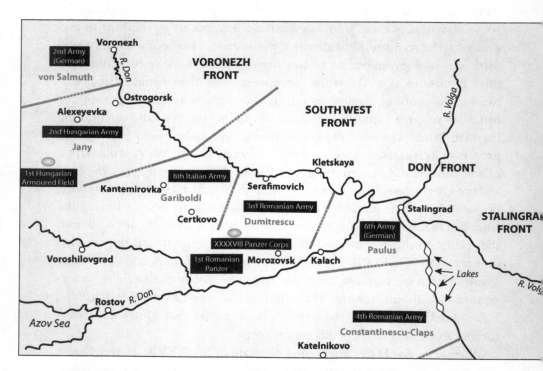

The Axis Don front: 18 November 1942 – the calm before the storm. (See page 153.)

CHAPTER 7

WINTER ON THE DON

The winter of 1942–43 was not the record-breaking weather from hell of the previous year, but for the poorly equipped Axis conscripts shivering in their trenches, that was scant consolation. The crews of XXXXVIII Panzer Corps may have been able to park their vehicles in dug-outs, and at least try to make themselves as warm and comfortable as possible, but this was a luxury denied to most of their comrades-in-arms. The Italian infantry divisions were especially ill-prepared, with all the newly arrived units desperately short of proper winter clothing, especially socks, warm felt boots and padded jackets. It didn't help that their supply system was incredibly inefficient, with almost everything sent from home likely to be stolen to feed the thriving black market. Lieutenant Bruno Zavagli, an officer in the *Alpini*, wrote:

> The black market has achieved full legitimacy in Rikovo … One freezes and trembles on the front and here, behind the lines, there's everything, but everything doesn't go further; the supplies remain here for some time, passing through predatory clutches that choose and plunder, reducing the amount until only the leftovers arrive at the front.

The results were stark. The 15,000 men of the Ravenna Infantry Division received winter coats for less than 50 per cent of their number, while the mountain troops of the Cuneense Division received only 3,000. Despite this, the *Alpini* tended to be better supplied than the infantry when it came to basics such as rations. A Cuneense officer, Veniero Marsan, arrived at the frontline and was despatched to liaise with the neighbouring infantry battalion from the Cosseria. Invited to stay for lunch by his brother officers, he was horrified to be fed soup so thin that it resembled warm water with a few scraps of meat.

He was too embarrassed to tell his hosts that when they had broth in his unit it was so thick with meat and vegetables that a spoon would stand up in it.

But in just about every other department, the *Alpini* fared badly. Prepared as they were to fight in the far-off snowy Caucasus Mountains, their main problems lay in weaponry and transport; they basically had little of either that was relevant for steppe fighting. When they boarded the trains back in Italy, they had been told they would be going with Army Group A to the mountainous south, so it was alpine boots, ropes and light equipment, with mules to carry small mountain-guns. Being diverted north and arriving instead on the Don, staring out across a seemingly never-ending flat expanse of river and grassland, they rightly felt unprepared. At least they had some warm clothing such as sheepskin-lined coats, but they still suffered from the same shortcomings as the infantry – personal weapons such as the Carcano rifle and Breda 30 light machine-gun that would fire in the cold only if heated over a fire beforehand, constant weapon jams as the special lubricants failed to arrive at the front, lack of artillery support with some sub-units being out of range of the guns, not enough ammunition for any of the weapon systems and, above all, not enough anti-tank guns to fight the feared Soviet T-34. The commander of the Germona Battalion in the Julia Division, Lieutenant-Colonel Rinaldo Dall'Armi, even wrote to Mussolini about the shortfalls:

> We arrived in Russia destined to go to the Caucasus, where our training, armaments, equipment and deployment would be natural, and where we could have competed sportingly with the best German and Romanian mountain troops. Suddenly we were redirected to the Don in flat territory and denied proper weapons – 1891 rifles and four laughable small cannon against Russian 34-ton tanks.
>
> There are only a few *alpini* – this is not human materiel with which one can play lightly.

The lack of modern anti-tank weapons was a severe handicap felt across all four Axis allied armies. The Hungarians and Romanians fared just as badly as the Italians, still being overwhelmingly equipped with ineffective 37mm and 47mm guns. The Germans were bombarded with pleas to supply better guns, and from October a small number did start to come through, but it still meant that as the snow began to fall, each Romanian infantry division could muster just one battery of 7.5cm PaK 40 – excellent weapons, but far too few in number. In Dumitrescu's 3rd Army, that added up to just forty-eight guns, each covering 2 miles of front, while in 4th Army, that distance was doubled.

Needless to say, this was greater than the weapon's actual range, and as the guns were horse-drawn rather than self-propelled, they effectively had to stay where they were first positioned, which was not exactly ideal given the fluid nature of the mechanised threat they were there to counter.

However, the soldiers did what soldiers do, they improvised. Lieutenant Nuto Revelli, a young officer in the 46th Company, Tirano Battalion, Tridentina Division, wrote:

> As usual, the anti-tank weapons available to us consisted of the 1891 rifle, some hand-grenades, and the agility of our legs. After two days, I already had a Russian parabellum [author's note: a superbly designed, drum-fed submachine-gun].

The Soviets were masters at playing on the unfairness of it all and specifically aimed a great deal of propaganda at the Italian forces. One of their 'best performers' was the leader of the Italian Communist Party, Palmiro Togliatti. Togliatti became well known to the 8th Army as he broadcast endless transmissions to his fellow countrymen:

> Every Italian soldier has the right to a pass allowing him to cross the Russian lines and turn himself in as a prisoner. Every soldier in the Red Army and every Soviet citizen is obliged to accompany him to the nearest Red Army command post. The commanders of the USSR guarantee the prisoner's life and will return him to his country at the end of the war. This is a message to all the Italians continuing to fight on the Germans' side – surrender!

Much as many of the listening soldiers desired nothing more than an end to the misery of the front, few, if any, believed the promise of Togliatti's words, having seen for themselves the 'guarantees' of Stalin's regime.

In essence, the *Ostheer*'s entire southern wing of some 2 million men (including their allies) was in a fairly precarious state. Case Blue was failing; the Red Army had not been decisively defeated in the second year of the campaign and the fabled Russian oil wealth had not been captured intact. Even worse, German military might in the south was split by hundreds of miles, with Army Group A at the end of its tremendously long supply lines in the foothills of the Caucasus and the Sixth Army being decimated on the Volga. As for the rest of Army Group B, it was now totally reliant on its Axis allies – and those same allies were seriously over-exposed. General Karl Strecker, the commander of the German XI Corps – Paulus' northern-most formation, which was adjacent to the Romanian 3rd Army – was specifically asked by his anxious Chief-of-Staff: 'Why is such a long sector held only by the Romanians and the other allies, Herr General?'

Strecker had no answer.[1]

The Red Army vs. 'the multi-national' army – Operation Uranus is born

When Istvan Balogh's captured diary was translated into Russian, it was delivered to G.F. Alexandrov, the Chief of the Department of Agitation and Propaganda for the Central Committee of the Communist Party of the USSR. He read it with mounting interest as the young Hungarian's hopeful June entries became open despair by September. This was exactly what Alexandrov and his bosses in the Kremlin were waiting for.

Days before Balogh's death, Generals Georgy Zhukov and Alexsandr Vasilevsky – the saviour of Moscow during the winter of 1941 and the Chief of the Soviet General Staff, respectively – had noted the major movement in Army Group B that placed the Axis allies to the north and south of Stalingrad, and in their minds a plan had begun to form that would become one of the Red Army's greatest offensives of the war. The two generals sketched out their idea and took it to Stalin. The Soviet dictator thought it workable and approved it. Operation Uranus, as the first phase would become known, envisaged two huge jaws crushing the allied Romanian armies north and south of Stalingrad and then snapping shut on the Don behind the German Sixth Army, trapping Paulus and all his men on the Volga. It was just the type of ambitious, combined-arms operation at which, in 1941, the *Wehrmacht* had excelled and the Soviets had conspicuously failed – but this was not 1941. This was a different Red Army led by different men, and the same applied to the *Ostheer*. In contrast to the growing stability in the upper echelons of the Soviet military hierarchy, all was in turmoil at OKW as Hitler increasingly took more and more personal control of tactical, as well as strategic, operations. His erstwhile subordinate, Franz Halder, was sacked as Chief of the General Staff in the autumn, and his place at the very top was taken by the more amenable Kurt Zeitzler.

In essence, Operation Uranus relied on three things: first, the STAVKA building up the necessary forces in secret so they could achieve surprise; second, being able swiftly to shatter the frontline defences of the allied

---

1 Later, Strecker's corps would be the very last to cease fighting in Stalingrad. On the morning of 2 February 1943 at 8.40 a.m., Strecker sent the following signal to Hitler: 'XI Army Corps with its six divisions has done its duty.'

armies; and third – crucially – overcoming the Axis panzer reserves that were bound to be in place. On this last point the success of the entire operation hung. If the Romanians, Hungarians and Italians held out for long enough then the Germans would have time to react and either escape the trap or launch their own counter-attack. The risk was huge, so the STAVKA did everything it could to find the answer to one simple question: would the Axis allies stand?

According to noted Russian Front historian Alexander Werth, the Soviets had initially been surprised by the toughness of the Romanian troops, especially given their record from the First World War was so poor. But since the terrible casualties at Odessa during the previous summer, matters seemed to have changed for the worse for the Romanians. Red Army raiding parties went out to deliberately capture Romanian soldiers for information – *Yazyky* (Tongues), as the Soviets called them – and those prisoners spoke of their growing hatred of Antonescu, the Germans and the war in general. With so many regular officers killed in Bessarabia, Bukovina, Odessa and the Ukraine, their replacements were mainly reservists, many of whom were poorly trained or elderly and lacked leadership skills and empathy with their men. This soured the atmosphere at the front, especially in the infantry divisions, with the men growing to resent their officers, who were described in a Red Army intelligence report as being 'very rude to their soldiers and they would often strike them for little or no reason'.

Those same officers also retained absurd privileges seemingly designed to cause disharmony in the ranks, such as being allowed personal servants and receiving much better quality rations. As the supply situation was so bad, this issue of food became a serious problem for morale. With deep snow on the ground and inadequate winter clothing, a private soldier received only half a mess tin of hot food per day along with 300 grammes of bread – barely enough to keep body and soul together. He saw his commander receive substantially more. The men did try to supplement this meagre ration with whatever they could buy from the local villagers or the black market, but their pitiful pay of just sixty Romanian Lei a month – equivalent to a handful of German marks – meant they were lucky if they could afford a pint of milk every other day. Thus, they did what hungry soldiers have always done: scavenge and steal if they felt they would not be caught. When men do that, the food they procure is often stale, badly prepared and hard to stomach – so bad, in fact, that men would fall ill with dysentery. Sensitised and suspicious as the Romanian military leadership already was, they saw shadows of sabotage behind every man in a latrine:

Russian agents have been carrying out poisonings in the rear areas to cause casualties among our personnel. (From an internal report from the 1st Romanian
Panzer Division on suspected Soviet espionage.)

For the Italians, whilst the Soviets noted that their military doctrine was one
that stressed the importance of the attack, the reality on the ground was that
assaults were rarely pressed home with much conviction and would usually
grind to a halt in about twenty minutes if resisted.

Balogh's entries in his diary confirmed the frame of mind in the ranks of
Hungary's 2nd Army.

Next, the Soviets had to train and then assemble the 1 million men and
thousands of tanks and artillery guns they estimated they would need for the
attack – all in total secrecy. To achieve this feat, the Soviets did not trust to
luck or good fortune but instead put together a comprehensive, co-ordinated
plan. This was *maskirovka* – deception taken to a strategic level and fully inte-
grated into operations. Operation Uranus was the first major instance of its
use in the campaign, after which achieving this level of operational surprise
on a grand scale increasingly became a feature of Soviet offensives for the
rest of the war. For the operation, whole formations were assembled and
then tested to the north in local fights against Army Group Centre. This
had the twin effect of training the new units in combat and confusing the
Germans, who saw a flurry of new enemy units appear and then disappear;
plus, it tied down reserves that could have been sent south. To cause even
more confusion, the Soviets also began to openly mass assault boats north
of Voronezh, while at the same time in their real attack sectors they made
sure the Germans saw them digging defensive trenches. It all added up
to a dilemma for the OKW, which suspected the anticipated Red Army
winter offensive would be against Army Group Centre and not against von
Weichs' men.

As it happened, the OKW would only be partly wrong. In reality, there
would have been no correct answer. Such was the almost magical recupera-
tive quality of the Red Army that it was preparing to launch not one, but two,
major offensives against the *Ostheer* almost simultaneously. Operation Uranus
was to be linked with the larger Operation Mars, which, like Uranus, was
planned by Zhukov. The Red Army would indeed attack von Kluge's army
group in a plan that was a truly audacious attempt to cut off and annihilate
the entire German Ninth Army around the city of Rzhev. To achieve this, the
Soviets concentrated 1.9 million men, 24,000 guns and mortars, 1,100 aircraft
and no fewer than 3,300 tanks. That is more tanks for one offensive than the

Ostheer had on the entire Russian Front. It was also many more than the 1,400 the STAVKA allocated to Operation Uranus (Uranus 'only' received 15,000 guns and 900 aircraft as well).

The scale of the envisaged operations were nothing if not grand. Just as the Soviet winter offensives of 1941 had saved Moscow and decimated the German Army in Russia, so Stalin now dreamt of his 1942 winter offensives dealing Hitler's forces a crushing blow by destroying his Axis allies and annihilating two of Nazi Germany's largest field armies – the Sixth and the Ninth.

All quiet on the Eastern Front

One of the many legends that has grown up around the stunning Soviet victory on the Don that winter was that the Axis forces were caught completely by surprise by Operation Uranus. This is simply untrue. Just as the lights burned long into the night around the planning tables in the Kremlin, so too did those in the offices on the Bendlerstrasse in Berlin.

Hitler, the OKW, OKH, Army Groups B and A (and most definitely the Sixth Army) all expected some sort of offensive, but they massively underestimated Soviet capability and intent and hugely overestimated the German forces' ability to resist. Their expectation was for a limited attack in the north against the Romanians, by relatively small forces, aimed at cutting the main railway into Stalingrad in an attempt to reduce the flow of vital supplies to the Sixth Army. The Germans did not believe the Romanians would be able, or willing, to put up a determined resistance, and so mobile reserves would be needed – hence, Hitler's personal decision to place Ferdinand Heim's panzer corps to their rear, ready to intervene. OKW thought that the Romanians would almost certainly give ground and maybe even lose the railway line, but then Heim's panzers would strike, seal off any breach and allow time for other German formations to move up and recapture the lost ground. It was not a perfect plan, but to the Germans it was the only possible solution given their general shortage of numbers. Berlin thought it was a gamble – but not a particularly big one. However, as events developed, it would be a fatal one.

What Berlin had not factored in was almost a complete accident of fate, one of those strange turns of events that seem so clear in retrospect but at the time happen without being noticed. The main link across all the southern Axis fronts was panzers – and more specifically, their types and lack of numbers. Everybody was aware there were simply not enough, and what they did have was a large number of two particular types that by this stage in the war were truly obsolete.

The main battle tank of Rodt's 22nd Panzer, Veress' and Lang's 1st Hungarian Armoured Field and Gherghe's 1st Romanian Panzer was the Czech-built PzKpfw 35(*t*) and PzKpfw 38(*t*). Both types were among the best tanks available in the 1930s, but by 1942 their day had passed.

In support of the some 280 tanks available, the reserves were also equipped with an even older concept – the light tank armed with either a machine-gun or small cannon. In this category was the Hungarian-built Toldi, Paolo Tarnassi's Ansaldo L3/33 (CV33) and Radu Korne's L3/35 (CV-3/35) tankettes – all vehicles that were already obsolete by 1940 and totally unsuitable to fight modern Soviet armour. A delusional Berlin was gambling on the 1st Romanian Panzer, the German 22nd Panzer and the 1st Hungarian Armoured Field being powerful armoured formations, which they weren't. Even the thirty or so modern PzKpfw IV tanks scattered across the San Giorgio and other battalions were not going to be enough for the battle ahead.

To the south of Stalingrad, the situation was no better for Constantinescu-Claps' 4th Army, and possibly worse. No thought at all was given to the possibility of a Soviet 'pincer' movement to encircle the city, so apart from Korne's small force, the only mobile reserve was the German 29th Motorised Division. As a motorised infantry formation, the unit had only a battalion of armour and not a regiment, but the troops who filled its ranks were battle-hardened veterans, recently re-equipped and rested and brought back up to full strength after the summer campaign. They would fight magnificently and almost win an impossible victory that could have saved the Romanians and the entire situation in the south, but they suffered from bad luck and the poor decision making that blighted the entire German response to the Soviet Uranus offensive.

This series of mistakes, based as it was on faulty thinking, was the genesis of the destruction of the Axis forces in Russia – and the accompanying annihilation of the Sixth Army at Stalingrad. The same mindset that would not believe the Red Army had both the ambition and forces to launch such an assault could not adapt to unfolding events in time to seize back the initiative. From the very start, the Germans and their Axis allies were on the back foot, reacting to Soviet moves with limited actions of their own and realising far too late the danger they were facing.

Soviet *maskirovka* vs. German Foreign Armies East

A not insignificant portion of the blame for this lies firmly and squarely at the doors of Germany's own military intelligence service, the *Fremde Heere*

Ost (Foreign Armies East – FHO) and its overrated head, Colonel Reinhard Gehlen. Gehlen, a small, dapper and precise man, had only taken over from his predecessor, Eberhard Kinzel, in the spring of 1942, but he was an insider who had been a senior figure in the service since July 1941. On succeeding to the post Gehlen had thoroughly overhauled the structure and organisation of FHO, but in its first really serious test, the failure to detect Soviet intentions that winter and warn German High Command was at least as significant a factor in the Red Army's success as their own *maskirovka* deception strategy. In fact, in early June 1942 just before the launch of Case Blue, Gehlen was confident enough to stand up in Berlin's War Academy and pronounce that the Soviet Army was seriously weakened:

> ... it is unlikely that the Russians will be able to cope with losses like those sustained at Vyazma and Bryansk again without great efforts ... and they will not be able to throw into battle again such voluminous reserves as during the winter of 1941–42.

This was wishful thinking of the worst kind, not supported by good intelligence or the history of the campaign. That same history should have been obvious to the head of German intelligence in the East – that the fighting on the Eastern Front had followed some general patterns since the start of Operation Barbarossa eighteen months earlier.

In brief, the *Wehrmacht* was a spring and summer force. It was not geared up in equipment, training or tactics for winter fighting in extremes of weather and climate. The Soviets, by necessity, were the opposite. This meant that the fighting in 1941/42 saw the *Wehrmacht* launch their main attack in the summer and then come to a juddering halt, exhausted, at the end of over-extended supply lines and with men and equipment worn out when winter arrived. The Red Army then launched a cold weather counter-offensive that engendered a crisis in Berlin. The Germans eventually halted the Red Army the following spring as the warm weather allowed them to bring their superior tactics and training to bear, and then they prepared to do it all over again in 1942/43.

This pattern was finally broken only after the monumental battle of Kursk during the summer of 1943, when the Soviets no longer had to wait for winter to go on the offensive. By then, the ascendance of the Red Army was gathering pace, and the *Ostheer* was correspondingly beginning its decline into oblivion. The Soviets could absorb the German summer attack and strike back immediately during the long, cloudless days of late summer and autumn. By 1944, it was the Red Army and not the *Ostheer* that could launch its main offensive in the summer. From then on, it was Moscow that dictated the pace of events on the battlefront and into the ruins of Berlin itself.[1]

North Africa

Despite the valiant efforts of the Eighth Army and the post-war British film industry to prove otherwise, the desert campaign in North Africa was something of a sideshow for the *Wehrmacht*. To prove it, one need look no further than the distribution of Germany's all-important panzer divisions. Of the twenty-seven in existence in late 1942, just two were with the *Afrika Korps*, with four or five divisions at any one time recuperating in occupied France. All the rest were deployed in the East.

In November 1942, despite this relative lack of importance, Berlin was forced to look up from its maps and situation reports from Stalingrad and the Caucasus and focus on the war in the desert. The reason was a battle won at an insignificant stop on the Cairo–El Alamein railway. In less than two weeks, beginning on 23 October 1942, Bernard Montgomery brilliantly led his British and Commonwealth forces to a resounding victory against the much-vaunted Erwin Rommel and his joint German/Italian army. Leaving the ground littered with hundreds of burning panzers and thousands of dead, the defeated Axis force fled west in a headlong retreat.

This defeat was gravely deepened when, just days later, on 8 November 1942, Operation Torch saw a British-US invasion force successfully land in French North Africa. This first incursion by US forces in the land war was a truly horrifying moment for Germany's military leaders, who remembered with dread the arrival of 'Black Jack' Pershing's 'dough-boys' in 1917 and the subsequent calamity that US intervention helped bring to Imperial Germany.

Overall, the timing could not have been worse for the *Wehrmacht* as the Red Army prepared for its planned offensives.

---

1 As for Gehlen, he would end the war as a Major General and would hand himself, his subordinates and his precious files over to US forces. The US military then granted him immunity from prosecution and imprisonment in return for him re-activating his old intelligence networks across Eastern Europe and the Soviet Union as the Cold War began. From 1956 to 1968, he was the head of West Germany's Federal Intelligence Service until he was forced to resign over embarrassing communist infiltration of the organisation. He died aged 77 in 1979.

The balance of forces

Secrecy was very important to Soviet preparation, and the precautions they took to preserve it were comprehensive. Under cover of darkness, villages and towns in the chosen launch areas were evacuated, their inhabitants moved out of their homes and transported away so troops moving up to the line could use their houses and barns to hide in during the day and avoid being observed by *Luftwaffe* reconnaissance aircraft. In the British Army, there is a saying: 'Time spent in reconnaissance is rarely wasted.' To prove this point Zhukov personally reconnoitred the key sectors, going forward with just a driver to see the land over which his troops would attack, even though the risk of being captured or killed was substantial.

Zhukov's counterpart in the south, Vasilevsky, pushed his men forward beyond a series of salt lakes so they had better jumping-off points – and both in the north and south, not even the Soviet Front and army commanders were told precisely what was going on.

Andrei Yeremenko's Stalingrad Front's part in the story[1] would be two-fold. With 430,000 men, 5,800 artillery guns and 650 tanks, its first task would be to contain the Sixth Army and attempt to prevent any of the troops, especially Paulus' three panzer divisions, from coming to the rescue of the Romanians. Second, with its southern 51st and 57th Armies, it was to form the southern pincer and smash through Constantinescu-Claps's 4th Romanians. In the days before the 'go' order was given, two mechanised corps and one cavalry corps were shipped silently across the Volga into bridgeheads on the western bank – watching, waiting and ready for the attack.

To the north, Rokossovsky's Don Front and Vatutin's Southwest Front would be the main assault forces, and they were mighty indeed. Nikolai Vatutin, a short, chubby-faced man with a rare flair for tank warfare, had 400,000 men, 6,500 artillery pieces,[2] some 730 tanks and 530 aircraft. Konstantin Rokossovsky had three armies, albeit smaller with almost 100,000 men fewer than Vatutin in total but still bringing 5,300 guns, 200 tanks and 260 aircraft to the battle.

The Axis opposition was dreadfully weak in comparison. To the north-west and south-east of Stalingrad, strung out for mile after mile of snowy steppe on or near the Don and Volga Rivers, sat two under-strength armies of peasant boys from Romania. Many were illiterate; barely one could point to where

---

1 A Red Army front was usually equal in size to a German Army.
2 Including 150 'Stalin's Organs', the much-feared Katyusha multi-barrelled rocket launcher, a lorry-mounted weapon that fired sixteen 132mm rockets.

they were on a map, and most had never before left their home districts. The vast majority were infantry conscripts, a large proportion of whom were fairly new to the line, having been through less than three months' training before being sent east to fill the yawning gaps torn out of their divisions in Bessarabia, Bukovina, the Crimea and Odessa. Officially, each division was meant to have one truck to every eighty men; unofficially, they were lucky to have one to 100. The resultant mobility gap was meant to be filled with traditional horsepower: one horse to every two men. In reality, too many of the horses were ending up in the infamous 'giddy-up soup' (slang for a soup made from horsemeat). As for the men, their ill-fitting woollen uniforms and poorly made boots, worn thin after miles of hard marching, were not suitable for the bitterly cold days and nights they had to endure. Most had picked up local clothing to try to keep the frostbite out — fur hats with ear-flaps, quilted jackets and felt boots, the eponymous *valenki* of the Russian villagers. If they could not get hold of these items, they would resort to stuffing straw and old newspapers inside their jackets and boots, anything to keep warm. Shivering for hours in their trenches, unable to move around for fear of the ever-present Red Army sniper, they dreamt of the daily ration runs — hot food! Unfortunately, as a corporal from the Rhenish German 305th Infantry Division observed in disgust:

> The Romanian field kitchens always prepared three different meals; one for the officers, one for the NCOs, and one for the men, who only ever got a little to eat.

An aristocratic Austrian officer, Lieutenant Graf Stolberg, found his innate *noblesse oblige* offended by the behaviour of the Romanian officers he saw:

> Above all the officers were no good ... they took no interest in their men.

For a *Wehrmacht* officer — indeed, for any officer of any army at any time in history — this was a grave charge. Evidence like this is just too frequent to ignore. Much as the martial pride of Romania would like this to be false testament, it is not. The fact is that with so many of the professional, experienced, pre-war officer and NCO corps already dead or invalided home after the 1941 campaign, the mass of front line divisions were in bad shape. They were often led at all levels by men who were not up to the task and, all-too commonly, downright neglectful of the soldiers they led. As the Red Army attacked this would lead to thousands of men abandoning their positions in desperate hope of escape as some of their commanders shamelessly tried to outrun them.

In the south, Constantinescu-Claps could field fewer than 76,000 men, with no tanks heavier than Korne's L3/35s, and a small number of anti-tank guns. His divisions were well below establishment after the summer fighting and the capture of the Crimea; his premier formations – the 5th and 8th Cavalry Divisions – were less than half strength; and while the 18th Infantry was still a powerful formation, the 1st Infantry was barely more than a good-sized regiment in number. The 2nd and 4th were not much better, either. Despite this, they were still expected to defend a stretch of front some 250 miles long with just thirty-three weakened infantry battalions. This was an impossible task. The men were widely spread, unable to provide one another with covering fire or deliver any defence in depth. The main line of resistance was often little more than a widely dispersed set of small foxholes set amid the snowy steppe, with two or three privates in each armed with nothing more formidable than bolt-action rifles, a handful of grenades and maybe a few Molotov cocktails. If the Soviets advanced, they would be able to overrun these lines in double-quick time, easily isolating each trench in turn and killing its defenders. Those same men would be unable to rely on their comrades for help and would end up dead in the bottom of their holes as Soviet forces literally rolled over them.

As for Dumitrescu's 3rd Romanian Army, at least it was a stronger proposition. Its line was some 150 miles shorter, meaning its sixty-nine infantry battalions had to cover only 1.5 miles each. It had more artillery than the 4th Army, so fire support was much better; plus, it just had more men – more than 90,000 more, in fact, including over 11,000 Germans. Red Army success in the north was not a foregone conclusion by any means.

The front holds its breath

Operation Mars was due to be launched first – in Moscow's eyes it was the priority operation – but as bad weather delayed it, Operation Uranus became the main focus. The Red Army was still learning its trade, though, and as the days went by it became clear to the STAVKA that not enough transport had been dedicated to the build-up, so it, too, was delayed. Nevertheless, in the days before H-hour, no fewer than 160,000 men, 14,000 vehicles, 10,000 horses, 6,000 guns and 430 tanks were quietly shipped across the Don into the bridgeheads opposite Petre Dumitrescu and his men – all at night. By the evening of 18 November, Zhukov judged they were ready. (See map, page 140.) History was about to be written.

CHAPTER 8

OPERATION URANUS
THE END OF THE ROMANIANS

'Fast Heinz' Guderian was never at a loss for something to say and amidst the leather-bound volumes he filled with his opinions on warfare, his view on quality versus quantity was a perfect summary of the situation the *Ostheer's* allies found themselves in as the Russian winter again began to bite in November 1942:

> It is better to have a few strong divisions than many partially equipped ones. The latter need a large quantity of wheeled vehicles, fuel and personnel which is quite disproportionate to their military effectiveness; they are actually a burden, both to command and supply.

Mussolini, Antonescu and Horthy would have been well advised to have read this critique before committing to Case Blue. All had fallen precisely into the trap that Guderian described so concisely, with Nazi cajoling, national rivalry and personal vanity having pushed them to commit a mass of men to the front they could never hope to train adequately, equip and then supply. It was now too late.

The storm was about to break. How would the four Axis armies fare?

The accepted version of the events that followed has a near-invincible Soviet war machine crashing through the paper-thin defences of the Axis lines, barely pausing for breath as the victors herded thousands of panic-stricken Axis conscripts in front of them across the steppe. Barely a drop of blood was spilled in anger as Romanians, Hungarians and Italians simply threw down their arms and ran away. That same narrative has the Soviet victory as pretty much inevitable from the start and only made greater when Hitler stepped in to condemn his own Sixth Army to oblivion through obsessive stupidity.

As with most legends, there is more than a grain of truth to this version of events, yet it is far from the whole story. In particular, it does the Axis allies a major disservice – their performance was far better than this picture paints and was peppered with often incredible bravery. With neither a panzer or anti-tank gun in sight, Romanian soldiers would leap onto the hulls of Soviet T-34 tanks with nothing more than hand-grenades and Molotov cocktails, destroying dozens of them – twenty-five by the Ploesti men of the 13th Infantry Division on the first day of the offensive alone – and defying massed infantry attacks armed only with rifles and a small number of machine-guns and mortars. The young Transylvanians of the 20th Infantry Division's 82nd Infantry Regiment would end up repulsing the attacks of two entire Red Army divisions, earning their unit the coveted *Mihai Viteazul* Order, as well as a number of citations and no fewer than fifty individual Iron Crosses from a grateful *Ostheer*.

On the other hand, the Soviets are paid too great a compliment in the Operation Uranus legend. Hugely successful as they were, their performance came perilously close to failing, and curiously, the much-vaunted German Army gets away pretty much scot-free, when in actual fact it was without a doubt the architect of its own disaster.

The offensive is launched

During the night of 18/19 November, fresh snow began to fall on the already freezing men of the Romanian 3rd Army. The ground was frozen solid, the whole landscape was white and the thermometer showed a temperature of minus 20°C.

It is unimaginably difficult for anyone who has never experienced it actually to understand what cold like that means for a human being. It utterly dominates your thinking. The one thing – indeed, the only thing – on your mind is surviving it. Any exposed bit of skin hurts, every breath knifes into your lungs and though after a while the pain in your fingers and toes disappears, it does so only because you know numbness is setting in followed by, if you're not careful, the 'black killer': frostbite. Even in top physical shape a man would soon begin to suffer, and the young Romanians were already weak from poor food and lack of sleep brought on by having to patrol and cover frontlines that were far too long for their numbers. The tiredness and mental exhaustion made the troops 'jumpy', so every noise they heard from the Soviet positions was an approaching assault and every engine a fleet of advancing tanks. Nervously, they would telephone to their commander: 'An attack is imminent, help us!' But no attack would come.

So when the duty officer at Sixth Army headquarters, Captain Behr, received a call from the German liaison officer with the Romanian IV Corps – Lieutenant Gerhard Stöck – at just after 5.00 a.m. on the morning of 19 November, he listened in bored resignation to Stöck's information that a cavalry patrol from the 1st Division had captured a Red Army officer, who, under interrogation, had told his captors that a major attack was about to begin in the Kletskaya sector. Behr had heard it all before and was not about to wake his boss, General Arthur Schmidt, on the basis of yet another 'cry wolf' report from the jumpy Romanians. So Behr told Stöck to relax and go back to his duty; he would note the call in his log.

On the other side of the Don, another phone call was being made, this one between the commander of the 65th Army, Pavel Batov, and his superior, Georgy Zhukov. Batov told Zhukov that in his sector thick snow was falling and visibility was down to less than 200 metres, so he proposed a delay. At the same time, another call was received from Issa Pliev, leading the 3rd Guards Cavalry Corps. Pliev's unit was crucial, as it would lead the charge – literally – against the Romanians at Kletskaya. Pliev told Zhukov his men had arrived at the Don bridges to begin crossing to their start line, only to find that all but one had been destroyed. Undeterred, the tough Ossetian with an unfortunate Hitler-style moustache informed Zhukov that they would cross on the frozen ice instead – tanks, artillery, horses etc. His mind made up, Zhukov told Batov the offensive would go ahead as planned.

The die was cast. The code word 'Syrene' was passed to the 3,500 artillery pieces on the waiting gun-lines, and minutes later, at 5.30 a.m. (German time; in Russian, it was two hours later), the battery commanders blew their trumpets as the signal to their gunners to open fire. The noise was deafening and woke up the men of the 22nd Panzer some 50 kilometres to the rear. Stöck was back on the phone to Behr even as the first shells exploded, and this time the captain did wake General Schmidt. No one panicked, and Stöck was told simply to keep monitoring the situation and report as necessary – difficult to do when approximately 21,000 shells were exploding all along the Romanian front every minute. However, all was not as it might seem. After the war, Moscow declared that 19 November would forever be commemorated as 'Artillery Day' in the Soviet Union in honour of the crushing bombardment that morning, but in reality, the enormous weight of explosives being hurled across the Don was not having the devastating impact the planners had hoped. The fire was too spread out, with most of it landing in the no-man's land behind the first Romanian defence line but in front of their reserve positions and all-important gun lines, and with visibility so poor, observers on the ground were unable to adjust the range by sight. The result was a massive wall of flame and shock waves that caused hundreds of casualties but was not the paralysing blow Zhukov wanted.

Fifty minutes later, the first Soviet infantry waves went into the attack and were met by steady fire from the Romanian trenches. Thousands of men from the 42-year-old Ivan Chistyakov's 21st Army near Kletskaya rushed forward, the brave young men of the 63rd, 76th, 96th and 293rd Rifle Divisions struggling to get a foothold among the trenches of their opposite numbers in the 5th, 6th and 13th Infantry Divisions. As for Pliev's cavalrymen, dismounted and moving swiftly through the snow, they came up against troops of the 1st Cavalry. The fighting was fierce, but the Romanians held; there was no panic, and they even counter-attacked. A second Soviet push, this time supported by Pliev's integral 4th Guards Tank Brigade, also came up short – the Ploesti men saw to that. So far so good for Dumitrescu's army, but now was the time they needed support. The Soviets were attacking in one echelon (with each rifle division of 5,000 men), having no fewer than nineteen of its twenty-seven rifle companies going forward at the same time. Now the T-34s were joining in, too, the drivers taking their steel hulls right over the top of the Romanian trenches and then spinning the track gears from left to right and back. The effect was terrifying. A small clutch of infantrymen would be huddled at the bottom of their hole in the ground, looking up in naked fear at the wet, mud-stained steel plate of the tank, the bolts covered in grease and dirt, the stench of oil and diesel overwhelming and the engine noise drilling into their heads. They screamed, waiting for the twenty-six tonnes of metal to collapse the walls of their haven and come crashing down on them, literally squashing them in the mud. But it didn't happen. The T-34s would spin on their tracks, their wide girth ripping up the deep snow and earth, yet the trench walls didn't give way. The reason? General Winter. The same icy cold that had been Russia's greatest ally the previous winter had now frozen the ground so hard that not even the weight of a T-34 could break it down. Romanian soldiers, who just hours before had been cursing the cold with all their bile were now thanking it as a saviour and were also using every weapon at hand to smash their attackers. Unfortunately for them, those weapons were few.

The four divisions facing the brunt of the attack had just six modern 75mm anti-tank guns each, and none was self-propelled. That meant the weapons could not be moved to the threat and instead had to wait for a tank to appear through the snow and fog; then it was a race to see who could fire the first killer shot. The Soviet shelling also took its toll, and several guns were hit and their crews killed, further reducing the ability to resist. This was the moment when the *Luftwaffe* was needed most. Weakened though it was, the German air arm in the East was still a fearsome force that could rule the skies at will. Squadrons of Heinkel He-111, Junkers Ju-88 and the feared Junkers Ju-87 Stuka dive-bomber were sitting in dispersal bays ready to go, but not one took to the air, as their commander, Wolfram von Richthofen, explained in his diary:

> Once again the Russians have made masterly use of the bad weather. Rain, snow and freezing fog are making all Luftwaffe operations on the Don impossible.

Khryukin, Rudenko and Krasovsky's Soviet Air Armies could not fly either, but that was not the point. The Germans' 'air artillery' could have bombed the Soviets in their jumping-off areas and wreaked havoc; instead, they were grounded. The offensive now hung in the balance, with both air forces neutralised and infantry and artillery slogging away. The only major asset either side had left to throw in was their panzer reserves.

Heim's XXXXVIII Panzer Corps vs.
Romanenko's 5th Tank Army

Forget the titles 'corps' versus 'army'. In reality, this should have been a pretty even contest, but up until now it had never happened. The Germans had concentrated armour in corps since the *Blitzkrieg* tactic was invented, but the Soviets had not done the same after putting Mikhail Tukhachevsky to death in the Lubianka back in 1937.[1]

---

[1] Marshal Mikhail Nikolayevich Tukhachevsky was an impoverished minor aristocrat who had converted early to Bolshevism and then been vital in helping win the Russian Civil War for the Bolsheviks. Made a Marshal of the Soviet Union at the tender age of 42 years, he became known as the 'Red Napoleon' on account of his ground-breaking theories on tank warfare. A ruthless and successful general, his reward was Stalin's jealous enmity. Secretly arrested for treason on 22 May 1937, partly on evidence fabricated by Reinhard Heydrich's Nazi SD agents, his archived confession was forensically tested after the fall of the Soviet Union and was found to be covered with dried blood spatter (communism has always been keen to use torture). Tukhachevsky and eight other senior generals were found guilty and sentenced to death. When told the verdict, Tukhachevsky was heard to say, 'I feel I'm dreaming.' An hour later, Captain Vasili Blokhin of the NKVD shot him in the back of the head. After the trial, five of the officers serving as judges were also summarily executed. Tukhachevsky's family was destroyed; his wife, Nina, and his brothers, Alexandr and Nikolai (both were instructors at a Soviet military academy), were all shot. Three of his sisters were sent to labour camps. His daughter was arrested when she reached adulthood and remained in the camps until Khrushchev declared the family innocent of all charges in 1957.

Tukhachevsky's theories on the mass employment of Soviet armour had died with him, and since Operation Barbarossa hit them, the Red Army had used its tanks in penny-packets. But times were changing, and now they were forming the six tank armies that would lead them to eventual victory in 1945.

That era was a world away in November 1942; at that time, the 5th Tank Army had been hurriedly created, an amalgam of armour, cavalry and infantry gathered together with no common doctrine or experience. What it did have was mass: Vasilli Butkov's 1st and Aleksei Rodin's 26th Tank Corps, the 8th Cavalry Corps and six full Rifle Divisions. This was true military power, and though it was new and inexperienced, it would not be easily defeated. At 7.00 a.m., it was committed and ran straight into one of the 3rd Army's two reserve divisions – the 7th Cavalry – attempting to reinforce the front, and the result was a dogfight. Held by the Romanian cavalrymen, the Soviet tankers swept out to the flanks and headlong into the 14th Infantry Division with barely a Romanian anti-tank gun in sight. The 14th was a border division made up of men from Iasi and Floresti in Moldavia – some of them former 'Soviet' citizens – and they fought back hard. Colonel Constantin Simionescu, of the 39th Infantry Regiment *Petru Rares*, was killed when personally leading a counter-attack, but his sacrifice was not enough; the 14th Infanty began to crumble. The danger was there – now was the time for panzers.

Ferdinand Heim was a man of action. No more than twenty minutes into the beginning of the Soviet bombardment that morning he ordered reconnaissance patrols towards Kletskaya and Bolshoye. His men radioed back – 'T-34s, lots of them'. Heim's mind was made up, and he ordered his corps north-east to hit Pliev's cavalry at Kletskaya and Bolshoye. From that moment on, absolutely nothing went right for the German general and his men.

The key to a panzer corps' power was mass attack – hundreds of tanks, self-propelled guns, artillery and mechanised infantry all acting as one, smashing into an opponent to hold him and then attacking his flanks and rear, destroying his ability to resist. Months later, the SS Panzer Corps would do exactly that in the classic counter-attack at Kharkov. Heim's massed force should have come from Lattmann's 14th and Rodt's 22nd Panzer and Radu Gherghe's 1st Romanians – well over 250 panzers in total. Where were they? The 14th was still bogged down in Stalingrad and had not been released, the Germans not considering the danger urgent enough.[1] As for Rodt, on receiving the call, his men rushed to their vehicles. The drivers hit their starter buttons and were rewarded with silence. The 22nd Panzer Division, one of Nazi Germany's elite units, was about to go through what can only be described as a moment of horror. During the shortages of the last few months, no fuel had been available for training. The effect was now coming home to roost – literally. The stooks of straw the tank crews had stolen from the villagers to try to insulate their precious vehicles against the cold would now be their downfall. The local mice had seen in them a potential home and nested en masse in the straw. Comfortable inside the tanks, the 'Soviet' rodents had gnawed through much of the electrical cabling. The result, at 7.00 a.m. on 19 November 1942 in southern Russia, was that the starter motors, turret rotating mechanisms and just about every other electrically driven component in the panzers was dead! A large number were totally out of action, and those that were serviceable began to slide haphazardly over the icy roads, all the division's track sleeves for winter driving having been lost too. Undaunted, Colonel von Oppeln-Bronikowski, commander of Panzer Regiment 204, pressed on, confident he would soon be joining up with his allies in the 1st Romanian Panzer.

That confidence was not misplaced. Several miles to Oppeln-Bronikowski's right, Radu Gherghe's German liaison team had received the radio message from Heim ordering them to move forward as fast as possible towards Bolshoye. No mice had interfered with the Romanians, and all of Gherghe's 106 serviceable panzers set off north, leaving another forty behind, still with the maintenance crews.

The 1st Romanian had never been so well prepared. Its 13,000 men were led by a cadre of experienced officers (men like Major Macrovici, the Divisional Operations Officer), NCOs and senior ranks. Also it was well equipped – with more than 300 machine-guns and forty mortars – and even though its eighty or so operational R-2 tanks were outclassed by the Soviet T-34, they now had just over twenty modern T-3 and 4 tanks. The men and machines were rested, and most of all the division was confident in its capabilities. In short, it was at its peak of readiness. As the first panzers left their protective dugouts and formed up on the roads, the division had no idea it was embarking on its 'death ride', which would see it fall to its nadir in less than a week.

As it was, having a shorter distance to travel, the advancing Romanians met the attacking Soviets first, the R-2s joining battle with the T-34s of the

---

1 As it happened, by the time the necessary order was given days later, most of the few panzers that Lattmann had remaining never even left the city.

19th Tank Brigade around the village of Sirkovsky. Initially, the Romanian tankers gained the upper hand and the Soviets withdrew, only to return in greater numbers. Tanks from both sides were hit and either caught on fire or blew up. The fighting ebbed back and forth, armour appearing out of the smoke and blinding snow, sometimes just a few yards from the enemy, and then disappearing again, pursued by the crack and thump of high-velocity armour-piercing rounds. Both sides tried to bring their artillery to bear and cause confusion. Such were the weather conditions that this was an almost impossible task, and most of the salvoes ended up ploughing the ground up around the village to minimal effect. After a few more hours of battle, both sides pulled back to regroup. Gherghe had lost a total of fourteen panzers completely destroyed, with another twelve damaged and out of action. Almost one-third of his division was now out of action.

All along the front the Soviets were now pushing forward hard, with the 21st, 65th and 5th Tank Armies locked in combat with II, IV and V Romanian Corps. The IV Corps 1st Cavalry and 13th Infantry now had some of the Romanian panzers on their flanks and were holding their ground against Batov's men. Ivan Chistyakov's 21st concentrated on attacking the V Corps just west of the shallow Sarisa Valley. The 5th and 6th Romanian Infantry Divisions (formed from men recruited from the wine-growing region around Focsani) were reinforced with several hundred ex-convicts sent direct from the country's prisons. All stood their ground, refusing to surrender the for-tified village of Raspopinskaya. Machine-gun and rifle fire kept the Soviet infantry at bay, whilst Romanian assault pioneers used improvised explosive charges to knock out any enemy tanks that ventured inside the village.

Consulting his maps and hearing the reports come in over the radio, Gherghe realised the main danger was now facing II Corps, and especially the embattled 14th Infantry Division. The 14th Infantry's three Dorobanti, Vânători and infantry regiments were already outnumbered and outgunned, when Romanenko then launched a frontal attack with the entire 8th Cavalry Corps. It was too much. The defensive trenches were overrun, and for the first time that morning, some Romanians ran away. A number of Gherghe's panz-ers arrived but were checked by the Soviet 1st Tank Corps as the Red Army cavalry destroyed the 14th Infantry's position. Within the space of a few short hours, they ripped an 8-mile hole between the II and V Corps that Gherghe's men were struggling to seal.

All was not lost for the Axis, though. Gherghe was banking on von Oppeln-Bronikowski's panzer regiment arriving and throwing the Soviets back – except it would not. Less than an hour after setting off, a new order had arrived over the radio for the commander of the 204th – 'STOP! Turn around and head northwest, not northeast!' The Chief of the German General Staff himself back at *Führer* HQ had decided that the main threat was not, in fact, from Kletskaya but from 5th Tank Army's right echelon bearing down from the bridgehead at Serafimovich. To Heim's total and utter fury, one of the cardinal rules of armoured warfare – concentration of massed force – was ignored as his main German panzer strike force had to leave the already-committed Romanians and head instead to Petschany. Whether the decision was correct from a strictly tactical perspective is not important; the fact is that it meant Heim's corps – the 3rd Army's only viable reserve – had been divided, and the 22nd Panzer (the German half) was effectively kept out of the fight for most of the crucial first day as it wasted hours changing direction without firing a shot. With no winter track sleeves and shuttling back and forth along icy tracks and rutted roads, more of Rodt's precious panzers ended up breaking down or sliding into snow-filled ditches; eventually, only 31 reached the assembly area that afternoon for the first assault. A further eleven were en route, but that still meant the division had lost sixty-two panzers (more than half its total strength) without a single round being fired. Even worse, it was now separated from its Romanian partner by a long distance, and the two would never effectively reunite. The XXXXVIII Panzer Corps was essentially a dead unit less than seven hours into Operation Uranus.

It was now past noon, and the Romanians had been under attack since before dawn. Ammunition was already beginning to run low; casualties among the ranks of corporals, sergeants, lieutenants and captains were high; and there was little sign of the expected panzer support, except for their own R-2s bravely continuing to fight. Dumitrescu had already committed his only cavalry reserves and was at a loss for what to do now. The 1st and 4th Soviet Tank Corps made the decision for him.

Sensing that Romanian resistance was starting to weaken, the Soviets renewed their assaults and finally smashed through the once solid defence of the 13th Infantry Division at Kletskaya. As the town was liberated by the Red Army that afternoon, the battered 14th Infantry on the 13th Infantry's left was almost annihilated, the remaining troops either raising their hands in surrender or dying in their trenches. Its sister division in IV Corps – the 9th Infantry – was routed from Bolshoye, despite receiving the support of at least some of Gherghe's panzers. Rampaging Soviet T-34s now charged forward and overran some of the Romanian gun lines to the rear. The 3rd Army was beginning to crack.

To the north-west at Petschany, von Oppeln-Bronikowski's panzers waiting in their designated assembly area realised they were now in the path of an entire Soviet tank corps. Not having anywhere near enough panzers to take them on and win, the quick-thinking German colonel hurriedly positioned his accompanying anti-tank battalion to form a defence around which his tanks could manoeuvre. The German gunners then proved just how useful they and their weapons would have been to the Romanians if they had had them. In a hectic engagement lasting over an hour, twenty-six T-34s were knocked out. The Soviet answer to this setback was simple and effective: they pulled back out of range and drove round the guns. Faced with possible encirclement, the 22nd Panzer Division had no option but to attempt to drive south and meet up with the 1st Romanian Panzer somewhere amidst the growing chaos.

Notwithstanding this setback for the Axis, as darkness closed in, the success of the offensive was still very much in the balance. True, the XXXXVIII Panzer Corps was misfiring, but the 1st Romanian Panzer was still in the field and fighting, as was the 22nd Panzer Division. Casualties amongst the Romanians had been extraordinarily high at more than 30,000 already – a third of the entire 3rd Army – with II Corps in particularly bad shape (its headquarters at Shirk had been overrun), while IV and V Corps were intact but badly mauled with several of their divisions ravaged. However, the Romanians had not just broken and fled as some Soviet, and German, estimates suggested; in fact, the majority had stood their ground and fought back. Russian casualties were correspondingly high, especially among the rifle and cavalry units, and the Red Army had made a host of its own mistakes – the 3rd Guards Cavalry Corps had ridden forward behind the lead rifle divisions of the 21st Army only to canter headlong into a minefield the infantry had not cleared properly. A large number of men and horses were killed. Meanwhile, on the Don, engineering units had not been positioned close enough to repair the demolished bridges, so everything had to be moved over the ice; fine for a marching man but less so for a tank weighing close to 30 tonnes.

Without doubt, though, the biggest advantage the Soviets had was the fact that the German military leadership at Army, Army Group and OKW levels were still unconvinced that Operation Uranus was anything other than a spoiling offensive, and they were reacting slowly and with little conviction. Paulus did indeed cancel his planned attempt to take what remained of Stalingrad, Operation Hubertus, and began to move units to the north-west, but with no great urgency; in fact, at 10.30 p.m. his Chief-of-Staff General Schmidt calmly went to bed asking to be woken only in case of an emergency. Schmidt's desultory attitude was mirrored at Dumitrescu's headquarters, where the aged general in command of Romania's most powerful field army simply sat at his desk and let the situation slip quietly out of his hands.

Day two – 20 November

Dumitrescu's near-dereliction of leadership was not mirrored by his subordinate, Mihail Lascar, the commander of the German-trained 6th Infantry Division. One of the few Romanian general officers held in high regard by his *Wehrmacht* counterparts, Lascar had spent the night frantically rounding up scattered units from his own and V Corps and drawing them into a hedgehog–type defence around Raspopinskaya. Every gun, cannon and mortar that could be found was manhandled into the new position, ammunition was distributed and the men were settled by experienced officers, NCOs and Lascar's German liaison team, including the redoubtable Lieutenant Gerhard Stöck. Lascar's plan was to stay where he was and wait for the relief force he believed the Germans would send. In the meantime, he and the 40,000 men he had gathered would stand where they were and force the Soviets to go round. He was without the men of the 1st Cavalry Division, though, who had run straight into their Soviet counterpart: the 5th Guards Cavalry Division. In scenes reminiscent of the previous century, groups of horsemen charged and counter-charged across the snowy steppe, swords, carbines and pistols flashing. The Romanians suffered badly, losing 150 killed and 300 captured. They were also cut off and forced to head south-west, where they were subordinated to Sixth Army in Stalingrad. This move saved them from encirclement at Raspopinskaya but doomed them to die in the fated city.

The lack of high-level German reaction continued, even as Lascar's men began to throw up barricades and pile what ammunition they had next to cannon and mortar positions. This erroneous belief was based partly on German arrogance – senior commanders still did not believe that the Red Army was capable of planning and launching large-scale mobile operations – and partly on a real-time lack of accurate intelligence. When II Corps headquarters had been overrun the previous evening, their accompanying German signals teams had been killed or scattered and all of their radio equipment destroyed. This effectively severed the link and passage of information between the Germans and most of the 3rd Army, including, crucially, Radu Gherghe's 1st Panzer, which was now totally out of contact and fighting blind. The last message the Romanian general had received from higher command was that the 22nd Panzer was at Petschany, so that's where he headed with his surviving panzers, only to run headlong into the Soviet 5th Tank Army advancing south-east to Kalach and the vital bridge over the Don. Colonel von Oppeln-Bronikowski was on the other, western side of this Soviet 'tank stream', so there was a slim chance that if the two panzer divisions acted together they could attack Romanenko's exposed flanks and save the day for the Axis. But with fewer than 100 panzers between them, negligible artillery, no air support and unable to communicate, Gherghe and his German counterpart were left with no other option except to attempt to save what remained of their battered units.

The 4th Romanian Army's turn

With all eyes on the Don to the north, everything was deceptively quiet to the south of Stalingrad, where the 4th Romanian Army waited in its trenches. Constantinescu-Claps, almost cadaverously thin (and fastidious about his appearance), said a silent prayer of thanks that he was not in Dumitrescu's place. The Romanian general knew his own army was far weaker than his northern neighbours, and there was no panzer corps sitting behind him to provide even a level of reassurance.

His opposite number, Andrei Yeremenko, was pacing up and down outside his own headquarters, nervously contemplating the offensive he was about to launch. The weather on his front was as bad as it had been for the northern attack the day before – freezing fog, snow and ice – and the Soviet general delayed the attack from dawn, much to a furious STAVKA's chagrin. But unlike Zeitzler and Heim, Moscow deferred to the man on the spot and confined itself to urging boldness. Four hours later, their calls were answered, and Yeremenko ordered his artillery to open fire. He had fewer guns than Zhukov, but they were better sited and their fire more accurate and concentrated. The result was devastating.

Complete lines of Romanian trenches collapsed under the weight of shellfire, burying alive the occupants by the hundred. The Romanian artillery bravely tried to respond with counter-battery fire but was swamped with high-explosives, and the Romanian gunners took terrible casualties. Soviet engineers had already crawled forward during the hours of darkness to clear safe lanes through the Romanian minefields, and now, after a forty-five-minute bombardment, Feodor Tolbukin's 57th and Nikolai Trufanov's 51st Armies stormed forward, the infantry leading. The main attack hit Lieutenant-General Corneliu Dragalina's VI Corps with its 1st, 2nd, 4th and 18th Infantry Divisions. Dragalina, the son of a First World War hero and an artillery officer by training, had received the Knight's Cross earlier in the summer in recognition of the valiant performance of his corps in Case Blue, and they now formed the greater part of 4th Army, despite the fact that they were seriously under strength and hemmed in on the open steppe between the Tsa Tsa and Sarpa Lakes. Dazed by the artillery barrage, Dragalina's men tried to resist but were overwhelmed far more quickly than the men of the 3rd Army. The Timisoara and Craiova men of the 1st and 2nd Romanian Infantry were the first to cave in, hundreds throwing down their weapons and almost gratefully marching into captivity. The Transylvanian Saxons of the 18th Infantry did not follow suit; instead, they fought back, but with other rifle divisions streaming out of range to their left and right they soon had no option but to retreat to avoid being surrounded – a withdrawal that soon became a rout.

In less than three hours, Constantinescu-Claps' line had been decisively breached. His VII Corps, with the 5th and 8th Cavalry Divisions, was still intact, as was his mixed IV Corps with the 297th and 371st German Infantry and his own Romanian 20th Infantry, but all else was gone, with thousands of Romanians fleeing in near-panic. Soviet morale was sky high; a wounded Russian soldier ordered to a dressing-station told his officer, 'I'm not leaving, I want to attack with my comrades.'

The situation worsened for the 4th Army when Yeremenko followed up his initial, startling success by releasing his mobile units to exploit the breakthrough and take up the charge. The tank units, those of Trofim Tanaschishin's 13th and Vasily Volsky's 4th Mechanized Corps, drove straight at Saty and Plodovitoye, respectively. These two small towns were miles behind the old front and sat astride the main southern railway line to Stalingrad. Reaching them would hammer another large nail into the Sixth Army's coffin.

Nothing was inevitable, though, and just as to the north with XXXXVIII Panzer Corps, the *Ostheer*'s leadership had the potential to stop the Red Army in its tracks. In the south, that potential lay in the fifty-five new panzers of the German 29th Motorised Infantry Division. Waiting in its divisional assembly area, the veteran Saxons of this first-rate formation reacted to the news of the Romanian collapse by mounting their vehicles and heading towards the sound of the guns. Their highly decorated commander, Hans-Georg Leyser, was a real firebrand and a man who knew how to get the best out of his men. Driving south from their bases at Beketovka, they met Tanaschishin's 13th head-on at about 1.00 p.m.

What happened next was a masterclass in how the *Wehrmacht* had conquered most of Europe in eighteen months. Spotting the Soviets through their binoculars, the Germans did not even reduce speed but instead went into a full-on panzer engagement. The panzer companies swung out to form armoured wedges, with the anti-tank guns pushing to the flanks and unlimbering at speed. Orders were given over the radio, and every commander knew his role, every man his own task. This was what well-trained, experienced and well-led panzer troops were capable of, and the effects on an enemy were devastating. Outnumbered, the Saxons proceeded to quickly wipe out the 13th, destroying all ninety of the corps' tanks. The German PzKpfw IV tanks then nosed through the burning hulks of T-34s to spot an extremely long train sitting motionless on the railway tracks some 400 yards away, steam clouds rising from its stationary locomotive. Troops were seen to be dismounting from the carriages, and Leyser realised it was Soviet infantry sent forward to reinforce the advance. He barked out the command, 'FIRE!' that sent dozens of high-explosive shells pouring into the men and the train. The slaughter was dreadful, the train destroyed. Asking permission to continue the counterattack, the general was dumbfounded when he received the extraordinary news that his request was denied and that he was instead ordered to retreat north and secure the rear of Sixth Army. This was yet another wrong decision by a German military command still unable to grasp the significance of what was happening at the battlefront. It sealed the fate of the Romanians of the 4th Army, and incidentally did the same for Leyser's command. The general would surrender the starving remnants of his superb division amidst Stalingrad's rubble on 31 January 1943.

Back in the 4th Army, Constantinescu-Claps now had only two intact infantry divisions left: the 4th and Nicolae Tataranu's 20th. The Bucharest men of the former were already committed to the struggle, desperately trying to hold a line to the rear of where the 1st and 2nd Divisions once were. As for the Transylvanians of the latter, they were tough fighters, their general one of only a handful of Romanians ever awarded the much-coveted Knight's Cross by their German allies, and despite having only a single 37mm anti-tank gun, they were determined to stand their ground.

For Yeremenko, the unfolding situation was much easier; he had crushed the 4th Army's largest corps and passed his own two mechanized corps through to exploit the gap and race to meet the northern pincer at Kalach exactly as planned. The counter-attack by Leyser's Saxons had been a rude shock, and Vasily Volsky was constantly on the radio calling for reinforcements, desperate to avoid Tanaschishin's unhappy fate. But overall, the operation so far was a brilliant success. Now it was time to sweep away the remaining Romanians so he could operate unhindered, and that meant Tataranu's stubborn 20th Infantry had to be defeated.

Several rifle and cavalry divisions were lined up for the attack, supported by a tank brigade, and then the order was given. The outnumbered Romanians did not give an inch and died where they stood. Fewer than fifty men from the 91st Infantry Regiment Alba Iulia-Regele Ferdinand I survived the day; from the 83rd Tribunul Solomon Baint, fewer than forty survived. The

Soviet T-34s wiped out the Pioneer Battalion and overran the 40th Artillery Regiment, cutting off most of the Romanians' support fire. With only a single infantry regiment remaining, Tataranu had no choice but to retreat to the rear.

The Romanian 3rd Army had been badly mauled on the previous day, but Dumitrescu's men were still in the field and resisting, despite taking thousands of casualties. Mihail Lascar had 40,000 men positioned around Raspopinskaya, and Radu Gherghe's 1st Romanian Panzer was still in action.

For Constantinescu-Claps's 4th, the picture was wholly different. As darkness settled at the end of their first day in the heart of the fighting, it was crystal clear that they had been decisively defeated. The front line was gone, and Soviet tanks and cavalry were now roaming throughout the army's rear area, destroying supplies and communications centres and fuel and ammunition dumps and generally obliterating all semblance of an organised military infrastructure. The once-proud 1st Infantry Division had more or less disappeared, and there were only 300 men left of the 2nd. The 4th was fighting for its life, and Constantinescu-Claps' link to his southern German neighbours was broken. It had been a particularly tragic day for Transylvania; the remaining ethnic Saxons of the 18th Infantry were almost encircled, and the 20th had been decimated. Chased north, Tataranu and his men would join their comrades from the 1st Cavalry Division in Stalingrad, where they would fight to the bitter end. In all, as the Romanians fell back towards Kotelnikovo in disarray, they left behind no fewer than 35,000 of their comrades, dead or captured – almost half the total strength the 4th Army had on that same morning.

Back in the north

The hole in the 3rd Army's front now stood at more than 40 miles as the rifle divisions rolled up the Romanian flanks, marching and fighting hard by day and night and giving their enemy no respite. Excellent generalship and command and control marshalled the follow-on formations and sent them west and south in a steady stream to pour over the still frozen Don. The 'Lascar Group', as it had now been officially entitled, was like a rock in a river, constantly in danger of being washed away but somehow clinging on. As for the 1st Romanian Panzer, it continued to make an absolute nuisance of itself, counter-attacking into the Soviet 124th Rifle Division and acting as a brake on Butkov and Rodin's 1st and 26th Tank Corps. The new PzKpfw III and PzKpfw IV tanks (the T-3 and T-4) with their heavier guns and thicker armour, were proving invaluable, but the old R-2s were taking heavy punishment. Gherghe lost another twenty on 20 November, of which some twelve could be repaired if his maintenance crews could work on them in safety without being suddenly attacked by Soviet troops.

By now, Dumitrescu had ceased to provide effective leadership to his troops, and as his army was rapidly decimated, he and his staff packed their bags, got into their staff cars and drove west to the airbase at Morozovskaya. The Italian liaison officer, Captain Giorgio Geddes of the Army Intelligence Service, saw the effects of the collapse in his own district behind the old frontlines:

> The roads were obstructed with all sorts of wreckage; the carcasses of dead horses, along with the metal frames of burnt-out trucks and overturned cannon. The corpses of dead soldiers lay in the bloodstained snow, thrashed by the relentless wind … our lips were chapped by the cold and our gums bleeding from lack of vitamins. We felt the end was near.

Day three – 21 November

The launch of Operation Uranus had not caught the German or Romanian commands by surprise. What had been a surprise was the scale and intensity of the attack. The Axis reaction, so far, had been piecemeal and ineffective, with divisions fighting singly and in an unco-ordinated way. This meant that the often-brave actions of units such as the 20th Romanian Infantry, the 1st Romanian Panzer and the German 29th Motorised were swallowed up in the altogether better controlled Soviet assault. Now, on the third day of the battle, the Germans were finally waking up to what they were facing, and they began to swing into action and fight back.

Paulus began to push Sixth Army units at the northern Soviet pincer in particular, and tanks and grenadiers from the 24th and 14th Panzer Divisions mounted counter-attacks against the 5th and 6th Guards Cavalry Divisions. This sounds far grander than it actually was. The reality on the ground was that these 'attacks' usually consisted of little more than a small number of panzers with some companies of very tired infantrymen driving into the advancing Red Army. The Soviet troops they encountered reacted brilliantly; they fired back, withdrew and then just went round the Germans, outflanking them and forcing them to retreat without firing another shot. Instead of sending small numbers, Paulus should have been frantically pulling everything together into a serious attack against Zhukov's northern pincer. The whole 5th Tank Army was horribly exposed and could have been cut off and encircled. Instead, battalions and regiments were sent where there should have been divisions and corps, and this left the Romanians scrabbling in the vacuum. The

7th Cavalry, as the 3rd Army's reserve, was flung forward into the Russian advance and lost all its artillery vainly trying to stem the advance.

To the south, where the collapse of the 4th Army was far more complete than its northern counterpart, the remnants of Corneliu Dragalina's VI Corps tried to defend a line of villages – Tundutovo, Gonchearovsky, Mal Derbety – backed up by Radu Korne's motley reserve force.

Korne was in many ways a cliché; a dashing aristocratic Romanian cavalryman with a distinguished and heroic career already behind him, he had a penchant for tall fur hats and immaculately oiled hair. Barbarossa had already brought him more glory to add to his medal haul from the First World War, and now he would once again step into the breach as he attempted to stem the drive of the Red Army's southern pincer. To do it, he collected every last unit and man he could find and melded them together into a formation. It included the 3rd Calasari and 4th Cavalry Regiments, batteries from the 3rd Horse and 7th Heavy Artillery, some light tankettes and groups of retreating infantrymen, as well as some construction gangs and headquarters staff. This was not an elite force by any means, but rather a forlorn hope. Even so, it was a force that could perhaps make a difference, and Korne threw himself and his command into a counter-attack towards the small town of Abganerovo near the main southern railway line. His men succeeded in taking and holding a strongpoint at Kraniy Geroy, but it was not enough to halt the Soviet push towards their target of Kalach on the Don River. Elsewhere on the 4th Army's former front, the Soviets had an almost free hand as the Romanian forces disintegrated.

Information for the Axis commanders on what was actually happening was very limited, with so many radio trucks destroyed and landline links being cut. Usual practice would have been for air reconnaissance to fill the gap, but the weather had been so bad this had been impossible. Finally, on 21 November, there were some breaks in the fog and blizzards, just enough to allow the Romanian 7th Fighter Group to operate some flights. Lieutenant Dicezare (a reservist) was one of the pilots, and as he scanned the steppe from his German-supplied Bf-109 fighter, he spotted a large Soviet column moving in the direction of his own Karpovka airfield. Flying closer to get a better look, he came under intense anti-aircraft fire, and his machine was hit in the fuel tank. He nursed his aircraft back to base and reported the threat. His fellow pilot, and former mountain soldier, Lieutenant Alexandru Serbanescu, was sent up to investigate, and he confirmed that the Soviet tanks were now only a few miles to their south and heading straight for the airfield. With no radio link, Dicezare, now with a cork plugging the bullet hole in his fuel tank, was sent to Morozovskaya to request help. Landing at the main *Luftwaffe* base, he informed General Ermil Gheorghiu of the situation and was promptly given two IAR JRS-79B (Romanian-built Savoia-Marchetti SM-79B) medium bombers to fly to Karpovka in an attempt to rescue as many personnel as possible. In the meantime, Serbanescu had assembled a defensive line at Karpovka, using the two airfield anti-aircraft batteries, the maintenance crews and even the aircraft by lifting their tails onto barrels to level the wings so that their machine-guns could be fired at the enemy. As soon as the first Soviet troops were sighted, the defenders unleashed a hail of fire in an attempt to convince them that there was a larger force of defenders than there actually was and buy time for the rescue flight to arrive. It worked. The Soviets held back, allowing enough time for the two rescue aircraft to land and pick up all of the personnel. All the heavy equipment, fuel and stores were abandoned.

To the north, the surviving bulk of the 3rd Army under Mihail Lascar was fighting for its life in its hurriedly fortified position around Raspopinskaya. Lascar called for help, knowing his men could hold for only a matter of days without resupplies of food, fuel and, most importantly, ammunition. Their only hope was that Gherghe and Rodt could finally unite their two panzer divisions and use their combined strength to break through. Communication between the two units was still very fragmented, and most of the time the two commanders had only a general idea of where the other was located. So von Oppeln-Bronikowski led his remaining panzers towards the village of Perelasovsky, hoping the Romanians would be following. Unfortunately for them both, the 1st Romanian Panzer was actually several miles west, near the neighbouring village of Bolshaya Donschynka. This was where Gherghe thought the Germans were, and he and his men drove into the village only to find it swarming with Soviet troops. Firing point blank into the *isbas* (peasants' houses), the Romanians managed to secure the village but were then left desperately short of fuel, food and ammunition. Luckily for them, the *Luftwaffe*'s 105th Transport Squadron managed to get through and land on an improvised airfield outside the village. The Romanian tankers gratefully unloaded jerrycans of fuel, crates of tank ammunition and machine-gun belts. But even as the aircraft were taking off to return to base, shells from Soviet artillery were beginning to land as more Red Army units stormed towards the Romanians in a determined attempt to stop them joining up with the 22nd Panzer Division. As Gherghe was deciding on a plan of action, his capable second-in-command, Colonel Alexandru Pastia, was injured by an exploding shell. Lacerated by shrapnel and bleeding heavily, he was mortally wounded, and this made up Gherghe's mind – the 1st Romanian Panzer was simply not strong enough to advance, and the only option was to retreat. The fate of Mihail Lascar and his men was sealed.

A new participant now arrived on the battlefront for the Romanian 3rd Army. Flown direct from the (strangely) continuing German offensive in the Caucasus, Colonel Walther Wenck – the Chief-of-Staff for the LVII Panzer Corps – had been ordered north to take over as Dumitrescu's new head of operations and to try to instill some sort of order in the chaos.[1]

Wenck, a typically taciturn, professional German officer, landed at Morozovskaya and was driven straight to a meeting with Dumitrescu, who was now based at *Luftwaffe* headquarters:

> I reported to General Dumitrescu, and through his interpreter, Lieutenant Iwansen, I was acquainted with the situation. It looked pretty desperate. The following morning I took off in a Fiesler Storch to fly out to the front in the Chir River bend. Of the Romanian formations there was not much left. Somewhere west of Kletskaya, still on the Don, units of Lascar's brave group were still holding out. The remainder of our allies were in headlong flight.

Wenck's summary of the Lascar Group was almost its epitaph.

Day four – 22 November

Sunday 22 November dawned cold, with blizzards once more sweeping across the steppe from the north. It was *Totensonntag* – in Germany, the Day of Remembrance for the war dead. In a setting that matched the sombreness of the day, on the land between the Don and Chir rivers carpeted with the dead, wounded and burning equipment of three battling countries, the struggle of the 3rd and 4th Romanian Armies was reaching its climax.

In the north, the Lascar Group was still a serious problem for the northern pincer movement, sitting as the group did across the Soviets' main line of advance. The Soviet rifle divisions Vatutin and Rokossovsky required to follow Romanenko's tanks and secure the flanks of the attack were instead forced to surround the obstinate Romanians to try to batter them into submission. The fighting was fierce, with Lascar encouraging his men as they clung to every trench and strongpoint. The main problem they faced (apart

---

1 Walther Wenck eventually rose to command the German Twelfth Army in 1945, which unsuccessfully tried to break through to an encircled Berlin. After surrendering at the end of the war, he was released from a POW camp in 1947 and went on to live a full life before dying in a car crash in 1982, aged 82 years.

from being entirely cut off and surrounded) was the lack of ammunition. The brave crews of the 105th Transport Squadron (the saviours of the 1st Romanian Panzer the previous day) managed to fly in some, but it was a fraction of what was needed as the encircled troopers desperately tried to fend off their Red Army opponents, who were equally determined to win the day.

By midday on 22 November, each defender in Raspopinskaya was down to just forty rounds of rifle ammunition, perhaps enough for one attack if they were lucky. Desperate to finish the battle and move on, the Soviet commanders offered Lascar a surrender proposal, but he refused, replying, 'We fight to the last man. We shall not surrender!' Full of bravado as this was, the ex-mountain soldier now knew no German relief force was coming to their rescue – the end was near. He decided a breakout that night, by all who were able, was the only option available to save at least some of his command. Hunched over a situation map at his headquarters in Golovsky, Lascar put a plan together for a two-pronged escape attempt. The Moldovans of the 15th Infantry Division would lead one attack, heading south-west to try to reach Bolshaya Donschynka, where Lascar thought Gherghe's panzers were still positioned. The second group had Lascar's own excellent 6th Infantry Division in the lead and aimed to break out towards Petschany and the 22nd Panzer Division – in fact it was the 22nd at Bolshaya Donschynka and Gherghe's Romanian panzers at Petschany. Lascar was going to remain and told his staff:

> If one of you survives these battles you must tell the story of our fight. I am a soldier and so shall remain at my post.

Privately, he then told his old friend, Colonel Cristea Stanescu, that when the Russians finally overwhelmed them, he would shoot himself rather than be taken alive.

As darkness began to fall in the late afternoon, the two columns formed up just outside Golovsky, under the overall control of the 1st Romanian Panzer's old commander, General Ioan Sion. A total of 15,000 men were going to attempt to escape; about the same number were going to stay, including several thousand wounded, and they would take their chances in captivity. Then, as if the situation were not bad enough, Soviet artillery began shelling the town and the surrounding area. After two hours, it was obvious that the barrage was to soften up the defenders for an all-out attack. General Lascar transmitted a last message back to his army commander informing Dumitrescu that he and his men had done everything that could be asked of them and more. He then left his HQ and headed off on foot to see what was happening outside. In the confusion, Mihail Lascar was surrounded by Soviet infantrymen and captured. He was soon joined by thousands of his men as the pocket collapsed.

As Golovsky fell, Sion led the by now 10-kilometre-long column of troops away from the fighting and out into the frozen steppe. Marching through the ice-cold night, the Romanians unbelievably managed to slip past the first Red Army patrols, and hopes began to rise that perhaps they would be saved. However, by the grey light of dawn that hope was dashed as tanks from a Soviet cavalry unit spotted the endless line of men and charged, launching high-explosive rounds and machine-gun fire into their ranks. In the ensuing panic, the breakout lost all cohesion as the Romanians, desperate to survive, ran frantically in all directions. The column fractured; some managed to carry on and reach Bolshaya Donschynka, where they linked up with the 22nd Panzer and were pressed into becoming additional 'Romanian panzer-grenadiers'. Among them was Ioan Sion, who, having successfully led as many of his men as possible out of Raspopinskaya and across the frozen steppe, finally ran out of luck two days later when he was killed in action holding off a Soviet attack. This indubitably brave officer then held the singular distinction of being officially the only Romanian general officer to be killed in combat during the war.

Another major group of survivors from Raspopinskaya, separated from their fellows after the tank attack, headed due west to try to reach the German lines. Marching on through the night and following morning with no hot food and with the penetrating cold taking its toll, they became exhausted, but nevertheless began to think that perhaps they had outrun the Soviet advance and would reach safety after all. It was not meant to be, and the following afternoon, a heavily armed Red Army column caught up with them and wiped them out in a one-sided fight. Hundreds were killed and even more captured.

The only real Axis success story from the demise of the Lascar Group was that of Major Gheorghe Rasconescu's 1st Battalion from the 6th Infantry's 15th Dorobanti Regiment Razboieni. Remembering everything their German instructors had told them two years earlier, almost the entire battalion, with all its equipment, reached the sanctuary of the western bank of the Chir River on 26 November. Exhausted and badly affected by frostbite and dysentery, Major Rasconescu and his men still succeeded in defending the important Oblivkavia airfield from attacks by the Red Army's 8th Cavalry Division until the beginning of December. Rasconescu was awarded the Knight's Cross by the *Ostheer* in recognition of his men's courage, and even more importantly he saved the battalion's hometown of Piatra Neamt from the grief of losing several hundred of its sons.

In the south, just as the final Romanian resistance of the Lascar Group was being suppressed, Constantinescu-Claps was beginning to accept the fact that he had lost control of the situation at the front. His infantry corps were either destroyed or scattered, and he could not maintain a solid defensive line. His only mobile force – Radu Korne's motley collection of cavalrymen, gunners and unemployed builders – was struggling manfully to hold back the armour and infantry of 4th and 13th Mechanised Corps, but was failing. Korne's men fought a fierce battle at Abganerovo when they advanced from their strong-point at Kraniy Geroy and tried to retake the town and its vital train station. The Romanians went forward bravely but were hit by a storm of fire from a large number of dug-in 7.62cm field guns, the famous Russian *Ratsch-Bumm*. Korne's men had no option but to fall back, leaving behind 300 dead and another 600 as Soviet prisoners.

Kalach

At the beginning of August, at the height of Case Blue, the German 16th and 24th Panzer Divisions had raced ahead of the advance to seize Kalach, a small town some 40 miles west of Stalingrad. What made Kalach a target of such importance was its imposing old road bridge over the Don River. Deciding to capture the bridge intact, Lieutenant Kleinjohann of the 16th Engineer Regiment led the men of his 3rd Company forward onto the bridge, even though it was on fire and the Soviets had placed demolition charges on it. Putting the fires out and cutting the wires to the charges, Kleinjohann succeeded in taking the bridge and thus closed the door behind the Red Army men now isolated and encircled on the western bank. That included nine rifle divisions and seven armoured and two motorised brigades, equipped with 1,000 tanks and 750 guns.

Now the Red Army was determined to turn the tables by liberating Kalach and cutting off the Sixth Army in Stalingrad.

The task was given to the 19th Tank Brigade and its commander, Lieutenant Colonel G.N. Filippov. This redoubtable officer hatched a bold plan to seize the all-important bridge by launching a direct attack. He had two captured German panzers in his unit, and he positioned them in the lead with the idea of driving them right onto the bridge and surprising the defenders. What he didn't know was that the Germans had established an assault engineer training school at Kalach, where specialist German and Romanian troops were taught how to destroy Soviet tanks. As thorough as ever, and keen to make the whole experience as real as possible, the Germans had numbers of captured Russian tanks at the school, so the local defence units were all too used to seeing T-34s driving around the area.

Those same protection troops were pitifully small in number. Crucial as the bridge was, it was guarded by just twenty-five personnel from the Todt Organisation[1] and a single 88mm Flak anti-aircraft gun that had only eight shells. So when Sergeant Wiemann, Filippov's Flak gunner, saw the two German panzers and a number of T-34s behind them, he thought it was normal. It was only when the tanks opened fire on the Todt men that he realised his mistake. Running to his gun, he and his bewildered crew managed to fire four rounds before they and the 88mm were destroyed. Three T-34s were burning furiously, but the Soviets had captured the bridge. Stalingrad was now officially cut off.

Day five – 23 November

As the Red Army staged, and filmed, a joyous meeting up of troops from the 4th Tank Army from the north and the 4th Mechanised Corps from the south, at the town of Sovyetskiym, the scale of the unfolding disaster was finally beginning to register with the Axis. In reality the two advancing Red Army columns had mistaken each other for the enemy and had opened fire. A number of tanks and more than 100 men were killed before they realised their mistake and ceased shooting.

With Lascar and his men filing disconsolately into captivity, the Soviet 3rd Guards Cavalry Corps attempted to get behind the still-fighting 1st Romanian Panzer and the 22nd Panzer Division. Reduced to a small number of tanks each, the two formations were separately forced to turn west to try to reach safety on the far bank of the River Chir. With them went the remnants of the 3rd Romanian Army, men from the 7th, 9th and 11th Infantry and the 7th Cavalry. Still nominally under Dumitrescu's command, they were subordinated to the newly formed German Army Group Hollidt, a miscellany of formations assembled in an attempt to hold the Chir against the advancing Soviets. Walther Wenck, now firmly in place as Dumitrescu's Chief-of-Staff, was also trying to muster a defence:

> I had to rely on the remnants of XXXXVIII Panzer Corps … which fought its way south-west. But I was not able to make contact with Heim's Panzer Corps until Heim had fought his way through to the southern bank of the Chir with 22nd Panzer Division.

---

1 A construction service originally headed by its founder, Dr Fritz Todt; it was used to build the Atlantic Wall, airfields and other strategic defences.

That same division was not what it had been just a few days earlier. Rodt had some forty serviceable panzers left; most of his artillery, engineers and service units were gone, and his 129th Panzergrenadier Regiment was almost obliterated. Indeed, the regiment's 1st Battalion was now led by a lieutenant – the only officer left alive. The new overall German commander in the south, Erich von Manstein, thought the division was 'a complete wreck'.

Manstein, formerly the Eleventh Army's commander, had been flown south from the planned offensive to take Leningrad to take control of the situation and lead the newly established *Heeresgruppe* Don (Army Group Don).

The 1st Romanian Panzer under Radu Gherghe was in much the same state as the 22nd Panzer. The division's catalogue of losses was horrific: 217 officers and NCOs and more than 6,000 soldiers killed, wounded or missing. This represented almost 70 per cent of the division's combat strength – 50 per cent of the machine-guns, all the mortars and all but two of its artillery guns were gone, as were 700 vital motor vehicles. As for its panzers, seventy-seven R-2s, ten T-3s and all eleven of its T-4s were lying burnt out on the Soviet side of the Chir. The pride and joy of the Kingdom of Romania's armoured might now consisted of nineteen R-2s and a single T-3. This was not going to stop any concerted Red Army attack, as Wenck well knew:

> I received orders direct from General Zeitzler … since Weichs's Army Group was more than busy … My main task, to start with, was to set up blocking units under energetic officers, which would hold the front along the Don and Chir … As for my own staff, I literally picked them up on the road … The old NCOs with experience of the Eastern Front were quite invaluable in all this, they adapted themselves quickly and could be used for any task.

Manstein knew Wenck of old, and his orders to him were simple:

> Wenck, you'll answer to me with your head if the Russians break through to Rostov from your sector. The Don-Chir front must be held … or not only Sixth Army but the whole of Army Group A in the Caucasus will be lost.

That meant more than 1 million men and their equipment and also the war.

As it was, the STAVKA initially believed they had trapped some 90,000 Germans in Stalingrad, and it took some time for them to become aware that the number was actually closer to 270,000. This included some 1,000 Croats and the same number of Italians, as well as about 12,000 Romanians, mainly from the 4th Army.

Of the rest of Constantinescu-Claps' men, only the aggressive defence of the Korne Detachment and another 'assembled' formation, the 'Pannwitz Detachment' – little more than a few mixed Romanian-German infantry companies, some assault guns and tanks and a Romanian heavy artillery battery led by the aristocratic German cavalryman Helmuth von Pannwitz – prevented Yeremenko's men from pushing further into a thoroughly disorganised German Fourth Panzer Army. In the light of this, the use of the phrase *Panzerschreck* (tank fright) by the German commander Hermann Hoth when he described how the Romanians had reacted to the Soviet offensives was particularly harsh and misleading. The 4th Romanian Army had collapsed, but it had not retreated en masse.

The OKW acknowledged this more than Hoth and in fact awarded coveted Knight's Crosses to Radu Korne (partly on account of his earlier actions in the Crimea and the Ukraine), and Colonel Ioan Hristea, the commanding officer of the 2nd Calasari Regiment, in recognition of Romanian bravery. General Corneliu Teodorini, already a Knight's Cross holder as the commanding officer of the 6th Cavalry Division, now earned the Oak Leaves to add to his earlier award. It is of note that all three led cavalry units whose men fought against overwhelming odds and held their ground.

The OKW was not alone in praising the Romanians. So did Wenck:

I had no communication lines ... and was only gradually able to form a picture of the situation of where the German blocking formations were engaged and where some Romanian units were still to be found.

The only reserves we could count on were the stream of men returning from leave. In order to collect together the stragglers from three armies who had lost their units ... we sometimes had to resort to drastic measures. I remember, for instance, persuading the commander of a *Wehrmacht* propaganda company in Morozovskaya to organise film shows at traffic junctions. The men attracted by the shows were then rounded-up, re-organised, and re-equipped. Mostly they did well in action.

On one occasion a Field Security sergeant came to me and reported discovering an abandoned '*fuel-dump belonging to no-one*'. We didn't need any juice ourselves, but we urgently needed vehicles to move our troops. So I ordered signposts to be put up everywhere along all the roads pointing '*To the fuel-issuing point*'. This brought us large numbers of lorries, staff cars and all manner of vehicles, all looking for fuel. At the dump we had reliable officers, who ensured the vehicles got the fuel they needed, but also screened them as to what they were doing – we secured so many vehicles complete with crews that our worst transport problems were solved.

Under the leadership of experienced officers and NCOs these new motley units acquitted themselves superbly during those critical months, and it was their courage and steadfastness that saved the situation on the Chir, halted the Soviet breakthroughs, and barred the road to Rostov.

These units were made up of everyone from *Luftwaffe* ground staff, *Reichsbahn* railway employees, Labour Servicemen and Todt Organisation construction teams to Cossacks, Hiwis and, above all, Romanians. Wenck was clear in his judgement that Germany's Axis allies were brave and steadfast when well led and properly equipped.

However, not all such desperate improvisations worked out quite so well. Giorgio Geddes, the Italian Intelligence captain, witnessed numbers of dishevelled, dejected and shell-shocked Germans and Romanians wandering aimlessly behind the lines:

Emaciated faces, tattered uniforms, without either officers or discipline, tortured by the ice, hungry and terrified by battles of one against ten.

In one tragic incident, Geddes watched, transfixed, as a Romanian machine-gunner took offence at the attempts of two German field-policemen to round them up and send them to collection points and instead shot them both dead, only to be shot seconds later by one of his own comrades.

Counting the cost – Romania

After the whirlwind unleashed by Operation Uranus abated on 24 November, the Romanians were finally able to evaluate the catastrophic events that had engulfed them and their armed forces in the East. It was a very, very grim picture.

Their 3rd and 4th Armies had been effectively destroyed. Of their twenty-two frontline divisions in Russia, no fewer than nine had been annihilated, with the 1st, 2nd and 18th Infantry Divisions of the 4th Army suffering 80 per cent losses. A further nine divisions had disintegrated and were scattered over the steppe. Only four were still in any sort of shape to carry out further operations. The most powerful military formation the Kingdom of Romania possessed – Petre Dumitrescu's 3rd Army – had been cut down to just 83,000 survivors (on the morning of Operation Uranus, it had more than twice that number). The 100 aircraft of the 1st Romanian Air Corps had been shot from the sky, losing 75 per cent of its force, its main base and the majority of its supplies and maintenance equipment.

The logistics and support personnel of both field armies had simply disappeared, with thousands of men lying dead and frozen in the snow or being rounded up by Soviet troops and marched east as future slave labour. The Moscow correspondent for the US-based United Press, Henry Shapiro, was taken to the battlefield around Serafimovich by his Soviet escorts, and he remembers seeing 'no end of corpses, both Germans and Romanians'. He also wrote:

> Well behind the fighting line there were now thousands of Romanians wandering the steppes, cursing the Germans, desperately looking for Russian feeding-points and anxious to be formally taken as POWs. Some individual stragglers would throw themselves on the mercy of local peasants, who treated them charitably, if only because they were not Germans. The Russians thought they were just poor peasants like themselves. Except for small groups of Iron Guard [author's note: the *Iron Guard* was Romania's home-grown fascist militia movement, much like the Italian Blackshirts] men who, here and there, put up a stiff fight, the Romanian soldiers were sick and tired of the War, and the prisoners I saw all said roughly the same thing – that this was Hitler's war and the Romanians had nothing to do on the Don.

Postscript – a tale of three generals

Mihail Lascar, ex-commanding general of the 6th Infantry Division and the hero of the defence of Raspopinskaya, was captured and then released in 1944, when Romania changed sides. He was given command of a pro-Soviet unit made up mainly of other former Romanian prisoners and survived the war, rising to fill senior appointments in the army and then the government. A report written at the end of 1942 by the Romanian Special Intelligence Service said of his conduct during Operation Uranus:

> ... in the hardest moments of the battle, General Lascar showed a high sense of duty by calmly coordinating the actions of 6th Infantry and the other units whose command he had assumed. He was an example for subordinates ... and when everything seemed lost he went among the soldiers even though he could have saved himself. He showed courage, dignity and patriotism.

Ferdinand Heim, the commander of XXXXVIII Panzer Corps, escaped the debacle on the Don only to face the full force of Hitler's wrath. General Schmundt, serving on Hitler's staff at the time, wrote, 'The Führer ordered General Heim to be relieved of his command immediately.'

Heim was arrested and narrowly avoided being sent to a concentration camp, only to be recalled to active duty in 1944 when sent to lead the defence of Boulogne against the D-Day invasion. Surrendering the port, Heim was then sent to England, where he was imprisoned with other German generals. Unknown to them, their conversations were being secretly recorded. Buried in the archives for decades, it took an investigation by the British *Daily Mail* newspaper in 2011 to unearth the tapes and publish their content. Ferdinand Heim, the supposedly 'good general' wronged by the evil Nazi leader, was heard not only admitting that he knew about the mass murder being perpetrated by the SS and others in the Soviet Union but also trying to persuade the others of a way to avoid being blamed:

> We must uphold the principle of only having carried out orders … We must stick to that principle if we are to create a more or less effective defence.

This, and other such comments, were the genesis of the post-war defence 'we were only following orders' used by so many in the German military to try to avoid taking responsibility for the horrors perpetrated by the regime they served.

Meanwhile, in Stalingrad, trapped amidst the rubble, were the German 384th Infantry Division and its aristocrat commander, Lieutenant-General Ecchard Freiherr von Gablenz. Bewildered by the turn of events and fearing the worst, he wrote a letter to his wife at home in Germany:

> I don't know how it is all going to end, and this is very difficult for me because I should be trying to inspire my subordinates with an unshakeable belief in victory.

Mars follows Saturn

With the *Ostheer* and its masters in Berlin scrabbling for a response to the encirclement of the Sixth Army, the STAVKA did not give them a moment's respite and instead launched Operation Mars against *Heeresgruppe Mitte* (Army Group Centre). The dreadful weather that had delayed the massive offensive had now abated, so with the skies over central Russia relatively clear and the ground hard enough for tanks, on 25 November, Zhukov threw his huge force at a German line stripped of reserves and heavy equipment that had all been sent to the south. Within days, the key city of Velikiye Luki was under siege, and the Germans were under intense pressure all along the front.

With Cologne in ruins, Stalingrad cut off, Rommel retreating in North Africa and Army Group Centre looking set to buckle, matters, unbelievably, became even worse when the Red Army renewed its assault on the beleaguered Demyansk Pocket in the north. Here was ample proof of the growing strength and expertise of the Red Army and its ability to launch more or less simultaneous offensives against all three of the *Ostheer's* army groups. In contrast, the dire situation highlighted the fact, obvious to all, that Nazi Germany was stretched beyond its resources. Hitler's gamble on winning a quick war in Europe and the Soviet Union had failed.

Incredibly, the *Wehrmacht* repelled the Demyansk assault (though it cost the virtual extinction of the 20,000-man Waffen-SS *Totenkopf* Death's Head Division), and in North Africa, the *Afrika Korps* managed to stabilise the situation.

As for Operation Mars, the experienced infantry divisions of Army Group Centre, under the determined leadership of some of Germany's finest surviving officers and NCOs, gave the Soviets a massive beating. Huge though the Soviet assault force was, it was ponderous and poorly co-ordinated. The same issues that had plagued Operation Uranus – ineffective artillery concentration, lack of integration between infantry and armour, insufficient communications – were all manifest in Operation Mars. However, whereas in the south the Soviets had been able to succeed, in Russia's 'middle' the situation was the opposite. The battle-scarred platoons and companies of *Landsers* who had somehow survived the retreat from Moscow the previous winter now stood their ground and poured an unending torrent of rifle and shellfire into the troops of the Red Army. The result was slaughter. By the time Velikiye Luki's Citadel finally fell, some 102,000 Soviet soldiers had been killed or wounded taking the city. In fact, by the time Operation Mars was abandoned in late January, the Red Army had lost more than 100,000 dead and twice that number wounded. Add to this hundreds of guns and aircraft and an incredible 1,600 tanks lost and it becomes a debacle. So bad was the result that the Soviets hushed up the whole operation for more than fifty years, while using propaganda to promote the magnificent success of Operation Uranus.

Operation Winter Storm – Manstein's gamble

With the Sixth Army encircled, the race was on. For the Red Army, the aim was to fortify the ring around the city and keep the enemy trapped. For the Germans, it was all about assembling the forces to get them out. The German rescue attempt, codenamed Operation Winter Storm, was launched on 12 December. The Fourth Panzer Army was the core of the attacking force, with the battered Romanian VI and VII Corps protecting the flanks of the advancing force. What they were all protecting – the leading Germans and the Romanians on left and right – was a lifeline for the city and its defenders, no fewer than 800 trucks heavily loaded with 3,000 tonnes of food, fuel, ammunition and other desperately needed supplies. Every panzer the Germans could spare was used, including the 6th Panzer Division, rushed from France, and the 17th Panzer Division, sent from its position as reserve for the Italian 8th Army. But it was still an under-strength force for the mammoth task it had been set, and if it failed, the fate of the Sixth Army was sealed.

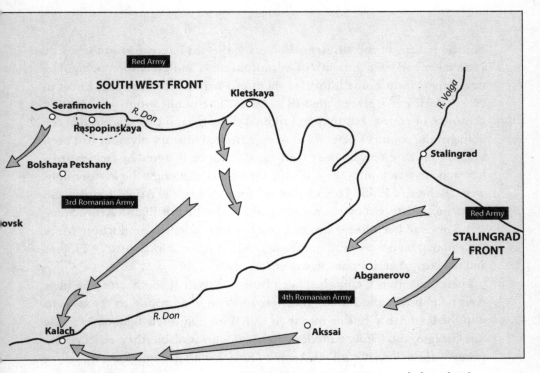

Operation Uranus 19–23 November 1942: The Soviet winter offensive to smash the 3rd and 4th Romanian Armies.

CHAPTER 9

THE ITALIANS TURN
'LITTLE' SATURN 'PHASE 1'

For the Italians of the 8th Army bordering the 3rd Romanian to the north, November had been a month of calamitous news and grave foreboding. The newspapers from home informed them of a major defeat for Axis forces in North Africa at a place called El Alamein. The publications were heavily censored, of course, but they still filtered through, and they told of disaster. Some of the country's best and most experienced infantry divisions had been lost, left in the desert by their German allies to be battered by British artillery and air-attack until they sullenly capitulated. Amongst the lost divisions were all three of Fascist Italy's armoured formations – the Ariete, Littorio and Centauro – defeated by the massed tanks of the British Eighth Army. Some 250 tanks had been lost – almost a year's worth of Italian production. More than 30,000 men were dead or missing, and the Italian North African Empire, and the army that defended it, was effectively lost.

Then Operation Uranus had been launched to their south, crushing their Axis neighbours and forcing their own line to bend round to the west to stop the Red Army getting into their rear. With only a few light tanks in the San Giorgio, and hardly a modern anti-tank gun available, they watched the advance of the Soviet 5th Tank Army to Kalach with genuine fear.

The third planet operation – Little Saturn

Operations Uranus and Mars were only ever segments of the overall plan dreamt up in Moscow by the Soviet high command. The Romanians had been destroyed, the German Sixth Army was trapped, the Demyansk Pocket was being squeezed and Army Group Centre was under attack. But the Soviets had not finished. Now it was time to destroy another Axis ally: the

Italians. Not only was it a useful goal in itself, but this would also further threaten both Army Groups Centre and South (especially the still-vulnerable troops in the Caucasus) and would almost certainly force Operation Winter Storm to be aborted and leave the Sixth Army abandoned.

Originally, Operation 'Little' Saturn was nothing of the sort. The STAVKA envisaged it to be the same as Operations Mars and Uranus – a massive, thunderbolt of an operation with big, meaty goals. However, as realisation dawned on Moscow just how big the Stalingrad pocket actually was, they showed commendable flexibility by deciding instead to limit Operation Saturn and ensure that the necessary supplies and reinforcements went south to finish the job; thus was born 'Little' Saturn.

Nikolai Vatutin was to be front and centre again, just as he had been with Operation Uranus,[1] this time in charge of three armies: the 6th, the 3rd Guards and the newly created 1st Guards. Between them they had 425,000 men, 5,000 artillery pieces and more than 600 tanks.

By contrast, Italo Gariboldi had just 216,000 men with fewer than 1,000 guns and just sixty tanks – and as we know, Paolo Tarnassi's armoured battalion had only twelve modern panzers, with the rest being light Italian-built tankettes, armed with ineffective 20mm guns, and a number of captured Czechoslovak and French vehicles.

The OKW knew the 8th Army was vulnerable and had originally placed the German 17th Panzer Division in reserve to their rear along with the German XXIX Infantry Corps – the 62nd and Arnold Szelinski's 298th Infantry Divisions[2] – interspersed among the ten Italian divisions, which were organised from south to north, right to left, as Francesco Zingales's XXXV Corps; the Torino, Pasubio and Duca d'Aosta (Lieutenant-Colonel Egon Zitnik's Croat Light Transport Brigade was attached to the Duca d'Aosta); then Giovanni Zanghieri's II Corps with the Sforzesca, Ravenna, and Cosseria; and finally the *Alpini*, with the Vicenza in reserve on 'security duties'.

To help the Germans establish a positive relationship with their Mediterranean allies, a short pamphlet was distributed to their officers containing a number of 'useful tips', such as this paragraph of patronising Teutonic sensitivity:

> You should treat them politely … Italians tire more easily than us and are more exuberant. You should not be superior towards our Italian allies who came here

---

1 Vatutin would be killed in an ambush by Ukrainian nationalist partisans from the Ukrainian People's Army (UPA) during 1944 near Kiev.
2 Szelinski was killed in action on 9 December before Operation 'Little' Saturn was launched.

fearlessly into hard and unfamiliar conditions to help us. Don't call them rude names and don't be sharp with them.

8th Army face the music

The weather on the morning of 16 December closely resembled that of 19 November, with a thick blanket of freezing fog covering the ground, along with heavy snow and sleet. Visibility was 100 yards at most, and all aircraft were grounded. It was a morning when the Italian sentries huddled deeper into their greatcoats and dreamt of their relief and a few minutes of blessed warmth back in their dug-outs, damp and miserable though they were. Most of the Italians on the Eastern Front were young men from the north of their country, so snow and ice were nothing new, but even so a Russian winter was a different proposition from those in the Po Valley. It did not help that the Italian supply system was grossly inefficient and riddled with corruption, so the winter coats, hats and boots that the men should have been wearing were actually keeping warm the black marketeers and anyone with the money to pay a bribe.

Through the mist, the horizon suddenly lit up with a sharp glow, and then a moment later came the dull booming … In a matter of seconds, the shells were landing all along the 8th Army's front as 20,000 rounds a minute rained down on the Italian trenches. It was not as devastating as might have been expected, though; just as Operation Uranus' opening bombardment had been less than battle-winning, the same applied to Operation 'Little' Saturn's owing to the necessity of keeping the impending operation a secret. This meant that the Soviet gunners had not been allowed to pre-register their targets and were now more or less firing semi-blind and hoping to score a hit. In these circumstances, it was down to their trained observers at the front, equipped with binoculars and a telephone back to the gun-line, to adjust the fire and bring the full weight of explosives to bear on the enemy. But with such terrible weather conditions, the observers were just as blind as their gunners. Not that this meant much to the Italian infantrymen, who felt the ground around them shake and tremble as they were showered with churned-up snow and stones. However, the sheer number of shells fired was so great that many were bound to find their targets regardless and obliterate trenches and foxholes, burying the dead occupants deep in the earth.

The infantry then launched their attack; 1st Guards commander, the Ukrainian Dimitri Lelyushenko, followed Red Army doctrine and kept his six Rifle divisions together as one huge block. Their main point of effort was aimed at Enrico Gazzale's 5th Cosseria Infantry Division and its neighbour,

Francesco Dupont's 3rd Ravenna. Dupont had replaced Edoardo Nebbia, who had been captured by the Soviets back in October. Both formations had spent the previous few days fending off repeated probing attacks that had sapped the men's strength and depleted precious ammunition stocks. Now the Genovese, Ligurians and Emilio-Romanese of the Cosseria and Ravenna were in the eye of the storm – and just like their Romanian 3rd Army counterparts, they did not run but fought back. The Cosseria had the German 318th Grenadier Regiment in its line as well, and together the Germans and Italians brought a withering fire to bear on the leading Soviet infantry, killing and wounding hundreds and driving the rest to ground. The offensive was not making any headway, replicating what had happened at the beginning of Operation Uranus on the 3rd Romanian's front a month earlier, only now the infantry who were holding out were Italian and not Romanian. They were doing their job, holding the enemy, delaying him long enough for reinforcements to come up in support. So where was the support?

Their artillery and mortars were not going to be of much use, hugely outgunned as they were and with shell stocks so low that permission had to be given by the regimental commander for a single round to be fired.

Giovannelli's Pasubio Division to their right was also under attack and could not help them, while away to the south, Karl Hollidt's cobbled-together Army Detachment (which included the remnants of the 3rd Romanian Army) had been hit that same morning by Feodor Kuznetsov's 3rd Guards Army in a fierce attack. Despite the pounding they had taken just two weeks earlier, the Romanians and their comrades from the German 62nd Infantry Division put up a stiff fight – the latter having been detached from supporting the Italian 8th a few weeks earlier. They were pushed back and took heavy casualties, but there was no Soviet breakthrough; equally, there would be no reinforcement from them for the Italian 8th. To the Cosseria's left were the *Alpini* of the Cuneense, separated from them by the narrow but deep and fast-flowing, Kalitva River, making any immediate reinforcement impossible. In any case, the *Alpini* had been under almost constant attack since the morning of 12 December – enough to pin them down in their trenches and cause a steady flow of casualties. A member of the Tridentina remembered it:

> The sky became red, on fire; following four bursts of *Katyusha* fire our village was in flames.

The Julia too had been in the thick of the fighting, losing almost 500 men killed in action and a staggering 3,000 to injury and frostbite.

The support job then had to fall to the 8th Army's reserves. The German 17th Panzer, which was intended to act as the mobile counterpunch for the ARMIR, was now miles to the south, about to join von Manstein's Operation Winter Storm offensive, and Gariboldi had only a single unit of any size available – the aged reservists of the 156th Vicenza Infantry Division on rear-area duties. Inadequately trained, in poor physical shape and without an artillery gun or a lorry available, it was impossible for the Vicenza's commander, Etelvoldo Pascolini, and his two under-strength regiments of middle-aged men to travel south in a hurry. Gariboldi asked the Germans for help, but the *Ostheer* had no reserves. The 8th Army's commander was at a loss. All of this meant the Cosseria and Ravenna were on their own.

Again, it was the Soviets who seized the initiative. With the impeccable timing and decision making that characterised the Red Army's southern offensives that winter, this was the moment when Nikolai Vatutin decided to throw the Red Army rule book on the fire. The tanks were going to attack, despite the fact that the infantry had not breached the enemy's line. This was a risky plan.

The tanks were meant to exploit a breakthrough, charging hard to get behind a broken defence and create confusion and mayhem as their mobility and firepower smashed command, control and back-up forces. But if the line held, then the tanks would be exposed on the open steppe and be vulnerable to well-sited anti-tank defences – this was the scenario played out so often, and so successfully, by Rommel in the Western Desert against the British before the arrival of Montgomery.

The Red Army 17th Tank Corps attacked

Wedges of T-34 tanks advanced from their bridgeheads with infantry perched precariously on their hulls, turrets turning seeking targets. Suddenly there was a huge explosion, followed by another and yet another. Tracks were blown off the advancing tanks; the 17th had driven straight into the Italian minefields. Red Army engineers had gone out and cleared lanes, but the markers had been lost in the artillery fire and subsequent infantry attacks. The attack stalled as the engineers went forward again, and that would have been the end if the Italians had possessed even a modest number of anti-tank guns. But they did not. The mines were cleared, and the tanks of the 17th went forward again. The men of the Cosseria and Ravenna had to resort to hand-grenades and Molotov cocktails to try to stop them – and they failed. Sensing the critical moment was being reached, Vatutin sent in his 18th and 25th Tank Corps as well, and there was no way of stopping them. Simple bravery was not enough; foxhole after foxhole was either crushed under track or isolated from its neighbours and attacked. Soviet infantry would crawl forward or run hunched up and then throw a grenade, and as always with grenades, they tended not to kill but to wound. The job would be finished with a burst of automatic fire or at the point of a bayonet.

The poorly equipped Italian infantry could not hope to stand up to that sort of pressure for long as the tanks rolled over them. The *Alpini* Corps, on the other side of the Kalitva, was now left alone (their turn would come later) as the Soviets drove hard to reach the open steppe and shatter the 8th Army's front.

By the morning of 19 December, the objective was achieved. The Ravenna and Cosseria had taken massive casualties and were exhausted, their lines comprehensively breached. Most of the survivors crossed the Kalitva and took refuge with the *Alpini*, watching in impotent horror as the Soviet war machine drove west.

This was the decisive breakthrough.

With all of the 8th Army's divisions basically in a straight line on the Don, and with no reserves in place, as soon as an exploitable gap did open, the game was over.

In a brilliantly executed operation, Vatutin's tanks did exactly that and fanned out behind the Italian front line, causing mayhem as they attacked dressing-stations, supply depots and maintenance areas. Threatened with encirclement, the four divisions still holding out had no choice but to abandon their posts and attempt to escape.

Egon Zitnik's Croats, on the extreme flank of the d'Aosta, were holding the two adjoining features known by their map spot heights as Hills 210 and 168 near the village of Hracin and had been under attack since the morning of 16 December. Cut off from any retreat, they were soon surrounded but continued to resist until they ran out of ammunition on 21 December, when they were finally overrun. There were no survivors, and the unit was totally destroyed.

Gariboldi now totally lost control as communications broke down, and he could do nothing except be a bystander as his army disintegrated in front of his eyes. The large Italian bases around Millerovo, 50 miles behind the Don, fell to the 1st Guards Army in the next few days, and then, on 24 December, both Tatinskaya and Morozovskaya were captured by the rampaging 3rd Guards Army. This spelled starvation for the Sixth Army, as these were the two main supply airfields.

With the front broken, large numbers of men from the Torino and Pasubio Infantry Divisions headed south-west, aiming for the main Italian supply centre at Kantemirovka on the railway line some 30 miles away. Unfortunately, this was also where the Soviet tanks were heading. The 17th Tank Corps' T-34s arrived before the fleeing Italians and forced the column to turn due south towards Cerkovo. Along their route, the Red Air Force wreaked havoc, bombing and strafing the Italians with impunity. Soviet ground troops, and even partisans, joined in, with the Italians unable to hit back as they had spiked and abandoned their artillery and mortars back on the Don. Somehow maintaining their discipline, some 7,000 men reached Cerkovo and dug in on the frozen steppe. There, with little more than small arms and a few salvaged infantry cannon and mortars, they successfully fought off further Red Army assaults until the Germans linked up with them some three weeks later.

In the pocket with them were several thousand Russian and Ukrainian helpers – *Hilfswillige* (willing helpers). This term covered anyone from ex–Red Army men who now fought with the Germans to those who carried ammunition, cleaned latrines and tended the sick and injured. However, no matter their exact role, all were justifiably terrified of being captured by the Red Army and the inevitable subsequent retribution this would herald. One such individual was Valentina Gorshkov, a nurse known to the Italian officer Giorgio Geddes, whom he had helped secure a job in the Torino Division's field hospital to escape deportation to Germany as forced labour. Surrounded at Cerkovo, Valentina and three companions had tried to flee on a sledge, only to be caught and handed over for trial to the NKVD. One of them, Elena Kudina, managed to escape during the proceedings and told both Geddes and Valentina's parents what had happened. Valentina herself was never heard of again, but her fate can be imagined.

As for the rest of XXXV Corps, thousands more never even made it as far as Cerkovo and were surrounded near a small town called Vertyakhovski, not far from the Don. Desperately trying to organise themselves into some sort of defensive force, they were pounded into submission by Red Army artillery and tanks.

Ragged bands of survivors were spread out over the steppe, all trying to escape to the west and most getting swept up by the advancing Red Army. One such group, led by a lieutenant-colonel and composed of almost 400 men from the Torino and Pasubio, were on foot and arrived in the tiny village of Alexeika-Losovskaya. Exhausted from their march, they settled down to snatch a few hours' sleep, only to be woken up by the sound of gunfire and cries of: 'The Russians! Run, they are killing everyone inside the houses!'

The Red Army had arrived, and their soldiers were attacking from behind a wall of hay bales. Some Italians bravely fired back, shouting a defiant 'Savoia!' before their senior officer loudly ordered them to stop, saying it was useless to resist without the support of heavy weapons. Taken prisoner, the men were herded together into a column to be marched east, while the officers were separated out and driven away to Boguchar along with their female Russian interpreters. None fared well and perhaps the civilian interpreters worst of all, as they were handed over to the NKVD to be interrogated and tried for treason, a charge for which there was only ever one verdict: the firing squad.

The greatest trek of all would be that of the 25,000 Piedmontese of the Sforzesca and Duca d'Aosta Divisions, who were joined by some Veronese and Mantuans of the Pasubio and even some 5,000 Germans. Cut off on the Don, they set out on an epic march south to reach the elusive safety of German lines. At first, just as with all the other 8th Army formations, they put up a remark-ably stiff resistance, giving the lie to the accusation that all Italians simply ran away at the first sign of the enemy. But again, as with their sister units, once their flank had been turned and the Soviets could get behind them they had no option but to retreat. The one card that Generals Mario Marrazini, the commanding officer of the Duca d'Aosta cavalrymen, and Umberto Utili, the XXV Corps Chief of Staff, had left to play was the 8th Army's surviving tank unit – the San Giorgio Armoured Battalion. Poorly equipped and few in number, it was no match for Vatutin's tank corps, but nevertheless, led by Paolo Tarnassi, the Italian tank crews fought bravely, battling away against huge odds, their main task to protect the vulnerable flanks of the retreating columns.[1]

For some thirty days, those columns, miles long, trudged through the snow and ice. The weather was horrendous, the thermometer regularly dipping down to minus 20°C. Food was scarce and fuel for cooking and warmth non-existent. To fall behind meant death from the cold. Air attacks were another constant danger, and one such raid claimed the life of the San Giorgio's com-mander, Tarnassi.[2] By that time, his tank battalion had been all but wiped out, having protected the retreating troops across the inhospitable steppe.

Finally, after marching for an incredible 250 miles, the cavalrymen and infantry reached the safety of the Donetz River and Voroshilovgrad. One of those who survived the journey was Eugenio Corti, a 21-year-old officer in the Pasubio. For Corti, the worst part of the whole trek was watching as, day after day, the wounded, frostbitten or just exhausted were left in the snow to die. He wrote a diary of his experiences, dedicating it to those left behind:

---

1 Utili would survive to return to Italy, where he would become a leading figure in the Italian Army after it sided with the Allied forces.
2 His death was reported in the *New York Times* newspaper on 15 January 1943.

This is one of the reasons I am writing today; so that everyone may know about your sacrifice my brothers, my thousands of brothers, who perished in that terrifying misery. But what chance do I have of receiving a more than ephemeral hearing if my voice is parched, after such treatment, and within me there is a desert? (From Corti's diary, published as the book *Few Returned*)

After a spell in the hospital recovering from his ordeal, Corti returned to his unit, at that time based in Salerno. With Fascist Italy on the brink of collapse, the young officer was worried his diary would be confiscated and his testament lost, so he wrapped it in a waterproof sheet and buried it, retrieving it only after the war had ended.

Leaving out the *Alpini*, some 130,000 Italians were caught up in the Operation 'Little' Saturn offensive. According to Italian sources, some 21,000 of those men died in the fighting or from cold and injury (to add to the 10,000 or so deaths in Operation Barbarossa and Case Blue) and another 64,000 were taken prisoner.[1] About 45,000 managed to escape, the majority of whom suffered from frostbite, hypothermia, hunger and wounds sustained in the battle. So appalling was the physical appearance of many of these men that when they were sent back to Italy they were often kept hidden in covered railway cars and unloaded only at night to avoid prying eyes.

By 25 December 1942, except for the Vicenza, the infantry and cavalry divisions of the Italian 8th Army had more or less ceased to exist as a fighting force. Fully 66 per cent of Fascist Italy's entire armed might on the Eastern Front had been wiped off the order of battle in just over a week. Even the *Alpini* were not exempt, the Julia in particular having been involved in some intense fighting. All that was left as more or less intact combat units were the three divisions of the *Alpini* Corps and their fearful Venetian comrades; their turn was about to come.

The ordeal continues for the Romanians

With the 8th Army visibly crumbling, Karl Hollidt's detachment was forced to pull back from the Chir River and retreat towards the *Luftwaffe* base and 3rd Romanian Army headquarters at Morozovskaya. The southern Romanian 11th Infantry Division was hit hard during the withdrawal, and its commander, Brigadier Savu Nedelea, was taken prisoner.[2] To try

---

1 Many of them were wounded and did not live more than a few hours after capture; in fact, only about one in six survived surrender and captivity and eventually returned to Italy.

2 Nedelea would remain a prisoner until 1946. He then returned to the army and served until retirement in 1948.

to stabilise the end of his line, Hollidt ordered the Romanian 7th Cavalry Division to hold the town of Chernigof. This would anchor his front and protect the supply depots still lying behind the town that the Germans desperately needed. The Romanian cavalrymen fought a series of bitter defensive battles against the attacking Soviets, Chernigof being reduced to a smoking ruin in the process. The cavalrymen held their positions, and when they finally retreated at the beginning of January, they were officially the last Axis troops to leave the Chir line. No fewer than twenty-eight members of the division were awarded the Iron Cross for bravery.

With the Chir line disintegrating, it was once again down to men like Walther Wenck and the much-derided 22nd Panzer Division to try to fend off disaster. By now, the division had been reduced to just six tanks, twelve armoured infantry-carriers and a single 88mm Flak gun, but under von Oppeln-Bronikowski (leading from the front in his battle-worn PzKpfw III), it became a force that struck the Soviets wherever possible. Wenck also created his own panzer battalion by collecting every serviceable or repairable panzer, self-propelled gun and armoured infantry-carrier he could find. He also took to 'borrowing' panzers from transports passing through the area, until von Manstein found out and stopped the practice. Unofficially, Wenck continued but used the tanks only in company strength so as not to arouse suspicion.

Muffled Thunderclap

Meanwhile, during Operation Winter Storm, von Manstein and Hoth somehow managed to get within 35 miles of Stalingrad, and then, using the codeword 'Thunderclap', von Manstein ordered Paulus to break out and proceed towards his position. It was the Sixth Army's last chance. General Paulus, the meticulous staff officer who operated 'by the book', asked for Hitler's permission. Hitler refused, and Paulus simply conceded. (By a quirk of fate, the general's wife, Elena, was Romanian.)

Seizing their chance, the Soviets counter-attacked, hitting Hoth and the dismally weak Romanian divisions with almost 150,000 men and more than 400 tanks. The tattered remnants of Constantinescu-Claps' 1st, 2nd, 4th and 18th Infantry Divisions were all but obliterated by Timofei Shapkin's 4th Cavalry Corps and the armour of the 7th Tank.[1] Claps' 5th and 8th Cavalry Divisions

---

1 Shapkin was lucky to have survived Stalin's Purges, as he was a 'Sotnik' – a Cossack squadron commander in General Denikin's white Russian 6th Don Cossack Regiment. Shapkin eventually joined the Red Army in 1920 and died of illness in March 1943.

– the General Popescu Group[1] – was nearly destroyed in the fights at Sharnutovsky with the Soviet 6th Mechanised Corps. Once more, casualties were appalling. Brigadier-General Thomas Hurley, a US general on a liaison mission to the Soviets, was encouraged to visit the battlefields and wrote a shocking report for President Roosevelt detailing what he had seen:

> The Romanian troops, judging by the dead we saw on the field and by the appearance of the prisoners, were far below the standard of the Soviet troops. The Romanians were equipped for the most part with second-rate arms and horse-drawn artillery. Throughout the entire salient we were hardly ever out of view of dead horses and dead Romanian soldiers.

By 29 December, with his flanks under threat and his panzer force exhausted, von Manstein abandoned Operation Winter Storm and with it the Sixth Army. What, now, for Paulus' beleaguered army?

Austrians and Romanians in the city of fire

One of the units fighting for its life in the Stalingrad Pocket was General Heinrich-Anton Deboi's Austrian 44th Hoch und Deutschmeister Infantry Division. The 44th was a formation with a long and illustrious history; it was no reserve division bolstered with conscripts and officered by elderly men whose only memories were of the trenches of the First World War. No, its ranks were filled with thousands of young Viennese volunteers, led by a cadre of professional officers and NCOs. They had fought across France, Poland and the western Soviet Union and were now part of Strecker's corps in Stalingrad.

The 2nd Battalion of its 132nd Grenadier Regiment was dug in on Kergachi Hill, a 400-foot feature in the north of the Stalingrad Pocket. At the beginning of December, G Company, one of the battalion's sub-units, had a strength of 55 men, down from its original total of more than 150. It then received another 30 men from a redundant veterinary unit (all the horses and dogs they treated had now become food), a few riflemen from Edler von Daniels's disbanded 376th Infantry Division and, finally, no fewer than 26 Romanians, mainly Transylvanians from the 20th Infantry. The company had six machine-guns and three light mortars and was dug into one-, two- and three-man foxholes defending the line. Ammunition was a huge problem.

---

1 Named after its leader, the 50-year-old Dumitru Popescu, commander of the 5th Cavalry Division, there were no fewer than five generals in the Romanian Army in the Second World War with the surname Popescu.

Each soldier received only eighty bullets to last a week. Many risked their lives to crawl forward in the darkness and strip dead Soviet soldiers of their weapons and ammunition. In response, the Russians would always try to take their dead with them, and they regularly fired parachute flares at night to try to catch the scavengers out in the open. If they were seen, the area would be raked with machine-gun fire.

The Red Army kept up a constant flow of harassing attacks against the Austrians and Romanians, wearing down the men and draining them of energy and the means to carry on fighting. Just days after being reinforced, a major offensive was launched against the division. G Company alone faced no fewer than forty T-34 tanks, all of which were carrying infantry. Without adequate anti-tank support, the Soviet armour literally rolled over them, but as on the Don, the ground was frozen so hard that the trench walls did not give way, and the men were not crushed under the tracks. The grenadiers, veterinarians and Romanians kept on fighting until nightfall, knocking out two T-34s with hand-grenades. In the dark, they stayed in their foxholes and trenches. Somehow, the regiment gathered together enough reserves to launch a counter-attack the next morning that pushed the Soviets back and relieved the stranded company. Casualties had been heavy, especially among the inexperienced replacements – a veterinarian with a rifle is still a veterinarian – but the line had somehow held. Exhausted, they were then told the daily bread ration had been cut again, from one-third of a loaf per man to one-fifth, with a small piece of sausage every few days and maybe some boiled horsemeat broth. This was not nearly enough to keep body and soul together in the face of the ferocity of a Russian winter. The result almost defied belief. On 21 December 1942, the first German soldiers in Stalingrad began to die from starvation. Their body fat burned away, and their skin grew pallid; young, previously fit and healthy men in their twenties began dying from hunger.

Christmas came and went in Stalingrad with the fighting unceasing. Casualties among the defenders rose alarmingly, with hunger increasingly taking a toll to rival bullets and shellfire. By early January, the 2nd Battalion of the Austrian/Romanian 44th Division could muster just three officers and 160 men from an establishment of more than 800. Within days, that was reduced to just one officer when the battalion's operations officer was killed in a counter-attack and the battalion commander put his pistol in his mouth and blew his own brains out in despair.

CHAPTER 10

THE LAST OF THE AXIS
HUNGARY'S 2ND ARMY

With the remnants of the Romanian 3rd and 4th Armies in retreat with Karl Hollidt's Army Detachment and Hermann Hoth's Fourth Panzer Army respectively, and the Italian 8th Army shattered beyond repair, with its survivors spread out between the Don and Donetz rivers, there remained only one Axis allied force of any size still intact at the front – Gustav Jány's 2nd Hungarian Army – and the three divisions of the Italian *Alpini* Corps lined up alongside them. The STAVKA had no intention of allowing this situation to continue.

The scope of Operation Saturn did not end with Vatutin's offensive against Gariboldi's Italians; that was the first stage, and now it was time for phase two. The plan was to launch yet another offensive. This would be the fifth separate, large-scale attack embarked on by the Red Army in just two months, this time aimed at breaking through the 220,000-strong Hungarian 2nd Army on its left and right flanks, encircling it on the Don and then sweeping out to the north and south to destroy the 125,000 men of von Salmuth's German Second Army and finish off the remaining Italians. For Moscow, this was the chance to bring the number of German and Axis armies crushed that winter to seven – the German Second, Sixth and Fourth Panzer and the Axis Romanian 3rd and 4th, Italian 8th and Hungarian 2nd – leaving just nine German and no Axis allied armies in the field. The war in the East would be transformed.

This was not an eventuality envisaged by the Hungarians.

As late as 7 January 1943, Jány's Chief-of-Staff, Lieutenant-General Gyula Kovacs, sent a reassuring message to Budapest informing them that a major Red Army offensive was considered most unlikely.

Considering the overall state of the Hungarian forces, this was more a fervent hope than anything more concrete. Those forces were in much the same parlous state as the other three Axis armies that had already been destroyed and suffered from all the same deficiencies – too few men holding a line that was too long, inadequate leadership and training standards and lack of equipment, especially anti-tank guns.[1] The field defences they had prepared on the Don were very basic, consisting mainly of wood-lined trenches and foxholes with barbed wire in places. There were not enough mines to lay extensive defences in depth and, of course, no guns to cover them anyway, so instead there were blocks of mines laid directly in front of major positions, with the *Magyars* hoping this would at least give them a modicum of protection.

The men shivered in their old summer uniforms and wrapped up in anything they could buy, barter or steal from the local civilians or unfortunate Russian prisoners. Covered in layers of clothing, they moved like fat old men, the lice burrowing down into their skin, spreading disease like wildfire. The food that got through was monotonous and low in calories, just about sufficient but little else. The soldiers' bodies burned up fat reserves in the cold and transformed young men into pale shadows of their former selves.

The Hungarian Army had re-organised their infantry into two-regiment so-called Light Divisions, which had not helped. True, the move had increased the number of formations available, but it had not increased the number of men, so each of the nine 'new' divisions on the Don line was smaller than its predecessor.

What was needed was a strong, mobile, preferably armoured reserve. Had anyone on the Don front heard that call before?

The Hungarian panzers

With the snow falling continuously as December neared its freezing end, Army Group B was staggering under repeated heavy attacks, and the world was watching the death-throes of its beleaguered Sixth Army. A demoralised von Weichs knew that part of the answer to his critically damaged front was the creation of a strategic reserve, powerful and mobile enough to be able to intervene anywhere along his fragmented line. This was a move with which a nervous Berlin wholeheartedly agreed. As a result, the OKH dispatched General of Mobile Troops Hans Kramer to assess the situation and advise both Berlin and von Weichs on the best way of achieving this vital goal.

Kramer himself was a successful panzer commander, despite suffering from chronic asthma. An energetic, wiry man, he would end the conflict with the

---

1 Even the comparatively well-equipped 1st Hungarian Armoured had only one anti-tank company with four obsolete 50mm guns and another four totally ineffective 20mm anti-tank rifles.

dubious distinction of becoming a British prisoner in both world wars, having been captured on the Western Front in the First World War and then again in the Second.

Now, on 28 December, Kramer boarded a Junkers Ju-52 transport aircraft at Lötzen with a direct order from General Zeitzler to fly to von Weichs' HQ at Straobjelsk and go and inspect the Hungarian panzer division, with a view to its forming the core of any reserve force. The Germans had been impressed by Budapest's creation of the 1st Hungarian Armoured Corps in November, with its two panzer divisions – the 1st and 2nd - and a cavalry division, seemingly equipped with additional artillery and tank battalions, and with even the cavalrymen getting four companies of light tanks. There were also, lingering in the minds of senior German officers, First World War memories of the brave and dashing nature of the Hungarian soldiery, so the OKH felt that the Hungarians were capable – but unsurprisingly, it was all a mirage.

On arrival in Straobjelsk, Kramer immediately reported to von Weichs and then travelled on to Jány's HQ at Alexeyevka on 30 December. After being introduced to the general and briefed by his staff, Kramer spent an enlightening afternoon with General Erwin von Witzleben, the senior German liaison officer to the *Magyars*. Von Witzleben did not pull his punches. All was not as favourable as Berlin perceived. What was desperately needed were German reinforcements and more modern weapons – in particular, of course, anti-tank guns that could actually destroy tanks. In von Witzleben's opinion, a Red Army offensive could not be ruled out, and if it did come, there was not much chance of the 2nd Army holding.[1]

Forewarned, Kramer journeyed on to the 1st Hungarian Armoured Field's headquarters at Nikolayevka and then to Marki, where most of the Hungarian tankers were physically based, and despite his fears, everything seemed in order. Reassured, he reported to Zeitzler that all was well and was rewarded by being named on the spot as the commander of Corps Kramer – Army Group B's new strategic reserve.

Headquartered in Alexeyevka, just south-west of the key road junction and supply base at Ostrogorsk, Corps Kramer was to consist of the German 26th and 168th Infantry Divisions, along with a small number of German panzers and self-propelled guns in the 190th, 242nd and 700th Panzer Detachments,

---

1 Von Witzleben was soon transferred back to the Reich, where he was to become involved in the growing anti-Hitler circles in the military. Designated as the new commander of the entire *Wehrmacht* if the 20 July bomb plot succeeded, when it failed he was arrested, tried, convicted and executed for treason on 7 August 1944 at Plötzensee Prison in Berlin.

while the backbone of the force were the 132 tanks, including PzKpfw 38(*t*), PzKpfw III and PzKpfw IVs (reluctantly given by the Germans), as well as a number of Toldi and 40M Nimrods from the 1st Hungarian Armoured Field. This, then, would be Jány's and von Weichs' reserve, a back-up for the frontline with Hungary's one and only operational panzer division at its core.

This 'new' panzer division, whether Budapest agreed or not, was almost identical in makeup to the 1st Romanian Panzer. The *Magyars* had poured just about everything they could muster into it – Lajos Veress begging, borrowing and even stealing whatever he could get his hands on to make the unit more effective. The whole formation was motorised, or at least horse-drawn, with the infantry and gunners being carried into battle in trucks. The reconnaissance battalion was equipped with fourteen 39M Csaba and eighteen 38M Toldi I/II light tanks, and the anti-aircraft battalion had four Toldi IIa and twelve 40M Nimrod self-propelled anti-aircraft guns. The armoured power was provided by the 30th Panzer Regiment. This made the division as strong as the 1st Romanian Panzer, but everyone had seen how that had fared two months earlier.

The *Ostheer*'s contribution to the corps, not based in Nikolayevka or in Marki with the *Magyars* tankers but instead co-located with the 2nd Army's headquarters in Alexeyevka, was not exactly lavish. The three so-called Panzer Detachments were all approximately company-sized and mainly equipped with PzKpfw 38(*t*) tanks, the same as those the 1st Armoured Field had and which had been found so inadequate by the Germans and the Axis allies everywhere on the Don that winter. The two infantry divisions – Friedrich Wiese's 26th and the Saxon 168th – were relatively static, and although the 26th in particular was a veteran formation, with a solid core of professional officers and NCOs, the long summer and autumn battles had significantly depleted its combat strength, and both units lacked sufficient transport. Overall, Corps Kramer was of limited capability.

Day one – 12 January

Unlike its predecessors, the Soviet offensive launched on the morning of 12 January 1943 was not heralded with a barrage by artillery and massed ranks of riflemen charging through cleared minefield lanes towards the Axis trenches. Instead, Filipp Golikov decided that his 347,000 Voronezh Front would initially restrict itself to nothing more than infantry probes out of the same Uryv bridgehead so fiercely contested in the autumn. Advancing cautiously, but in numbers, the lead rifle divisions of the Soviet 40th Army engaged the

Hungarian III Corps 7th Light Division and the German 429th Grenadier Regiment next to them in the line. The Germans and the 7th Light Division's 35th Regiment held their positions, but the division's other regiment – the 4th – did not show the same resolve. As trenches began to fall, their defenders killed or wounded, some Hungarians threw their rifles away and raised their hands. What began with a handful of men spread like a chain reaction, and in no time at all, the regiment ceased to exist. Surprised, but always willing to seize the advantage, the Soviet infantry pushed on, causing chaos behind the frontline as white-smocked riflemen suddenly appeared behind reserve units, on artillery lines and at depots and storage centres. Confusion reigned at III Corps head-quarters as Deszo Laszlo's 7th Light Division disintegrated, and they ordered a retreat to avoid the corps being encircled on the Don.[1] Falling back, a 3-mile-wide gap now opened up between them and their IV Corps neighbours.

This was the first crucial moment of the offensive. With few integral reserves of his own, Jány needed Corps Kramer to come to the rescue quickly and restore the front. Unfortunately for the 2nd Army, the Germans did not agree. After all, to the north, Maks Reiter, one of the few Latvian generals in the Red Army, had attacked von Salmuth's weak Second Army with his Bryansk Front, but the Germans were holding, despite the fact that more than half of the Second Army's infantry strength was six new divisions freshly raised and sent to the front in mid-1942. Poorly trained in comparison with older units, they had suffered badly in the summer fighting. The 385th Infantry Division, for example, lost five of its six battalion commanders and half of its company commanders in just six weeks. To OKW's mind, therefore, the Hungarians had a local difficulty, and they should sort it by themselves. Corps Kramer would stay put.

Filipp Golikov had no such reservations, and as darkness fell he ordered a full assault to be launched at dawn the next day.

Day two – 13 January

It was still dark when Kirill Moskalenko's 40th Army struck out from the north side of the Uryv bridgehead. The Ukrainian general and his staff had worked feverishly through the night, bringing up more troops, ammunition and tanks; preparing the artillery; and issuing the necessary orders. Now his men charged headlong into the VII Corps's 20th Light Division and the

---

1   Laszlo would go on to win the Knight's Cross in 1945 as commanding officer of the Hungarian 1st Army.

remaining German infantrymen of the 429th Grenadier Regiment. The Hungarians and Germans were under extreme pressure, trenches falling and the line faltering, so III Corps deputy commander, Otto Abt, authorised a counter-attack by a scratch force of four *Magyar* infantry battalions and the panzers of Corps Kramer's 700th Detachment. The resultant fighting was intense; hundreds were killed and wounded on both sides, and by the end of the day, the 700th had only four PzKpfw 38(*t*) tanks left, and the Hungarian infantry units had been decimated. Unable to do more, they were pushed back under relentless pressure, but they did not run.

The commander of the 429th Grenadier Regiment wrote in his after-action report:

> The Hungarian troops fought very well, and the reason for the failure of their counter-attack attempt lay with the helplessness of their units against enemy armour and the freezing weather.

Nevertheless, by nightfall on 13 January, the gap in the Hungarian lines had widened to more than 6 miles, and it was now some 7 miles deep.

Day three – 14 January

Pavel Rybalko, a master of tank warfare and a follower of Tukhachevsky's doctrine of deep operations, and his powerful 3rd Tank Army, had until then been confined to merely pinning down Jány's left wing, but now they went over to the offensive. In what had become standard practice, the 12th and 15th Tank Corps drove forward with bunches of riflemen mounted on the T-34s, firing as they advanced on the Hungarians of József Heszlényi's IV Corps.[1] Ulaszlo Solymossy's 12th Light Division bore the brunt of the assault, with the Soviet 18th Rifle Corps bludgeoning the 18th and 48th Regiments and heading towards Ostrogorsk. With major tank and infantry units breaking through the line, the IV and VII Hungarian Corps now began to split away from each other, much as the III Hungarian Corps had done the previous day. The temperature had now

---

1 On 8 May 1945, Heszlényi, along with his son József Heszlényi Jr, who served on his father's staff, was captured by US troops. The general, a Knight's Cross recipient, was then handed over to the Soviets. He committed suicide by slashing his own wrists with a razor blade on 2 June 1945. On 19 January 1946, a communist-dominated military tribunal posthumously demoted and dishonourably discharged him from the Hungarian Army.

plummeted to minus 30°C, the icy wind whipping the snow into the faces of the men struggling to escape the Soviet onslaught.

With the defensive lines lost, and no major counter-attack appearing on the horizon, the Hungarians stumbled backwards through heavy fog to try to reach the Gyevica River and Ostrogorsk. The Russians followed, running amok among rear area units and supply troops but occasionally hitting front line soldiers who fought back and kept the Soviet tanks and infantry at bay. Now, just as in that fateful week in late November farther south with the Romanians, a small number of powerful anti-tank guns could have made all the difference. Just thirty 75mm guns operated by well-trained crews and the trucks to move them around could have smashed Rybalko's inexperienced tank force. Instead, the *Magyars* had the Swiss-manufactured 20mm Solothurn s18-1100 anti-tank rifle, an automatic, magazine-fed weapon that could not penetrate the armour of a T-34 even at very close range. The 3rd Tank advanced 12 miles that day, and yet more Hungarian pleas to allow the 1st Armoured Field to intervene went unheeded.

This left each of 2nd Army's three corps to more or less fight their own battles, as Jány, like Dumitrescu, Constantinescu-Claps and Gariboldi before him, lost the ability to influence what was going on at the front.

Day four – 15 January

In the north, the STAVKA admitted defeat and ordered Operation Mars to be abandoned. With hundreds of thousands of men dead or wounded and masses of equipment lost, the Red Army had suffered a significant setback. This should have brought blessed relief to the Axis forces farther south, but as it happened, it worsened their plight as supplies destined for Mars were now diverted to Operation Saturn.

With the additional fuel and ammunition, the Soviet advance could continue unabated; infantry, tanks and artillery were hitting the Hungarians and not giving them a moment's respite to reorganise. The III Corps had lost the 7th Light Division, and its remaining two divisions were being pushed north away from their fellows and into the arms of the equally hard-pressed German Second Army. By the end of the day, they were more or less cut off from Jány, and they became a de facto part of von Salmuth's force. Here, the 6th and 9th Light Divisions showed their mettle and bravely stood their ground for the next ten days, helping to stave off the Soviet-planned encirclement of the Second Army and then retreating with it back to the temporary safety of the Olym River.

Von Weichs belatedly sanctioned the release of the Saxons of the 168th Infantry for action against the southern Red Army prong, and the easterners went forward strongly, their artillery firing accurate barrages that significantly slowed down the Soviets but did not stop them. A far larger force would be needed for that to be achieved.

The Alpini are surrounded

With the *Magyars* being pushed backwards and the front line disintegrating, the threat now was of the Red Army advancing into the gaps and encircling any troops who could not keep up with the 2nd Army's retreat. In particular danger were the Italians of the *Alpini* Corps and the Vicenza Division as they had been facing south, warding off attacks from the direction of their old supply base at Kantemirovka. As the VII Corps fell back in disorder, their flank was exposed, and the threat of being cut off loomed.

Nevertheless, the commanding officer of the corps, Gabriele Nasci, was under strict instructions not to move, having received a direct order to that effect from von Weichs at Army Group B:

> To leave the Don line without orders from Army Group is absolutely forbidden.
>
> I will make you personally responsible to execute this order.

The *Alpini* held and were surrounded.

Day five – 16 January

The day dawned as cold as usual, with no lifting of the blanket of freezing fog covering the steppe. The conditions meant the *Luftwaffe* could not operate to support the ground troops, nor could the Hungarian pilots, left frustrated just a few miles away at the 2nd Air Brigade base at Ilovskaya.

Golikov, supported by Vatutin's Southwest Front, took advantage and continued to attack with no let up in the furious pace of operations. The OKW, yet again caught by surprise, as it had been by Operation Uranus, was finally waking up to the unfolding disaster and scrambled to respond but was gravely hampered by events along the entire length of the Russian Front. The Red Army was attacking yet again on the Volkhov River in the far north to try to free Leningrad from its marathon siege. Army Group A was still streaming back as fast as it could from the Caucasus before its escape door in Rostov was shut. In the Stalingrad Pocket, the vital Pitomnik airfield fell, leaving only Gumrak and its inadequate facilities to act as a lifeline for the Sixth Army.

The only reserves available anywhere near the action were the few still-uncommitted troops of Corps Kramer and specifically the panzers and grenadiers of the 1st Hungarian Armoured Field. So, an incredible five days after Operation Saturn had hit them, with two *Magyar* divisions more or less destroyed, all three corps separated from one another and the line disintegrating, the OKW signalled the 'GO!' order to Veress and his men at Nikolayevka.

The Charge of the Magyars!

It was going to be a straight fight: the cavalryman Lajos Veress and his 130 Hungarian tanks versus Pavel Rybalko's 56,000 men and 200 panzers, backed up by another 100 tanks from Kirill Moskalenko's 40th Army.

This would not be like the 22nd Panzer disaster; no hungry mice had bedded down in the *Magyars'* panzers, and the enemy was so close that any lack of track sleeves made no difference. The young Hungarian tank crews received their orders, sprinted from their dug-outs to their armoured vehicles, started the engines and formed up. Hundreds of infantry climbed aboard the waiting trucks, sitting double-lined, back-to-back, on the cold, hard, wooden-plank seating, with their rifles between their knees. The clinking of glass was often heard; with so few anti-tank guns available, improvisation was the only option, and crates of Molotov cocktails had been prepared and were pushed under the seats ready to be used. Veress needed every advantage he could get, and weight of explosives was one. His 1st and 5th motorised artillery battalions formed up and headed off to pre-reconnoitred gun lines. There, the division's twenty-four 105mm guns were prepared, each gun crew sighting their weapons on mapped-out targets, and the ammunition was manhandled into place and readied for firing.

Veress led his men north-east, driving past 2nd Army HQ at Alexeyevka and on towards Ostrogorsk. His PzKpfw 38(*t*) tanks confronted the Soviets on open ground, the T-34s immediately scoring hits with their heavier guns. The small force of PzKpfw IV tanks with Veress fought back with some success. As they had been trained, the Hungarians sped out to the left and right flanks as fast as they could, churning up the snow with their tracks as they then spun back into the fight. Facing the thinner side-armour of the T-34s, they poured armour-piercing shot into the Soviets. Now it was the Russian tanks' turn to burn. Tank after tank was hit, slewing to a halt; black, oily smoke billowing out; panicked crewmen escaping through the hatches to be shot down in the snow. The *Magyar* artillery opened fire, raining down shells to hit tanks and infantry alike and, even more importantly, to try to block the beleaguered Soviet spearhead troops, cutting them off from reinforcement.

The attempt failed. The weight of fire was not heavy enough, and the Soviets rallied. Rybalko's corps commanders – Zenkovich and Koptsov – were competent professionals who knew what they were doing. Calling in their own artillery for counter-battery fire, the Hungarian gun lines soon began to take hits – guns and crews destroyed by the salvoes. Through the smoke on the field, fresh Soviet tank companies pressed forward. Veress had no choice but to order the retreat. Just as had happened to Gherghe's 1st Romanian's, the 1st Hungarian's counter-attack to save their army had failed.

A large number of Hungarian panzers had been lost, and now Veress was swamped by desperate pleas from corps and divisional commanders, all begging for help to save their units from imminent destruction. Realising two of the key towns were Ilovskaya and its airbase and the army HQ at Alexeyevka, Veress took the risky decision to split his forces between them. Did he have another choice? Probably not. His force was not strong enough to restrain the advancing Soviet spearheads; now it was about buying time for a withdrawal.

The Soviet 18th Rifle Corps, still fresh from defeating the 12th Light Division, now turned on Jeno Felkl's 10th Light Division, capturing all its artillery and causing panic in its ranks. Falling back in utter confusion, the 10th was herded by the 40th Army towards Ostrogorsk, where it was joined by the IV Corps's 13th Light Division and the majority of the Saxons of the 168th Infantry Division. Pounded by Soviet artillery and harried by tank and cavalry squadrons, they were all soon surrounded. Heeding calls for aid, Veress (along with other parts of Corps Kramer) counter-attacked the Soviets, hoping to reach Ostrogorsk and break their comrades out. The *Magyar* tankers managed to struggle forward a few miles but were not strong enough and had to fall back that evening.

Day six – 17 January

Jány poured over his maps and came to much the same conclusions as had Veress about which were the crucial points that needed to be held, adding Ostrogorsk and Nikolayevka to the list. Most of them were on the main railway line, and all were vital road junctions. Holding them meant he could bring up supplies and reinforcements (if he could source any!) and disrupt the Soviets long enough to give him a chance to establish a viable defence farther west. On the Soviet side, Golikov and Vatutin were of the same opinion as their Hungarian opponent. The lynchpin was Alexeyevka; if it were taken by the Soviets, Jány's plan would fail and, with it, his army.

Realising that most of József Heszlényi's corps was already there anyway, Jány formally ordered the IV Corps to fall back north to Ostrogorsk and dig in. Erno Gyimesi's VII Corps – the 19th, 20th and 23rd Light Divisions – was in the best shape of all three of Jány's Corps but was too slow and lacking in transport to be used. In any case, the divisions were in danger of being encircled themselves. The main battle would happen without them, so Jány ordered them to fall back towards the Oskol Valley some 100 miles west of the Don, which they reached on 25 January, having suffered terrible losses and having fought a rearguard action the whole way, including against the seemingly omnipresent Ivan Ivanov's 18th Rifle Corps.

Veress himself fell back on Alexeyevka, positioning half his armour to defend the town and sending the rest a few miles north to the airfield at Ilovskaya. There they joined up with Hungarian Air Force personnel, ground crew and anti-aircraft teams and prepared to face the oncoming Soviets of the 40th Army. The first Russians arrived about noon, and soon a full-scale battle was going on, shells and bullets zipping across the now-abandoned airstrip. With no cover, the attacking Soviets could not move forward, and they did not have enough forward artillery to silence the defences. They pulled away, leaving several tanks burning and a number of dead infantrymen in the snow. Foiled in his dash to take the airfield, Moskalenko sent troops south to break the link with the defenders of Alexeyevka. Jány and Veress could do nothing about that. Darkness was falling, and the Hungarians were not nearly as adept at night fighting as the Soviets. By late evening, Alexeyevka had been isolated, all communications had been cut and Jány no longer had anything more than intermittent contact with any of his units outside the town.

The *Alpini* nightmare begins

With the Hungarians in headlong retreat, the neighbouring Germans of the XXIV Corps in tatters and the Red Army already many miles behind them and on all sides, the *Alpini* finally received permission from 8th Army HQ to leave their lines and try to break out west at 11.00 a.m. on 17 January. The message ended with the words: 'God be with you.'

And so began what can only be described as an ordeal for the men of Nasci's four divisions, with Pascolini's Vicenza now an 'official' part of the corps. Over the next ten days, they would march almost 150 miles in temperatures that often plummeted to minus 20°C and fight a whole series of pitched battles and innumerable skirmishes – all without any resupply, reinforcement or support, and while running out of food and ammunition. It was an ordeal most would not survive.

At first, the withdrawal managed to maintain some sort of order, with the three *Alpini* Divisions leading, followed closely by the Vicenza and behind them, strung out over miles of open steppe, thousands upon thousands of personnel – Italian service troops, survivors from the Torino and Pasubio, Romanians from 3rd Army, a large number of panic-stricken Hungarians and several thousand Germans, the latter being about the only ones capable of any sort of continued resistance. However, all too soon problems with communications and the constant harrying from the Red Army would cause the withdrawal to fall into chaos and confusion.

The *Festung* curse

On 18 January, it became official: the 2nd Army was in dire straits. Everyone knew it because Hitler had declared Ostrogorsk a *Festung* (Fortress) – a defined military term the Nazi dictator had coined meaning that the named location was to be defended to the last man and the last round. There was to be no retreat and no surrender. Designating a city or town a *Festung* was a clear sign of desperation, and it never helped; in fact, it was usually a positive hindrance, denying commanders operational flexibility and the freedom to manoeuvre. Needless to say, the new title meant nothing to the men shivering in the foxholes around Ostrogorsk as Soviet artillery shells continued to strike, their own guns able to do little as ammunition stocks began to run dangerously low.

Some 15 miles to the south-west, a lightning thrust by Soviet forces almost took Alexeyevka by storm, and only a counter-attack by the 1st Hungarian's remaining panzers saved the situation and threw the Soviets back.

Over the next few days, Moskalenko and Rybalko continued to keep the pressure on the *Magyars*, artillery and local assaults grinding the life out of the remaining defenders and sapping their will to resist, but in truth, their main focus had moved north and south towards the German Second Army and the Italian *Alpini*, respectively. Leaving several corps behind to finish off the Hungarians, the Voronezh and Southwest Fronts set their sights on other targets.

Sixth Army's death throes

Back in Stalingrad, on 19 January 1943, Paulus, a practising Roman Catholic, had given strict instructions that no soldier was allowed to commit suicide, but he need not have worried. Starvation, disease and the Red Army were killing plenty.

The only officer left alive in the 2nd Battalion of the 44th Division's 132nd Grenadier Regiment was a platoon commander from the Romanian-manned

G Company. His company, his regiment, his division – indeed, his entire army – was bleeding to death in the snow-covered rubble that was once a thriving industrial city on the Volga River. The young Austrian grenadier lieutenant knew the situation was hopeless. His position was surrounded, and the defensive line had collapsed. There would be no miraculous escape, no cavalry coming over the hill to save them. Gathering together the last thirteen men of his command – Austrians, Germans and Romanians – he explained his plan and sent a final radio message to his divisional headquarters. They divided up their remaining bullets and hand-grenades, took last lingering looks at photographs of loved ones and letters from home and then, shambling forward like arthritic old men, climbed out of their bunker and attacked. There was a pause, a hail of gunfire, and then silence. None survived.

Fighting retreat of the *Alpini*

Struggling through the snow, Nasci's *Alpini* were in trouble; they soon realised that they not only had to fight out of encirclement, but also every mile of their way back to the west. Umberto Ricagno's Julia Division felt the brunt of this reality first as it attempted to throw the Russians out of the tiny village of Novaya Postoyalovka. Along with some of their comrades from the Cuneense, the Julia fought for thirty long hours to take it from its Soviet defenders so their retreat could continue. A young *Alpini* officer, Lieutenant Egisto Corradi, saw a Russian tank run over one of the Italians' few artillery guns before aiming directly at him. He flung himself into a shallow ditch only to look up at the underside of the tank as it drove over him:

> *This vehicle must be filled* ... 'That's all I read! It was an American Sherman tank, maybe it was out of order, or hit. It stopped about thirty paces beyond. We were on top of it immediately and we beat savagely on the metal with our guns. We yelled – '*Come out!*', they responded '*Niet!*', we were like drunks, full of pride and rage.

The Italians solved the problem by setting fire to several stooks of hay they placed around the tank, causing the terrified crew to emerge rapidly.

Casualties among the attackers were horrific, and even worse, the lack of transport meant that the majority of the wounded who couldn't walk any more had to be abandoned. The terrible march continued. Second Lieutenant Veniero Marsan of the Cuneense described the toll it took on his orderly, Ottavio:

At a certain point Ottavio simply stopped walking; he sat down in the snow and wouldn't move. I told him to get up, and I told him that if he stayed where he was he would die. There was no response. I slapped his face, I yelled at him, I told him to get up, to get moving, to save himself. There was no response, he was immobile, like a statue … we took him to an *isba* where there were at least twenty other soldiers lying on the floor, also suffering from various degrees of exposure. We knew the men were beyond suffering, and would die very quickly in that state.

Ottavio and his fellows were not alone as the corps struggled on, leaving the steppe littered with the dead, wounded and frostbitten.

Alexeyevka and Ostrogorsk

With Rybalko's tanks sent north, the 1st Hungarian Armoured managed to both hold Alexeyevka and break through to Fortress Ostrogorsk, reaching it on 21 January. Troops spread out through the town, gathering up the wounded – especially the stretcher cases – and loading them onto waiting trucks. The dead were left where they lay. Then it was time to go. Ostrogorsk was going to be evacuated, despite Hitler's directive. In fact, Hitler had been persuaded that a new line was required in the Oskol Valley to the west (where most of the VII Corps was already headed) and had grudgingly agreed to the withdrawal. With Veress' panzers and motorised infantry acting as a mobile rearguard, the survivors from Ostrogorsk, and anyone else they could collect, started to head west.

Suddenly, it was all over. Alexeyevka was abandoned the following day, and the Hungarian 2nd Army officially ceased to act as an independent command. Jány and his staff packed their equipment and papers into staff cars, and any other transport they could lay their hands on, and began to move out. Clerks and signallers rushed around burning all the papers that could not be taken and using axes and hammers to smash anything else that would not burn and had to be left behind.

With Budapest's consent, the OKW decreed that all Hungarians still in the Ostrogorsk-Ilovskaya-Alexeyevka area would come under Hans Kramer's command. Much like Wenck with the 3rd Romanian, Kramer used a cadre of experienced German officers and NCOs – the *Alte Hasen* (Old Hares), the German Army term for veterans of the front – to round up dispersed survivors and marshal them into some sort of order. Thousands of Hungarians were spread out over the steppe to the west of the old Don line, many being picked up and herded east by the victorious Soviets. Those who escaped that particular fate were pressed into temporary units, handed whatever weapons were available and sent straight back into action against the advancing Red Army columns. Kramer's plan was simple: head west through Budyenny, then Noviy Oskol, and reach the new line in the Oskol Valley. Despite the odds, he somehow managed to achieve his plan. All together, some 12,000 Hungarians who had not given up and were still fighting were brought under command, where they were grouped with Veress' tank crews, who continued to perform minor miracles with the few panzers remaining. By the end of January, Operation Saturn was over for the Hungarians. A new headquarters had been established in the rear, and all the *Magyars* left standing were pulled out of the line and sent there to be reorganised. The 1st Hungarian Armoured Field was the very last formation to go, finally leaving the front on 9 February. By then, it had just six panzers in working order.

Hans Kramer outlasted the 1st Armoured by a single day, receiving his marching orders on 10 January from his replacement, the Austrian Knight's Cross winner Erich Raus. As was common German practice, with any non-standard formations being named after their commander, Corps Kramer now became Corps Raus. Kramer went to North Africa and was promptly captured by the British.

'I have a son' – abandoning the *Alpini*

Back on the frozen steppe, the nightmare of the *Alpini* continued. By late January, the corps was a shadow of its former self. The Julia was all but destroyed, its few survivors joining with the remnants of Emilio Battisti's Cuneense to try to keep up with Luigi Reverberi's Tridentina, which was still battling westwards. However, their luck finally ran out on 27 January near the village of Valuiki, where the majority were again surrounded by Red Army troops, including squadrons of mounted Cossacks. In a last act of defiance, members of the Cuneense's 1st *Alpini* Regiment burned the regimental flags to keep them out of Russian hands before laying down their weapons (the few who had any by that stage) and going into captivity. Among those prisoners were three divisional commanders: the Julia's Ricagno, the Cuneense's Battisti and the Vicenza's Pascolini. Not among them, however, were the Cuneense Lieutenant-Colonels Scrimin, Bellani and Vertone, the former two being the commander and second-in-command of the 2nd *Alpini* Regiment. Days earlier, these senior officers had made the unbelievable decision to abandon their own men and try to break out by themselves. Apparently, with Battisti's

permission, they requisitioned a horse and sled and set off west. They asked
the Russian-speaking Veniero Marsan to accompany them as an interpreter,
but the shocked junior officer had pointedly refused, believing their behaviour was morally reprehensible and tantamount to desertion. Bellani excused
himself by saying, 'I have a son, and I haven't the heart to think I might not
see him again.'

Did Bellani think that no one else had a son, or daughter or brothers, mothers and fathers? As it turned out, their behaviour did them no good anyway,
as they were captured very shortly afterwards and sent to the prison camp at
Khrinovoje, an especially grim hellhole even by Soviet gulag standards. All
three died there.

The Battle of Nikolayevka

Roughly 10 miles north of Valuiki, in a shallow valley bisected by the railroad,
was Nikolayevka, the former headquarters of the 1st Hungarian Armoured
Field. Newly liberated and now garrisoned by at least two regiments of Red
Army infantry with artillery and even some tanks, Nikolayevka held the key
to the escape of what remained of the *Alpini* Corps. If the Italians could take
it, then the way was open for them, and they would have finally broken out of
the encirclement. Reverberi's Tridentina was now the only cohesive combat
force left, and as his men settled down for the night in the nearby hamlets of
Tereshkov and Arnautovo, the stocky mountain general planned his assault for
the following morning of 26 January.

Par for the course by now, nothing went as hoped for by the Italians. The
Soviets seized the initiative and struck first, attacking Arnautovo that same
night, infantry being fired in by supporting mortars and artillery until they
got close and the fighting became hand-to-hand. Among the *isbas*, men wres-
tled on the ground as Russians and Italians stabbed, shot and gouged one
another, the dead piling up in the narrow lanes. But the *Alpini* held, and the
Russians broke off their attack just before dawn. This allowed Reverberi to
try to concentrate on Nikolayevka, and his assault force crested the brow
above the town and charged down the long slope towards it as the sky above
them was lightening. That force was pitifully weak, consisting as it did of
three much-reduced alpine battalions supported by three German-manned
armoured vehicles.

The Soviet defenders were in no mood to give up and put up a wall of fire
into which the *Alpini* ran. Both sides understood the significance of the battle;
for the Russians, it meant victory and for the Italians, it meant survival. The

Soviets counter-attacked, but the *Alpini* pressed on, entering the streets and clearing the buildings with hand-grenades and machine-guns as they doggedly fought on. But by late afternoon, the Russians were still clinging on, and it was beginning to get dark.

Reverberi went forward to see the situation for himself and realised it was now or never for what remained of his command. Climbing on top of one of the three still-operational German panzers, the general waved his arms around like a mad man, shouting as loud as he could at his men, 'Avanti, Tridentina, avanti! Avanti, Tridentina, avanti!' ('Forward, Tridentina, forward!')

This personal display of leadership carried the day, and his men rallied and charged forward once more, taking the town and killing the remaining Soviet defenders. With Nikolayevka in *Alpini* hands, thousands of Italians, Germans, Romanians and Hungarians were saved and stumbled into the safety of the *Ostheer* lines.

That safety was only transitory, though, as the *Alpini* were forced to carry on retreating west well into February. Nuto Revelli said of the endless trudge:

> We are falling apart, sick, more or less frostbitten with non-stop diarrhoea … now we are just a mass of disarmed men … we aren't good for anything.

The cost of defeat

The Hungarian 2nd Army consisted of ten divisions, organised into three corps of nine light infantry divisions, with the 1st Armoured in reserve as the tenth, and on the morning of 12 January 1943, the official ration return listed 228,011 officers, NCOs and men. In two weeks of ferocious fighting, well over half that total number were lost – killed, wounded or missing (the majority of the latter ending up as prisoners-of-war, perhaps as many as 70,000). József Heszlényi's IV Corps was the worst hit. Jeno Felkl's 10th and Laszlo Hillosy-Kuthy's 13th were all but gone after being surrounded at Ostrogorsk, while Ulászló Solymussy's 12th Light had been utterly annihilated along with Deszo Laszlo's 7th Division. Erno Gyimesi's VII Corps had fared best, but its dead still littered almost 100 miles of steppe west of the Don as the survivors limped to the Oskol Valley. All together, the 2nd lost more than 140,000 men, including 2,000 trained officers who were irreplaceable at this stage of the war.

Almost as bad were the losses in war materiel. The figures were staggering. The Hungarians lost 146,000 rifles, 2,900 machine-guns, 460 anti-tank guns and rifles, 400 mortars and another 400 artillery pieces, along with 56,000 horses, 16,000 carts and wagons and 6,600 motor vehicles – plus no fewer than 530 field kitchens. The army's survivors were unarmed, immobile and could not even be fed! Hungarian industry had toiled for years to produce the equipment needed to keep the 2nd Army in the field, and now it was lost to the steppe and the Soviets.

For the Hungarian nation and its leaders in Budapest, the news from the front was catastrophic. It took weeks for people to understand what had happened and begin to consider the implications for their nation. The reality was stark: the fighting on the Don was the worst military disaster Hungary had suffered since the Battle of Mohacs was lost to the Ottoman Turks in 1526, and it was one the Hungarian armed forces did not recover from for the rest of the Second World War. Its immediate effect was the withdrawal of all Hungarian troops from the front line, and the *Magyars* would play no further part on the Eastern Front (apart from rear area security duties in the Ukraine) until 1944.

Alpini losses

The bravery shown by thousands of young alpine troopers during their epic break-out was of the very highest calibre and gives the lie to the hackneyed stereotype of the lack of Italian military valour. However, such courage does not come without a price, and the *Alpini* paid theirs in full that January. Umberto Ricagno's Julia, no stranger to appalling casualties having lost 5,000 men in the Pindus Gorges in Greece back in 1940, was hardest hit; only some 2,300 men made it out from the original 12,000 in the ranks before the withdrawal. Captain Ugo Reitani, from its artillery regiment, was one of the lucky ones, having started the campaign with 230 men, 160 mules and enough guns and equipment to fill an entire train on the way to Russia, he now found himself in charge of

> ... fourteen men, thirteen mules, a few empty rifles, a few handguns and the rage we have ...

The previously 16,000-strong Cuneense and Tridentina were decimated, the latter reduced to fewer than 4,500 men, of whom their equally brave commanding officer, Luigi Reverberi, said:

> My officers and alpini have been heroic, but so many are missing. Mine, in comparison to those of the other divisions who are prisoners for the most part, are dead or wounded. In just one day at Nikolayevka I lost forty officers.

Amongst those officers was the corps Chief-of-Staff, Giulio Martinat. A veteran of Ethiopia and Albania, he was awarded a Knight's Cross by the Germans for his bravery during the Nikolayevka battle. In 1950, his hometown of Perrero in Piedmont erected a monument in his honour. For the prisoners Reverberi spoke of, the agony of retracing their steps east awaited them, followed by a lingering death for most in captivity.

The Stalingrad agony finally ends

The sacrifice of the men trapped in Stalingrad, and those who fought so hard on the Don, was not matched by their leaders. On 31 January 1943, General Friedrich Paulus was promoted to Field Marshal, the highest rank in the German military, in the clear expectation from Hitler that he would then commit suicide rather then become the first ever German to hold that rank and go into captivity alive. The Nazi dictator said to his staff:

> In peacetime Germany about eighteen to twenty thousand people a year choose to commit suicide, even without being in such a position. Here is a man who sees fifty or sixty thousand of his soldiers die defending themselves bravely to the end. How can he surrender himself to the bolshevists?

Paulus' response was emphatic:

> It looks like an invitation to commit suicide, but I will not do this favour for him ... I have no intention of shooting myself for this Bohemian corporal.

After innumerable acts of bowing and scraping to Hitler that had condemned his men to despair and death, this was beyond ironic. If he had defied his *Führer* earlier, perhaps tens of thousands of his soldiers might have survived. We will never know. As it was, Paulus finally surrendered that same day in the basement of the Univermaag Department Store in the city centre. Suffering from dysentery and a nervous breakdown, he was led away to sign the declaration of capitulation. Friedrich Paulus would survive – as would almost every other German senior officer taken prisoner – and joined the Soviet-sponsored National Committee for a Free Germany, appealing to his fellow countrymen to join him and Moscow.

On 1 February 1943, Adolf Hitler ordered the following communiqué to be broadcast across the Third Reich:

The Battle for Stalingrad has ended. True to its oath to its last breath, Sixth Army, under the exemplary leadership of Field Marshal Paulus, has succumbed to the overwhelming strength of the enemy and to unfavourable circumstances. The enemy's two demands for capitulation were proudly rejected. The last battle was fought under a swastika flag from the highest ruin in Stalingrad.

In Germany, three days of national mourning were declared, and in an act insensitive even by Nazi standards, the official 'funeral oration' for the Sixth Army was broadcast on the radio by Hermann Goering – a man whose incompetent fingerprints were all over the Stalingrad disaster, having promised that his *Luftwaffe* could deliver 300 tonnes of supplies to the Sixth Army every day during its encirclement. The average was actually less than 100 tonnes.

As a final piece of pathos, as Stalingrad fell, some German and allied soldiers tried to escape across the snowbound steppe. As late as mid-February, *Luftwaffe* reconnaissance flights reported seeing groups or even individuals struggling west through the snow. In the end, only a single man reached safety – Sergeant Nieweg, an anti-aircraft gunner. By the time he stumbled into the German lines, he was half-dead from exhaustion, starvation and frostbite. He was taken straight to a field dressing station for medical treatment but was killed just twenty-four hours later during a Soviet mortar bombardment.

Chapter 11

Counting the cost of the Don

The effect of the Don defeat for Nazi Germany and her allies was profound. Almost one in ten of the entire *Ostheer* had been killed or captured at Stalingrad. Some 15,000 Germans died during the five days of Operation Uranus to encircle the city, with another 147,000 being killed before the final surrender. The 89,000 Germans and Austrians who survived Stalingrad had to trudge wearily into Soviet captivity. They were joined by 3,000 Romanians (mostly survivors of the ill-fated 20th Infantry and 1st Cavalry Divisions) and a few hundred Italians and Croats. The Croats were all that was left of the 369th Regiment. Trapped in Stalingrad, they had fought alongside the Germans, almost 1,000 of them being flown to safety along with other wounded. Attached to General von Lenski's German 24th Panzer Division as additional infantry, by the end of January there were only a few hundred left alive and fighting. They disappeared in the last few days, either to the grave or captivity.

For the majority of prisoners, weakened as most were by starvation and disease, the harsh treatment they were to receive in the POW camps meant death. A secret NKVD report from the spring of 1943 acknowledged that no fewer than 55,000 prisoners captured during the Don fighting – Germans, Austrians, Italians, Romanians, Hungarians and Croats – had already died in the camps by the middle of April. In the end, just 5,000 of Paulus' men went home after the war finally ended. They were joined by some 10,000 Italians from the original 64,000 taken prisoner, similar numbers of Romanians and Hungarians and some 200 Croats, who were promptly re-arrested upon repatriation by Yugoslavia's new Communist government. Their ordeal would continue.

As for Field Marshal Paulus, still very much alive; he famously appeared as a witness for the prosecution at the Nuremberg Trials and responded to a journalist's question about the other Stalingrad prisoners by telling him to inform their mothers, wives and children that they were well – the last betrayal of so many. Paulus himself would never see his Romanian wife, Elena, again, as she stayed in West Germany after the war and he remained in the East, seen as he was by many as a traitor to the men he had led to disaster. He died in 1957, just two years after the last of those men was released from captivity in the Soviet Union.

The Ostheer and Luftwaffe are decimated

When the German/Austrian Sixth Army was wiped off the *Wehrmacht*'s Order of Battle, Germany lost its first entire field army since the Battle of Jena in 1806 against Napoleon. It also lost most of the Fourth Panzer Army and 89,000 men of von Salmuth's Second Army. Alongside a Field Marshal, Germany lost twenty-two generals and another 2,500 experienced officers. No fewer than five of the *Panzerwaffe*'s twenty-seven panzer divisions were destroyed (as Paulus signed the document of surrender, the Germans could muster just 495 panzers along the entire length of the Eastern Front), and while the 14th, 16th and 24th Panzers would be rebuilt, the ill-starred 22nd and 27th were disbanded and never re-formed. The OKH calculated that the army had lost fifty divisions' worth of military hardware in the seventeen months from the start of Operation Barbarossa up to the beginning of Operation Uranus and an incredible forty-five divisions' worth in the following four months. Ammunition was also now a big worry in Berlin. Stocks were already low going into the summer campaign, but so fierce had been the fighting in Stalingrad that the situation was now near-critical. In just one month, the Sixth Army had fired 23 million bullets, 753,000 mortar bombs, 576,000 anti-tank rounds and 117,000 cannon shells and had also used 178,000 grenades and 15,000 mines. Germany's armaments industry and war economy – the future of which was the stated reason for Case Blue in the first place – could not keep up with that level of expenditure. The situation worsened as neutral countries like Portugal and Turkey began to back away from supplying the Reich with raw materials, including the tungsten and chrome it so desperately needed.

Stalingrad was not just an unmitigated disaster for the German Army either. The *Luftwaffe* also suffered gravely. Starved of resources in the run-up to Case Blue and fighting on four fronts, Stalingrad was the point at which Germany's once-vaunted air arm began a rapid decline. Hundreds of fighters and bombers were lost, and the air-transport fleet, so vital in a war being fought across thousands of miles, lost more than 500 aircraft and their crews - seventy-two aircraft alone were lost when the Tatinskaya airbase fell to the Soviet 3rd Guards Army. The *Luftwaffe* never recovered. Losses in experienced, technical ground crew – the *Luftwaffe*'s so-called black men – were high and made worse by Goering's new policy of creating ground troops from supposedly underemployed staff. Thousands of personnel who could have been used to help rebuild the *Luftwaffe* were instead diverted into Field Divisions as half-trained infantrymen. Even for Goering, this was a stupid idea. For the Red Army, it was manna from heaven, and it consistently targeted the *Luftwaffe* units as weak links until the end of the war.

Moscow's blood price

Not that Moscow got off lightly; in fact, the casualty count for them was even worse. The figures are enormous and difficult to comprehend. Across the 'planet operations' of Mars, Uranus and 'Little' Saturn in the final quarter of 1942 and the beginning of 1943, the Soviet Union lost 515,508 men killed or missing and an additional 941,896 wounded – a total of some 1.5 million men in only three months. They lost more than 300,000 defending Stalingrad in the autumn and another 150,000 killed over the Christmas period. On Rokossovsky's Don Front alone, 46,000 were killed and 123,000 wounded in the final stages of the offensives from the beginning of the New Year until operations were temporarily suspended in early February. He also lost more than 2,000 tanks and almost 4,000 artillery guns while expending 24 million bullets, 990,000 mortar rounds and 911,000 artillery shells. However, despite this terrible toll, the crucial difference between the two nations was that the Soviet Union could sustain these losses and replace them whilst Nazi Germany simply could not. Reinhard Gehlen was wrong: The Russian bear was not at the end of its tether. The Nazi eagle was.

In an age when public support for war is often the deciding factor in victory or defeat, it is telling to read the conclusion of a report compiled by the SS on civilian morale and attitudes in Germany after the Don campaign: 'Universally there is a conviction that Stalingrad represents a turning point in the War.'

CHAPTER 12

AFTER THE DON
THE AXIS REGROUPS

The failure of Operation Barbarossa in the snows in front of Moscow in 1941 condemned the Germans and their allies to at least another year of fighting in the Soviet Union and probably a lot more. This in turn meant attrition in troops and equipment on a scale so vast that even Berlin could not keep up. Hence, the Third Reich's only hope of maintaining any sort of parity with the Soviets lay with Bucharest, Budapest and Rome, and that hope died under the tracks, hooves and boots of the Red Army on the Don as it ground the Axis into the dirt. It was a catastrophe from which Nazi Germany and her allies never recovered. The arguments over quality versus quantity and the relative combat power of Hungarian, Italian or Romanian divisions can be argued over *ad infinitum*, but what is undeniable is that in the vastness of the Soviet Union, sheer numbers played a crucial part, and the men and equipment the *Ostheer* needed to win were lost that winter.

What, now, for those same allies? The *Wehrmacht*'s Erich von Manstein understood the magnitude of the campaign – in particular, the impact it had on the allied forces:

In conclusion, we cast a final glance at the full course and outcome of the 1942–43 winter campaign in south Russia, we must begin by acknowledging the successes attained on the Soviet side, the magnitude of which was incontestable. The Russians had contrived to encircle and destroy the German Sixth Army, the strongest we had in the field. They had, moreover, swept four allied armies clean off the map. *Many brave members of the latter had fallen in battle* [author's italics] and considerable numbers had gone into captivity. What allied troops remained had disintegrated, and had sooner or later to be withdrawn for good from the zone of operations.

Manstein was never one to hand out praise lightly; indeed, his remarks and commentary were often very caustic, so it is of note that he paid even a modest tribute to the performance of Germany's allies.

The home fronts

In the allied Axis countries, the news from the Don hit like a hurricane. Across the wide plains of Hungary and Romania, and in the cities and towns of northern Italy and the Danube, hundreds of thousands of families received the dreaded news that a loved one – father, brother, son – was dead, wounded or missing. It was worst among the close-knit mountain folk of the Carpathians, Dolomites and Apennines, where whole communities were robbed of a future as their young men perished together on the far-off steppe. The young *Alpini* officer Nuto Revelli had been wounded in the fighting but survived. Repatriated home to Italy, he spoke of his train journey through villages and towns in the recruiting areas of the Julia Division:

> In every station there's a small crowd of women dressed in black, already marked by mourning, imploring us for news. They show us photographs of their relative; they want to know the fate of the Julia Division. We only know the Julia almost vanished completely on the Russian Front. We don't know what to say.

Previously passive populations became increasingly restless and vocal in their opposition to the path their leaders had set them on. The clamour of battle and defeat in southern Russia was most definitely heard in the halls of government in Budapest, Bucharest and Rome.

Italy

As Nuto Revelli was travelling home following the Don disaster, a shocked Benito Mussolini was trying to come to terms with his grandiose ambitions in Russia going up in so much smoke. Back in the Ukraine, Giorgio Geddes was a part of the effort to reorganise:

> It had to be decided whether to move the 8th Army north, towards Gomel, or to repatriate it for good. While Hitler and the Duce were deciding, what remained of the Italian 8th Army, quartered in the Don region and still operational, would be passed under the command of von Mackensen's [author's note: the monocled Prussian aristocrat and panzer commander Eberhard von

Mackensen] First Panzer Army, despite the now-terrible relations between the
Germans and the Italians.

Unsurprisingly, given the impact of Operation 'Little' Saturn, the decision was
made to withdraw almost every surviving Italian from the Soviet Union. The
8th Army was then ignominiously disbanded, its divisions either broken up or
re-formed away from battle zones. Italy would play no further military role
on the Russian Front.

For Fascist Italy, the prospects for the war, so bright in 1940/41, were now
very bleak. The *Regia Marina* (Italian Navy) intended to rule the waves of the
Mediterranean, but was now mostly at the bottom of that same sea; the *Regio
Aeronautica*, long seen as the darling of Italy's armed forces, had been shot
from the skies, its pitiable remnants pulled back to protect the Italian mainland from Allied bombers. The nation's African Empire, carved out at such a
huge toll in blood and treasure, was mostly in the hands of the British, and the
army that had defended it was a shadow of its former self.

However, despite its poor showing, Italy had achieved about as much as
it could for the Axis war effort; it had mobilised almost as many men as the
British (4.5 million Italians vs. 4.6 million Britons) and had squeezed its
weakened industrial and agricultural base to within an inch of its life. Now, all
Il Duce's bluff and bombast could not hide the stark reality of Italy's situation
as the country slid towards invasion and defeat. In the industrial heartlands
of the north, thousands of workers stopped work and marched in the streets
demanding 'peace and liberty'. The vast Fiat works in Turin stood idle, and
the economic powerhouse of Milan came to a standstill. Almost 300,000
Italians had already died in the fighting, the economy was in ruins and hunger
was widespread as first Sicily fell and then the Allies began to advance north
towards Rome from their beachheads in the south.

The result was inevitable.

The diminutive Italian monarch Victor Emmanuel III, desperate to keep
his throne, dismissed *Il Duce* and installed a new government under Marshal
Pietro Badoglio. Then, despite the Marshal's loud and repeated protestations
to Berlin, Italy's three-and-a-half-year war against the Allies came to an
end when it switched sides on 13 October 1943. Nazi Germany's original
European Fascist ally was now a 'co-belligerent' with the Allies, i.e. an enemy
of Germany. In an operation of unbelievable speed across southern Europe
and the Balkans, hundreds of thousands of Italians were disarmed by their
ex-German comrades, with large numbers of these hapless men rounded
up and sent to the Reich as forced labour. To help make sure things went

peacefully, the *Wehrmacht* massacred 5,000 men of the 33rd Acqui Infantry Division on the Greek island of Cephalonia as an example. This event became the historical base for Louis de Bernière's famous novel *Captain Corelli's Mandolin*, which was turned into a successful Hollywood film starring Nicholas Cage and Penelope Cruz.

The Germans then rescued the imprisoned and embittered Mussolini from his mountain-top captivity in a daring raid by *Fallschirmjager* so that the former dictator could establish a new Fascist Republic in the still-occupied north of Italy.

For Italians, the agony would continue right up to the final German surrender, with bloody fighting in the north matched by an equally bloody near–civil war in the rest of Italy among fascists, monarchists, socialists and communists. More than 100,000 additional Italians would die in this phase of the war, many at the hands of their fellow countrymen – including Mussolini himself, shot with his mistress, Clara Petacci, both hung by their feet from a garage in Milan as the crowds cheered.

Romania – the biggest domino

Romania did not follow the same path as Italy in withdrawing all its remaining troops back to the homeland after the Don fighting. The pitiful remnants of the Romanian 3rd and 4th Armies were indeed brought back to the kingdom to be re-formed, but no fewer than eight entire divisions with tens of thousands of men remained in southern Russia – the 10th Infantry and the 1st and 4th Mountain Divisions in the Crimea, as well as the 19th Infantry, 6th and 9th Cavalry and 2nd and 3rd Mountain Divisions in the Kuban. When news of the Don calamity came through to these units, their morale plummeted, and the Germans, wary of their reaction, withdrew them from front line roles and relegated them to coastal defence and anti-partisan duties. This move, intended to soften the blow, actually made the position worse, and unit discipline began to unravel as men fell prey to boredom, alcohol and lethargy.

In Romania, dissatisfaction with Antonescu reached new heights, and young King Michael now began to plan how and when to remove the *Conducator* and seek peace with the Soviet Union and the Western Allies.

In the meantime, the army had to take stock and try to salvage whatever it could from the wreckage left after Operations Uranus and 'Little' Saturn. Most important was the need to recreate a viable armoured force. The small number of 1st Romanian Panzer Division vehicles still operational at the front were designated as the Nistor Armoured Group to carry on the fighting (they were also sent one new R-2 as a pathetic reinforcement), while the remainder of the division, mostly its support and supply sub-units, as well as a cadre of experienced officers and NCOs, was withdrawn home in January 1943 to start the reorganisation process.

Radu Gherghe had survived the fighting in Russia and now took charge of the reconstitution of his beloved division – a mammoth task. In a desperate attempt to rebuild its panzer force, Bucharest ordered that basically any vehicle with tracks was to be used regardless of whether it was obsolete, damaged, armoured or, in some cases, even capable of moving under its own steam. The retired Renault R-35s were brought back into service, as were the obsolete FT tankettes. A number of R-2s recovered from the battlefield were repaired and repainted. Improvisation was the order of the day, with 'new' models created such as the TACAM-R2, a self-propelled gun created by mounting a captured Soviet 76.2mm ZiS-3 gun on the chassis of an R-2 tank. The Germans were also pressurised into supplying a number of PzKpfw IV tanks and Sturmgeschütz III assault guns to add to the fifty repaired R-2 tanks.

On 20 March, as spring turned to summer, Gherghe departed, having been promoted to head the I Corps.[1] Gerghe was replaced by the division's original commander, Nicolae Stoenescu, and under his guidance the surviving Romanian tankers continued the painful process of rebuilding throughout the rest of 1943 and into 1944. Antonescu sought to help by passing the 'Law for the Organisation of the Armed Forces' in October 1943, which set out the creation of a new Mechanised Troops Command under which all armoured units would now be grouped. The 1st Romanian Panzer was officially on the books.

But grand as it sounded, laws do not produce tanks, and during 1943 and into early 1944, Bucharest was able to contribute only two relatively small armoured groups to the Eastern Front; although having said that, the fact that it sent any at all was miraculous. The first was the so-called Cantemir Group – the successor to the Nistor Armoured Group – which consisted of nothing more than a few companies of obsolete tanks, some artillery and several battalions of motorised infantry. The Cantemir Group fought alongside the Germans in southern Russia as an independent unit.

The second force was actually the larger of the two, composed of a full battalion of some forty R-2 tanks dispatched to reinforce the five Romanian units in the Kuban.

Both units acquitted themselves well despite their lack of combat power, but unsurprisingly, by the time they were brought home in March 1944, they

---

1 In 1944, he would become a German POW when Romania switched sides before dying peacefully in 1959.

had only ten tanks between them still in operational condition. The rest, and hundreds of men, had been abandoned in Russia. Nevertheless, the survivors were married up with Stoenescu's re-forming unit in what was now grandiosely entitled the 1st Panzer 'Greater Romania'. With the division nearing combat readiness, the Defence Ministry again decided that Stoenescu was not the man to lead it into battle (he could be forgiven for becoming paranoid, or perhaps he was relieved) and instead appointed the Knight's Cross–wearing Radu Korne. Promoted to general following his daring and tenacious leadership of the improvised detachment that bore his name during Operation Uranus, Korne was now given orders to take his sixty tanks and assault guns east to Moldavia to await the advancing Red Army.

The rot sets in

A month later, when the Red Army attacked to liberate the Crimea in April 1944, the previously reliable Wallachs and Danube men who manned the 10th Infantry Division gave up the ghost. The division collapsed almost overnight, the troops no longer willing to fight and die in a war they did not believe in anymore. The OKW's reaction, far swifter than the hesitancy that characterised the Don campaign, was to withdraw it – along with the rest of the remaining Romanian divisions in Russia – to join the re-formed 3rd and 4th Armies now in Bessarabia, preparing to defend the lands they had won back in 1941 at the beginning of Operation Barbarossa.

Defend the homeland!

Now, more than three years after Barbarossa's launch, the chastened and battered *Ostheer* could spare only the small and ill-equipped Eighth Army and, in a quirk of fate, the re-established Sixth, to join the Romanians in the region. All the formations were in woeful shape, and when the Soviet thunderbolt struck in August, the entirely predictable happened: the Romanian formations disintegrated, with thousands of men surrendering without a struggle. That could not be said for Korne and his men of the 1st Panzer 'Greater Romania', who mounted their vehicles, loaded their weapons and drove straight at the Red Army. With the front disappearing and gaps opening up everywhere, the Romanian tankers struggled from one counter-attack to another, making the Soviets pay a heavy price for their advance but taking dreadful casualties themselves at the same time.

The Red Army was now firmly on Romanian soil, and it was clear that the game was up, and everyone knew it – everyone except Antonescu.

The Romanian strongman refused to budge from his alliance with Berlin. In a meeting with the king on the morning of 23 August in the palace, with the front broken in Moldavia and Bessarabia, the air force destroyed and the army visibly crumbling, he replied to the monarch's demands to make peace with the following:

> We shall try to hold the fortified line of Focsani-Oancea-Bolgrad with the battalions of recruits I have posted there along with other troops from within the country … should we fail to hold the enemy on this line we will withdraw to the mountains and will try to hold them there. We cannot abandon the Germans.

King Michael had no alternative. With a pre-arranged signal, he called in his personal adjutant, who arrested the *Conducator* on the spot and locked him in a strong room where the king's father used to store his precious stamp collection.

That night, the king broadcast over the radio to the nation:

> Romanians, in this most difficult hour of our history I have decided, in full understanding with my people, that there is only one way to save the country from total catastrophe; our withdrawal from the alliance with the Axis powers and the immediate cessation of the war with the United Nations. [Author's note: at that time, Britain, the USA and the Soviet Union were known collectively as the United Nations.] … From this moment the fighting and any hostile act against the Soviet armies ceases, as does also the state of war with Great Britain and the United States …

At a stroke, it was all finally over – or at least that was the intent. The remaining German forces in Romania were left isolated and in danger of encirclement and destruction; plus, Nazi Germany had now lost Ploesti and, with it, its last major source of oil. From now on, the *Wehrmacht* was increasingly immobile, its aircraft grounded, its ships and U-boats trapped in port and the army without tanks and trucks. Troops travelled on foot, bicycles or horses.

As the fuel-starved Germans fled west, the Romanians uneasily faced their enemies-turned-allies: the Red Army. Still unsure of their new comrades' loyalty, the Soviets interned the majority of the country's armed forces, including most of the 1st Romanian Panzer, in hastily established prisoner-of-war camps. Radu Korne, no Nazi but a Knight's Cross winner, was unsurprisingly relieved of his command on the grounds of being 'politically unreliable' – the accepted code at the time for being a potential opponent to the communists, both Soviet and Romanian. The second-in-command of the division's 1st Panzer Regiment, Lieutenant Colonel Gherghe Matei, was eventually released and put in charge of a small portion of the division, some 1,000 men with a number of tanks and assault guns, and sent along with the rest of the re-formed Romanian Army to fight the Germans and their Hungarian allies in Transylvania, where the Soviets used them as little more than cannon fodder.

For Romania, the Transylvanian campaign was an unmitigated disaster that almost rivalled the Don. With so many of its men already killed or maimed by the war, another 170,000 casualties were now added to the 615,000 already suffered on the Russian Front since 1941, many of whom were still in Soviet POW camps from which few would ever return.

As for the Romanian panzer arm, the armistice protocol signed a while later ended their brief existence as the 1st Panzer 'Greater Romania', and they, along with their training division, the Armoured Training Centre and the whole Mechanised Troops Command, were all disbanded en bloc. The only exception was the so-called 2nd Romanian Tank Regiment – in reality, a small battalion – which was sent, like Gherghe Matei's unit, to the front to fight the Germans. Ordered to Slovakia in early 1945 and assigned to a Red Army tank corps, it was treated with often open contempt by its Soviet 'brothers-in-arms', despite the unit being cited for bravery and courageous conduct on no fewer than four separate occasions by the Soviet High Command. Starved of supplies and reinforcements, and repeatedly sent to where the fighting was fiercest, the Romanians lost more than 90 per cent of their vehicles and 50 per cent of their men in just two months. The regiment was finally disbanded at the end of March 1945, and with it went the last vestiges of Romania's ever-fragile armoured power.

The reluctant Axis allies – Finland and Bulgaria

For a full two and a half years, the Finns had not moved from the positions they had reached in late 1941 – basically, their pre–Winter War border. Having achieved their war aims, Marshal Mannerheim and his government had decided to sit and watch as the *Ostheer* and Red Army tore themselves to pieces along some 1,000 miles of front. However, over the years, inactivity had become sloth, and the once-adept and much-lauded Finnish military had not used the time it had been given constructively. Just as in 1939, the Finns had few tanks, aircraft or heavy guns and were now totally reliant on the static defences of the Mannerheim Line, with its miles of trenches and concrete pillboxes, to keep the Red Army at bay. This was the Maginot Line all over again.[1]

In June 1944, the Soviets proved to Helsinki that the Mannerheim Line was as fallible as every other line of static defences ever built, as they attacked with almost 500,000 men equipped with hundreds of tanks and supported by thousands of artillery pieces. The Finns, tied to the line, robbed of their legendary mobility and committed to a battle of attrition they could not hope to win, crumpled under the onslaught and went into retreat. For the very first time in the war, some of their units even panicked and fled. Casualties were very heavy, and by the end of August, the Finns realised the end was in sight. Desperate to avoid total defeat and an inevitably hostile occupation, Mannerheim asked Moscow for a cease-fire, and once agreed, it came into effect on 5 September 1944. Part of the price the Kremlin extracted was the obligation on the part of the Finns to expel all German forces from their soil immediately, and although this was mostly achieved remarkably peacefully, there was always going to be trouble. In the ensuing chaos, fighting did break out, and men who had been comrades-in-arms a few weeks earlier now ended up killing one another. The Finnish dead joined 90,000 of their fellow countrymen who had already been lost during the war.

The Bulgars had matched the Finns in keeping out of the campaign in the East and had managed to preserve intact the vast majority of the forces they had when Operation Barbarossa was originally launched. This refusal by the Bulgarians to send troops to Russia was reiterated to Hitler by Tsar Boris at a very stormy meeting at Hitler's headquarters in the pine forests of Rastenburg in East Prussia during August 1943. Within two weeks of this refusal, the Tsar was dead from alleged heart failure.

His loss was a serious blow for Bulgaria. Tsar Boris had been popularly known among his people as the 'Unifier' for bringing the disputed province of Macedonia back into Bulgaria at the beginning of the war. He was one of those rare individuals who stood up to Hitler's demands and fanatical hectoring, and in his case, it was not just his refusal to send troops East but also his steadfast opposition to handing over his country's 50,000 Jews to the Nazis, an act that saved them from the Holocaust. Because of this, many suspected a Nazi-inspired poison plot to remove him and install a more pliant regime

---

1 The famed French defensive network built at vast expense to prevent another German invasion after the First World War. The fortifications were named after the Defence Minister who had instigated its construction – André Maginot. He died of typhus contracted from eating bad oysters, whilst his military brainchild would fail in spectacular fashion in 1940 when the *Blitzkreig* simply bypassed the line.

under his 6-year-old son, Simeon II. If this was the intent, then it was a failure. The new Tsar's (or rather, regency's) policy towards Russia remained the same – inactivity – and his twenty-three divisions made no move to the east. This was just as well as they lacked just about everything a modern army required. They were even short of horses. The Bulgarian Army did have one armoured brigade, equipped with sixty German-supplied tanks – the ubiquitous, obsolete 'workhorse' of the Axis allies, the PzKpfw 38(*t*), along with a small number of heavier PzKpfw IVs – plus another sixty French-built Renault R-35s (the same vehicle the Romanian Army had retired in late 1941 before being forced to reactivate them after the Don when they were 'panzer-poor').

As the Red Army approached the Bulgarian border a year after the Tsar's death, the mood of panic in the country was palpable. The Bulgarian Communist Party seized the initiative and launched a coup against the Prime Minister, Konstantin Muraviev, on 9 September 1944, even as Soviet tanks were driving at top speed towards Sofia. The monarchy was swept away forever as a pro-communist 'Government of the Fatherland Front' under Kimon Georgiev took power. The new administration immediately made peace with Moscow and switched sides, and almost overnight the old guard in the armed forces disappeared as army formations were rebranded as People's Liberation Brigades, staffed with Soviet-style 'political commissars'. The Soviets ensured control of their new allies by taking direct command of the Bulgar troops, and, as with the Romanians, they tended to use them as 'cannon fodder', sending them where the fighting with the Germans was the hardest. First, they were tasked to try to halt the withdrawal of German Army Group E from Greece and then to pursue the retreating *Wehrmacht* all the way into Austria. There, on 13 May 1945, they met British troops advancing from the west as the fighting in Europe finally ended. Behind them, the Bulgarian Army left 32,000 of their comrades killed, wounded or missing. The recompense they received from Moscow for this bloody sacrifice was more than fifty years of communist repression and corruption.

Croatia and Slovakia – the end of independence

As independent countries, Croatia and Slovakia would both outlive the fighting on the Don by less than three years.

For Croatia, a beautiful land of pebble beaches, scented pine forests and snow-topped mountains, the unspeakable barbarity of Anté Pavelic's *Ustase* regime had been feeding the growing strength of Josip Tito's Partisan army since the country's creation. As Pavelic's murderous thugs massacred Jews, Serb villagers,

Muslim farmers and artisans, they were physically undermining the very foundations of their own puppet state. During autumn 1943, the Italian surrender removed a significant support to Zagreb's terrorist government, and with the civil war raging, Pavelic needed every man he could lay his hands on to fight at home. Sending any more to the East was simply out of the question. He had already lost several thousand of his very best fighters in the doomed 369th and the Light Transport Brigade, and he was not about to repeat that mistake.

When the *Wehrmacht* finally abandoned the Balkans between late 1944 and early 1945, the Croatian dictator showed his true colours and fled to General Francisco Franco's Fascist Spain to save his own wretched skin from the justice he so richly deserved. Without him, his genocidal regime of extremists, opportunists and acolytes collapsed. Croatia ceased to exist. The victorious communists liberated their own country, without Soviet help, and reunified Serbia, Montenegro, Slovenia, Croatia, Bosnia and Herzegovina back into Yugoslavia. That reunification would hold for fifty years before the hatreds that had burned so deeply in the Second World War reignited in the 1990s.

The Slovaks were the exception for the Axis allies in being part of Case Blue but not on the Don or in Stalingrad. They were actually positioned in the Caucasus, officially attached to the German Seventeenth Army, one of the *Wehrmacht*'s finest. Retreating like everyone else to avoid being cut off, the previously reliable Slovaks were now less than enthusiastic about both the war and their junior role. In one incident, a Slovak officer, Lieutenant Pavel Marcely, and his entire rifle company of some 100 men deserted to the Red Army. Soon, this disillusionment became nothing less than a contagion, and the once illustrious Slovak 1st Division alone lost 2,731 men, who defected to the Red Army during the fighting at Melitopol, east of Odessa. This was despite a *Wehrmacht* report from their liaison team in Slovakia's capital, Bratislava, that stated:

> ... the Slovakian people are proud that Slovakian soldiers are holding their ground so bravely, even in the difficult winter ... co-operation with the Germans was extremely good.

Exactly where this fantasy came from is anyone's guess. The reality was that another Axis ally was beginning to realise the victory party was over and that the reckoning was coming.

However, the OKW was far more sceptical and withdrew the Slovaks from the frontline, assigning them instead to second-rate rear area security duties. Robbed of trust in their fighting capabilities, morale tumbled even further among the Slovak riflemen, and by early 1944, the Germans were worried enough to disarm them completely and use them instead as construction brigades to dig trenches and maintain roads. For fighting soldiers, this was utter humiliation and was met with disgust at home. Alarmed like every other Axis ally by the remorseless advance of the Red Army, the Slovaks began to organise new divisions – three in total – to help defend their homeland. This process was still underway when a partisan-inspired national uprising started in late August 1944. The Germans rushed to crush it, dissolving all the new Slovak Army units to stop them from joining the insurrection, and that was the end of both the infant country's army and the state.

In the heat of August and September 1944, Nazi Germany had lost France and no fewer than three of its foremost allies: Romania, Bulgaria and Slovakia. Berlin was holding onto Hungary by a thread, and Croatia was now more of a handicap than an advantage, soaking up men and equipment desperately needed elsewhere. The situation left the *Ostheer* dangerously exposed in the south, where it was stripped of any meaningful support apart from the reluctant *Magyars*. The Axis collapse that autumn was almost as big a disaster for the Germans as the Don battles of 1942/43. Outdated and ill-equipped Bulgaria's twenty-plus divisions might have been, but they alone would have been a powerful boost for the seriously ailing *Wehrmacht*, even more so if joined by hundreds of thousands of armed Romanians and Slovaks.

As it was, Nazi Germany would face the last eight months of the Second World War with Hungary as its only remaining ally of any significance. It would not be significant enough.

Hungary – last man standing

The Romanians were not the only country whose previous armoured strength lay in ruins in early 1943; it was the same for their mortal enemies in Hungary. Having lost thousands of men and more than 120 armoured vehicles in the fighting, the battered remnants of the 1st Armoured Field were withdrawn from Russia, to be used as a foundation to try to build the dreamt-of armoured corps of two *Magyar* panzer divisions. They would now be supplemented by eight Assault Artillery Battalions, very much modelled on the emerging self-propelled gun detachments the Germans were adopting to try to remedy the shortcomings in the *Panzerwaffe*. To fill the ranks of these new formations, Budapest had been developing and ordering a number of new vehicles from its embryonic weapons industries.

First and foremost amongst these vehicles was the much-anticipated Turan tank. This had not been ready for the Don battles, yet even before its eventual delivery, it was recognised that tank design had advanced rapidly and a heavier tank was needed with more armour and more fire power – thus, the Turan II. Also built was the 40/43M Zrinyi II, a self-propelled (SP) assault gun armed with a 105mm MAVAG 40/43 L20.5 howitzer with a range of more than 7 miles.[1]

Just as with the Turan, Budapest handed the production of the new vehicle over to the manufacturer Weiss. The first Zrinyi II and Turan II vehicles rolled off the production lines in August 1943. The tanks were delivered to the 2nd Armoured and 1st Cavalry Divisions and the self-propelled guns to the 1st and 10th Assault Artillery Battalions, although the *Magyar* tank crews and cavalrymen were not exactly impressed with their new armoured machines. One Turan commander wrote of his new tank:

> We tried shooting at a knocked out T-34/85 [author's note: a later version armed with an 85mm gun in place of the 76mm] with the main 40mm gun. The 40mm anti-tank shell penetrated just the underside part of the T-34/85 from 20 metres! Against the turret this shell was totally useless.

Basically, Hungary's armoured answer, the much-vaunted Turan, was outdated before it ever fired a shot in anger. This did not bode well for when they went into action for the very first time almost eight months later, when ordered to take part in the *Ostheer*'s major counter-attack in Ukrainian Galicia.

On 17 April, departing from Solotwina to Kolomea (a town originally taken by the Hungarians in July 1941), the 100 new Turan tanks struggled forward through the densely wooded mountains of the area, the roads still waterlogged from the spring melt. Predictably, they came up against the very tank they were designed to defeat – the ageing but still-superb T-34. The *Magyar* tankers were hit hard. By the time the attack was called off on 26 July, more than thirty Turan Is and IIs had been destroyed in combat. After two years and more in development and production, it was a disaster.

Nevertheless, the Zrinyi SP guns and Turan tanks fought on during the battles around Ottynia in Ukrainian Galicia in July and onward farther north into Polish Galicia in September. Then, with the Red Army about to cross the borders of Hungary, all were pulled back south to defend the homeland. By that time, Hungarian heavy industry, starved of raw materials, manpower and

---

1 The Zrinyi was named after a *Magyar* folk hero, Count Nikolaus Zrinyi, who fought the invading Turks and died bravely in 1566 at the Battle of Szigetvar.

energy, had almost ground to a halt, and the flow of completed Turans and Zrinyis had become a mere trickle. The key Weiss factories were also working on a new medium/heavy tank, the 44M Tas named after a *Magyar* chieftain from the ninth century. In the end, only a prototype of the 44M Tas was ever completed, and this was destroyed in a bombing raid by the USAAF on 27 July 1944. Hungary's indigenous tank industry was a conspicuous failure, with fewer than 400 Turan tanks ever reaching the front. This was approximately the same number of tanks that Germany produced every three weeks in 1944.

Invasion

The rolling plains and well-kept villages and towns of eastern Hungary now became one huge battlefield. Far to the north, Adolf Hitler was in the depths of his own paranoia and growing madness, and nothing could dissuade him from an almost pointless defence of Hungary. Pouring men and equipment into this desperate fight could in no way be seen as an honourable attempt to stand by a friend – Hitler was totally incapable of such an emotion. Rather, it was an illusory bid by the Nazi leader to attempt to hold onto the country's oil production facilities to try to keep at least a number of his diminishing tank force mobile. The result can be imagined – disaster and havoc on an epic scale for such a small nation. As artillery, tank and infantry fire swept westwards, the production and supply of food collapsed, leading to widespread hunger and near-starvation, especially in the cities. In the capital, the official daily ration fell to just 556 calories per person, one-fifth of the universally acknowledged amount an average person requires to survive and stay healthy. The Hungarian industrial base, pushed to its limits to equip the armed forces, ended up being stripped by an incredibly ungrateful Third Reich when, in an act of outrageous national theft, the Nazis dismantled more than 500 Hungarian factories and shipped their contents to Germany. As it turned out, much of this would be in the Reich for only a few months before being captured by the Soviets, who transported it east – but not back to Hungary.

With the outcome of the fighting becoming more obvious by the day, Regent Miklos Horthy decided to follow the example of his hated Romanian neighbours and sue for peace and an end to Hungary's part in one of the most destructive wars in its long history. This time, though, unlike with Romania, the Germans were ready.

On 15 October, a warm Sunday afternoon, Horthy spoke to his nation in a pre-recorded broadcast:

Hungary was forced into the war against the Allies by German pressure ... Today it is obvious to any sober-minded person that the German Reich has lost the War. We shall not become the Reich's rearguard combat zone. We have agreed to abandon further participation in the fight against the Soviet Union.

Peace at last. The fact that it was not was largely due to one man – an Austrian Waffen-SS officer named Otto Skorzeny.[1] Skorzeny was a hugely flamboyant egotist who became one of Hitler's favourites after his involvement in the raid that rescued Mussolini – an operation whose success he has always been credited with leading despite the fact that it was a *Fallschirmjager* operation and not a Waffen-SS one. Regardless, now in Budapest, he proved his worth by effectively reversing the Horthy broadcast. Leading a mixed force of SS troopers and panzers, he surrounded the government Citadel and bluffed the elderly Horthy into believing he had a large force at his disposal that would reduce the city to rubble if he did not surrender. He also informed Horthy that he had kidnapped his surviving playboy son, Miklos Junior, and that his safety could be guaranteed only by his father's acquiescence. Still bereft at the loss of his eldest son István in Russia, Horthy could not bear to lose his only surviving boy and surrendered.

The tangible result was the sudden broadcast of martial music over Hungary's national radio and then the announcement of a 'mistake' – Hungary was still an ally of Germany, and the war would continue.

By the beginning of 1945, Hungary was in ruins and Budapest a charnel house. The siege of the capital finally came to a bloody end when the last surviving Waffen-SS cavalrymen of the trapped Florian Geyer and Maria Theresa Divisions tried to break out to the west. Of the thousands of men trapped in the city, only some 700 actually escaped to safety. As the curtain came down on the capital's tragedy, Hungary finally left the Axis and switched sides, officially declaring war on Germany on 31 December 1944. Just as with all her 'new friends', Moscow extracted a lot from the *Magyars*, putting Hungarian troops into the line to fight the retreating Germans and those thousands of their countrymen who refused to change their allegiance. Among the latter were the few remaining men of the Hungarian 2nd Armoured Division – the last remnants of their once-proud panzer arm – who fought to the bitter end, finally surrendering to the Red Army in the Austrian Steiermark at the end of April 1945.

---

1 In a twist of historical fate, Austria – originally *Ostarrichi* (the Eastern Command), had originally been created in ad 955 by the Saxon King Otto as a defensive buffer against the same *Magyars* Skorzeny now faced.

CHAPTER 13

AFTERMATH

It must be remembered that to be captured by the Red Army during the Second World War was a life-threatening event, a fact that the Germans and their Axis allies were well aware of. More than 11 million German soldiers were taken prisoner during the conflict, but despite the fact that the majority of the *Wehrmacht* fought on the Russian Front, only just over 3 million of them surrendered to the Red Army. Especially as the war was coming to an end, the priority for every German in uniform who could drive, run, walk or crawl was to head west and give himself up to the British or Americans – or even the French. This reaction was not exactly a surprise.

At dinner on the second evening of the Allied Powers Tehran Conference in 1943, Stalin proposed a toast to the 'execution of fifty thousand or perhaps a hundred thousand of the German command staff' at a table with the US president, Franklin D. Roosevelt, and the British prime minister, Winston S. Churchill. Churchill was outraged, and his response was as forthright and combative as one would expect:

> I would rather be taken out into the garden here and now and be shot myself than sully my own and my country's honour with such infamy.

Roosevelt, a brilliant man but one often taken in and outmatched by the Soviet dictator, joked that perhaps they could make do with just shooting 49,000. Churchill did not see the funny side, and neither did the more than 1 million German prisoners-of-war who died in Soviet captivity or equally the tens of thousands of anti-communist Russians, Ukrainians, Cossacks, Caucasians and Balts who were handed over at Judenburg and Odessa to be summarily shot.

From the Axis allies, the numbers were smaller but equally as stark: a total of 309,000 Romanians, more than 80,000 Hungarians and 70,000 Italians. All were sent east to a lingering death in Soviet captivity. Survival was a near-miracle. Only 16,000 Italians came out alive, and the percentages for the other nationalities were just as bad. The Soviets did not stop when they occupied a country either; indeed, their work had only just begun.

In Hungary during the five years after the war, more than 600,000 civilians and former soldiers were rounded up by the Red Army and sent to forced labour camps for no given reason. One eyewitness, a *Magyar* doctor named Zoltan Toth who was captured in Budapest in 1945, stated:

> If the Russians spotted a prisoner with good, useable boots, they took him out
> of the line, put a bullet in his head and pulled off his boots.

Those who lived did so through determination, willpower and, often, simple good fortune. The German officer and aristocrat Count Heinrich von Einsiedel was sent home from the Soviet Union in one of the earliest transports after Stalin's amnesty for 'good prisoners' in 1950, and he described his fellow prisoners as follows:

> Starved, emaciated skeletons; human wrecks convulsed with dysentery due to
> a lack of food, gaunt figures with trembling limbs, expressionless grey faces and
> dim eyes which brightened up only at the sight of bread or a cigarette.

However, horror at the Soviet Union's treatment of its defenceless prisoners must be balanced by the truly monstrous behaviour of the Nazis towards their own Soviet captives and the Russian people themselves, and the Axis allies must bear their share of that blame. The figures are appalling; the Germans and their allies captured some 5.7 million prisoners during the fighting, the majority in 1941 and 1942. These men were systematically starved, neglected, beaten, worked to death in conditions that are almost impossible to comprehend and summarily executed. The result was that no fewer than 3.3 million died in captivity, and they were joined by more than 20 million of their civilian countrymen, women and children, with enormous numbers deliberately left to die through lack of food, as detailed in Germany's aptly named *Der Backeplan* or *Hungerplan* (Hunger Plan). The brainchild of the German economist Herbert Backe, the plan called for the annihilation of what was perceived by the German regime as a superfluous population through the extreme reduction of the rations allocated to Soviet civilians in the cities and among the farming population. This inhumanity does not excuse Moscow's killing of hundreds of thousands of prisoners and enemy civilians, but it does at least put it in some sort of context.

The Axis allies, murder and the Holocaust

The Holocaust was a crime of such magnitude, of such horror, that even now, some seventy years later, it still has the ability to chill the blood and numb the mind. Anti-Semitism has a long and dark history in Europe, but turning that disgusting 'tradition' into industrialised murder was overwhelmingly the work of two men – Adolf Hitler and his acolyte, head of the SS Heinrich Himmler, a man who, much like his master, was riddled with hypocrisy and murderous complexity. In late October 1941, with Operation Barbarossa stalled after the Ukrainian summer battles, Himmler attended a weekend hunting party at the lodge of the Reich's vain and pompous Foreign Minister, Joachim von Ribbentrop. There, Himmler remarked to his masseur and companion, Felix Kersten:

> How can you find any pleasure, Herr Kersten, in shooting from behind cover at poor creatures browsing on the edge of a wood; innocent, defenceless and unsuspecting? Properly considered, it is pure murder.

At the very same time he was uttering these words, squads of SS men acting under his orders were murdering 4,927 Jewish men and women and 4,273 Jewish children at Kaunas in occupied Lithuania – a known fact thanks to the extremely accurate records kept by the Nazis on their own atrocities. The juxtaposition of such comments in Himmler's own warped mind is thankfully beyond my understanding.

Himmler also complained to Kersten about the guest of honour at Schönhof, Count Ciano, the Foreign Minister of Italy, who was proving himself an excellent marksman:

> I wish the Italians had been such good shots in Africa, where there's no danger the Italians are heroes.

This from a man who never had the courage to face an enemy in battle and whose reaction the one and only time he ever witnessed a massacre he had ordered was to be violently sick.

While the weight of post-war approbation has focused on Nazi Germany, and understandably so, there is no escaping the fact that most member states of the Axis alliance also committed war crimes, although their participation or acquiescence in the greatest crime of all, the Holocaust, was markedly different from ally to ally.

Fascist Italy was not an anti-Semitic state in the way Nazi Germany was, and Mussolini resisted Hitler's demands to hand over Italian Jews. The chaos of the war and the German occupation changed all this, but even so, the majority of the country's 45,000 Jews survived, and only some 8,000 were murdered.

The Bulgarians, to their eternal credit, totally refused to hand over their 50,000 Jewish countrymen to the clutches of the Nazis, even to the extent of Bulgarian citizens lying in the road to stop German convoys trying to round up Jews. However, they were unable, and sometimes unwilling, to extend that same protection to non-Bulgarian Jews in the lands they acquired from Yugoslavia and Greece. Those Jews were shipped off to be murdered. They also showed no scruples when dealing with their traditional foes, the Macedonian Greeks, who were beaten, shot or hanged for the slightest infraction and very much treated en masse as 'enemies of the state'.

The Slovaks had no such qualms with genocide. Some 70,000 from the 90,000 Jewish population were murdered by the Nazis without any complaints from Bratislava.

For Romania and Hungary, the anti-Jewish terror was a story of ambivalence. Within their own borders, the two nations tended to view their large Jewish populations with hostility, dislike and official discrimination but stopped a long way short of outright extermination. This kept them relatively safe from the Nazis for most of the war, but this attitude did not extend to Jews they found elsewhere. This was especially true for the Romanians, who took an active part in the slaughter in the Soviet Union and in Bessarabia. On 12 November 1945, Lieutenant Colonel Traian Borescu – Chief of the Chancellory of the State Intelligence Agency, the enormously powerful Romanian Special Information Service (SIS) – testified in the newly established Bucharest People's Court about the loathsome activities of *Einsatzkommando II* B (Task Force II B, a sub-unit of *Einsatzgruppe* D [Task Group D]).[1] Borescu admitted that an entire company of Romanians from the SIS were subordinated to *Einstazkommando II* B, a unit whose 'speciality'

---

1 There were four *Einsatzgruppen* that followed the *Wehrmacht* into the Soviet Union after Operation Barbarossa – A, B, C and D – and all were created for a single purpose: the physical extermination of 'enemies of the Reich', usually by mass shooting. It is estimated that they murdered almost 1.5 million people, mostly Jews.

was to push its defenceless victims into a suitably large building, such as a warehouse or barn, and then drill holes in the walls, place machine-guns into the holes and open fire. After the shooting had stopped, the buildings were set on fire, killing any survivors and destroying the evidence – no doubt what the Nazis would term a 'neat solution'.

Borescu's testimony went further, detailing how the Romanian authorities also murdered Jews in primitive camps set up in the Soviet Union behind the advancing 3rd and 4th Armies – an extension of the *Einsatzgruppe* approach to the mass killings of Jews. The historian Raul Hilberg recorded:

> … at Bogdanovca, the largest and most lethal camp, the killings began on the 21st of December 1941. At first four thousand to five thousand sick and infirm Jews [author's note: mostly from the villages and towns around Odessa] were placed in several stables, covered with straw, sprinkled with gasoline and then torched.

As for Hungary, with its very large Jewish population, a gripping struggle for survival was fought out between the truly heroic Swedish diplomat Raoul Gustav Wallenberg and the man who, more than any other, came to epitomise Nazi evil: Adolf Eichmann. Eichmann, a colonel in the SS, headed the anonymously named RSHA Sub-Department IV-B4. A small section of the Third Reich's security apparatus tasked with overseeing Jewish affairs, which over time became the driving administrative force behind the 'Final Solution'. The Nazi system was organised in such a way that tens of thousands of bureaucrats and petty functionaries were involved in the machinery of mass murder without ever having to physically pull a trigger, yet still being responsible for human extermination on an industrial scale. Eichmann was the head of this system, and his weapons were officialdom and an efficient rail network. These two combined to allow him to deport the Jewish populations of most of Europe to the death camps of Auschwitz-Birkenau, Treblinka, Sobibor, Belzec and Chelmno. There, on arrival, families would be 'sorted' into who would live and who would die by officials like Dr Josef Mengele, with the vast majority herded like so much human cattle into the waiting gas chambers. By 1944, Hungary's Jews were some of the last left alive in Europe, and Eichmann was determined to get them.

Hitherto protected by Horthy, an old-fashioned anti-Semite but no mass murderer, the Nazis felt that the time was ripe for the Holocaust to engulf Hungary, and Eichmann arrived in Budapest, forcing the local civil service into submission and beginning the deportations. To its credit, the Hungarian Army refused to bow to the odious SS bully and sabotaged his efforts at every turn.

In this they were helped by Wallenberg, who single-handedly saved thousands of Hungarian Jews by giving them fake Swedish passports and declaring them to be his fellow countrymen and therefore neutrals whom the Nazis could not touch. Wallenberg was utterly fearless, handing out the life-saving documents to every Jew he could find, including to the outstretched hands of those already locked up in cattle-trucks ready to be sent north to their deaths. The Scandinavian would then calmly instruct the train commander and driver to stop and allow 'his fellow Swedes' to go free. Wallenberg's reward was to be honoured by Israel alongside Oskar Schindler and others who saved Jews during the war. One, Alice Breuer, a doctor Wallenberg saved not once but twice, was standing on the banks of the Danube in front of a fascist militia firing squad when she heard a powerful voice ring out, 'These are Swedish citizens! Release them immediately and return their belongings to them!'

Incredibly, the firing squad did not open fire:

> To our astonishment the executioners obeyed him. He seemed very tall indeed, and strong. He radiated power and dignity. There was truly a kind of divine aura about him on that night.

This gratitude, though, did not extend to the Soviets, who arrested Wallenberg, kidnapped him and secretly imprisoned him for the rest of his life. The man who probably ordered that arrest was the late Soviet Premier Leonid Brezhnev, then an influential political officer with the Red Army. Brezhnev's reason was likely greed, as he had a lifelong passion for motor cars and wanted Wallenberg's rare US-built Studebaker. Having arrested him, his own rise in the Communist Party effectively condemned Wallenberg to death inside the wire, probably in the 1960s after two decades of imprisonment.

Another man who hindered Eichmann's attempts at Jewish extirpation in Hungary was a total surprise – SS Major Kurt Becher. Although Becher was not a hero like Wallenberg, he heartily disliked Eichmann, and like many of his fellow Nazi officials, was totally corrupt. As an old friend of Himmler, Becher was sent to Hungary to try to buy 20,000 horses for the Waffen-SS divisions fighting on the Russian Front. Whilst negotiating the deal, he was approached by the Weiss family, owners of the largest industrial corporation in the country and responsible for a high percentage of Hungary's tank and ammunition production. Fearing their importance to Hungary's war effort was not enough to protect them from Eichmann and his train timetables, the family offered Becher virtual ownership of their factories if he could help them escape. With the greed and hypocrisy worthy of an SS officer, Becher accepted the bribe and arranged for no fewer than forty-eight members of the Weiss family to be flown to neutral Portugal and safety. Eichmann was furious, calling it a *schweinerei* (a pig-dirty trick), which no doubt pleased Becher even more!

Despite Wallenberg's heroics, and those of many other ordinary men and women determined to act like decent human beings, the end result for the Jews of Hungary and Romania was as bloody and final as for the two countries' armies on the Don. Nazi Germany's death camps ended up taking more than 250,000 Romanian Jews (estimates suggest that number may be as high as 350,000) and more than 500,000 Hungarians (5 per cent of the country's entire pre-war population).

Violence and chaos

The closing stages of any war are usually the bloodiest and most chaotic. As law and order within society break down, the defeated look to settle scores before it's too late and the victors take their revenge. Given the magnitude and scale of the Second World War, it was always likely that this would mean horrendous bloodletting in 1945 and beyond – and indeed, this was to be.

The Croatian and Bosnian wars of the 1990s and the ongoing African civil wars of the last decade and more have reminded the world of an ugly fact: that rape in war is sometimes not just a horrific aberration committed by men in the aftermath of combat, but can also itself be a weapon of war and terror. No army in the Second World War was wholly innocent of sex crime. A Ukrainian doctor who specialised in abortions, Doctor Sarezkii, was arrested by the German authorities in the summer of 1942 and charged with 'illegal practices' (abortion was unlawful at the time). In his defence, the doctor prepared a written report of his own activities that documented a massive rise in the demand for abortions following the Axis occupation as a result of the advancing troops raping local women. The rate then dropped off equally dramatically following a German decree that pregnant women were exempt from deportation as forced labour up until the new child's second birthday. We can only marvel at the strength and stoicism of these women in such terrible circumstances.

Having said all were guilty to some degree, there is no escaping the fact that it was the Red Army that perpetrated sexual violence on an industrial scale. Bulgaria was the first Axis ally to be invaded, and it escaped relatively untouched – a result of the close kinship felt between Bulgars and Russians and the fact that Bulgaria had not taken part in the invasion of the Soviet

Union. Romania was next, and at first the civilian population fared poorly, until Antonescu was deposed and the country switched sides, at which point things calmed down dramatically. For Hungary, its botched defection and dogged defence of the capital spelt disaster for the nation's womenfolk. When the advancing Red Army took Csakvar, a small town of some 5,000 people in Fejer County west of Budapest, the soldiery ran amok, raping every woman and girl they could find between the ages of twelve and sixty. An eyewitness and victim, 21-year-old Alaine Polacz, was attacked so savagely she suffered spinal injuries that threatened to condemn her to life in a wheelchair. Her ordeal lasted days, and she wrote of it:

> This had nothing to do with embraces or sex … it was simply aggression … this was going on throughout the entire country.

When the Communist Party seized power in Hungary, it decided to ignore the atrocities, fearing any discussion or investigation would embarrass its masters in Moscow. This means accurate figures are difficult to gauge; however, hospital admission records from the time suggest that anywhere between 50,000 to 200,000 Hungarian women were raped between 1944 and 1945. The effect on Hungary's male population can only be guessed at as they were forced to stand by and watch as their wives, mothers and daughters were ravaged. One visible sign of the fissures it created in Hungarian society was the massive increase in the rate of divorce in the three years after the war. Couples had simply seen and endured too much to remain married.

Marital breakdown was not the only change in the societies of the Axis allies following the war. As the *Magyar* writer Istvan Bibo wrote:

> For the first time since 1514 the rigid social system in the country started to move, and move in the direction of greater freedom.

Before the war, some 40 per cent of Hungary's peasants were landless, and hugely powerful aristocratic landowners still held power, much as they had for centuries. This all changed, with the estates broken up and land redistributed, although sometimes at the expense of others, such as the Jews whose property was shared out when they were deported and never returned to them or their relatives, whether or not they survived.

It was not just the countryside that witnessed social and economic upheaval. Industrial workers, sensing the power so tantalisingly close to being in their grasp, downed tools and went on mass strikes. In Turin, the home of the infantry division destroyed on the Don and bearing the city's name, the workers took over the Fiat complex and began to hunt down their bosses. The managing director only just escaped with his life by running down a fire escape. Armed workers started to patrol the factory floor as a form of 'workers' militia', and all management was barred on pain of death. Across Italy, high-profile right-wing business leaders were murdered, including the well-known Christian Democrat industrialists Giuseppe Verderi and Arnaldo Vischi, the latter one of the most important businessmen in the Emilia-Romagna region. It was this region, home to the Cosseria and Ravenna Divisions, which became a particular hotbed for this sort of violence. No fewer than 103 of the area's landowners were murdered by disgruntled peasants after the war, including the infamous case of 6 July 1945, when every member of the powerful Manzoi family was shot dead at the family villa in Lugo near Ravenna. The murdered included the three Manzoi brothers, their mother, the housemaid and even their dog. Everyone knew the villagers responsible, but silence reigned.

The long, dark night

On a chilly autumn Moscow evening in early October 1944, two old adversaries sat talking over an after-dinner drink in the Kremlin. Both were imperialists, both master politicians and both determined to try to shape the post-war world to their own nation's advantage. A simple piece of plain white paper was passed between them – a 'naughty document', as Churchill described his own handiwork – and on it he listed five countries (three of them Axis allies) with percentages against each:

- Romania 90% Soviet, 10% 'others',
- Bulgaria 75:25,
- Hungary and Yugoslavia 50:50,
- Greece 90% Britain, 10% Soviet

The numbers indicated the level of influence each would have in that respective land. Stalin studied the page, smiled and marked it himself with a big blue tick. The fate of nations had been decided in minutes.

As the Red Army rolled through country after country, some conquering, others liberating, Stalinist communism came with it, and that meant coercion and rigged elections to make sure Moscow's will would be done. In October 1946, the communists 'won' 70 per cent of the vote in Bulgaria; the following month, it was another 70 per cent in Romania, and then the victories became even more miraculous. Poland in January 1947 – 80 per cent; Czechoslovakia in May 1948 – 89 per cent; and, finally, the last Axis ally, Hungary, a literally incredible 96 per cent in May 1949. Alongside the massive poll-rigging came full-scale repression. Hungary was swept by a wave of government-held 'people's tribunals', with no fewer than 1.3 million individuals charged with all manner of offences, mainly political claptrap, between 1948 and 1953. Some 700,000 would be convicted – a full 7 per cent of the entire population punished to control them and their neighbours. One man caught up in this utterly corrupt process of 'judicial cleansing' was Gustav Jány.

Previously commander of the 2nd Army, he had been awarded the Knight's Cross by a grateful *Ostheer* in March 1943, proving it did not blame him for the disaster that had overtaken his army on the Don that winter. He had then returned to Hungary later that same year for a well-earned retirement. He survived the war only to be put on trial by the new government for 'war crimes'. The main indictment was for 'causing the deaths of 140,000 Hungarian soldiers in January 1943 at Voronezh by means of his irresponsible generalship'. On 6 October 1947, unsurprisingly, the court, heavily influenced by the country's Soviet occupiers, found him guilty, and he was sentenced to death. On 27 November, TASS, the Soviet state news service, carried a brief statement that announced the sentence had been carried out.

There was one Axis national ally that disappeared without a trace: Pavelic's Croatia. As a country, the Croatia of the *Ustase* was without a shadow of a doubt built on the blood of the innocent. Established with large populations of Christian Orthodox Serbs, Jews and Bosnian Muslims within its borders, the new state's founding principle was Croat racial supremacy – to be achieved through discrimination, terror and outright extermination. When forced conversions, torture, shootings and burnings did not work fast enough, Pavelic copied his German mentors and set up concentration camps to do his work, the most infamous being at Jasenovac. There is fierce controversy over just how many people were murdered in that dreaded place, but no one disputes that it was a minimum of 100,000, and it may have been as many as several hundred thousand – that was from a non-Croat populace of only 3 million people. Jasenovac, and the genocidal state it represented, plumbed the same depths of barbarity as its Nazi mentors.

The future

Two years ago, I took my wife and children on holiday to the beautiful Mediterranean island of Sicily. There, on the sun-drenched northern coast near the ancient Norman port and citadel of Cefalu, I sat and relaxed, doing nothing more strenuous than work on my tan. To pass the time, the hotel entertainment staff organised a game of water polo in the swimming pool for the guests. Within minutes, the two teams had sorted themselves out; on one side was a mixed bunch of Germans and Italians, and the other was exclusively Russians. As the only Englishman there, I let the rerun of the 'Little' Saturn offensive happen without me – and I'm very glad I did, as the two teams forgot the ball and tore into each other with gusto. That someone did not die I consider a miracle.

But do things change? Sometimes, and for us, only time will tell. Friedrich Wilhelm Heinz, a German veteran of the First World War, returned from the front to a homeland riven by chaos, hyperinflation and mass unemployment and said, 'Everyone told us the war was over. That was a laugh; we ourselves were the War.'

Heinz went on to become a senior leader of the Brownshirt Nazi stormtroopers.

APPENDICES

APPENDIX A: Romanian Army Order of Battle, Eastern Front, November 1942

Romanian Orders of Battle at the Eastern Front, November 1942		
Army	**Corps & Divisions**	
3 Army *(Dumitrescu)* at the *Don Front* north of *Stalingrad* Reserves: Heim's Corps, 7, 15 Cavalry Division	IV Corps	1 Cavalry 13 Infantry
	V Corps	5, 6 Infantry
	II Corps	9, 14 Infantry
	I Corps	7, 11 Infantry
4 Army *(Constantinescu-Claps)* in the *Kalkyk Steppe* south of *Stalingrad* Reserves: German 16, 29 Motorised Infantry Division	VII Corps	5, 8 Cavalry
	VI Corps	1, 2, 4, 18 Infantry
	IV Corps (German-led)	20 Romanian Infantry German 297, 371 Infantry Division

APPENDIX B: Romanian Infantry Divisions and Recruiting Areas

1st Infantry Division: Timisoara
85th Infantry Regiment:
93rd Infantry Regiment Closca: Arad
5th *Vanatori* Regiment: Timisoara
1st Artillery Regiment Regele Carol I: Timisioara
38th Artillery Regiment: Timisioara

2nd Infantry Division: Craiova
1st *Dorobanti* Regiment Dolj: Craiova
26th *Dorobanti* Regiment *Rovine*: Caracal
31st *Dorobanti* Regiment Calafat: Calafat
9th Artillery Regiment: Craiova
14th Artillery Regiment: Craiova

3rd Infantry Division: Pitesti
4th *Dorobanti* Regiment Arges: Pitesti
30th *Dorobanti* Regiment Muscel: Campulung Muscel
1st *Vanatori* Regiment Principele Mostenitor Ferdinand: Pitesti
6th Artillery Regiment: Pitesti
15th Artillery Regiment: Salcia

4th Infantry Division: Bucharest
5th *Dorobanti* Regiment Vlasca: Giurgiu
20th Infantry Regiment Teleorman: Targu Magurele
21st Infantry Regiment Ilfov: Bucharest
2nd Artillery Regiment: Bucharest
10th Artillery Regiment: Giurgiu

5th Infantry Division: Buzau
8th *Dorobanti* Regiment Buzau: Buzau
9th *Dorobanti* Regiment Ramnicu Sarat: Ramnicu Sarat
32nd *Dorobanti* Regiment Mircea: Ploiesti
7th Artillery Regiment: Buzau
28th Artillery Regiment: Ramnicu Sarat

6th Infantry Division: Focsani
10th *Dorobanti* Regiment Putna: Focsani
15th *Dorobanti* Regiment Razboieni: Piatra Neamt
27th *Dorobanti* Regiment Bacau: Bacau
11th Artillery Regiment: Focsani
16th Artillery Regiment: Bacau

7th Infantry Division: Roman
14th *Dorobanti* Regiment Roman: Roman
16th *Dorobanti* Regiment Baia–Maresal Josef Pilsudski: Falticeni
37th Infantry Regiment Alexandru cel Bun: Botosani
4th Artillery Regiment:
8th Artillery Regiment: Botosani

8th Infantry Division: Cernauti
29th Infantry Regiment Dragos: Dorohoi
7th *Vanatori* Regiment Eremia Movila:
8th *Vanatori* Regiment Grigore Ghica: Lipcani
12th Artillery Regiment: Cernauti
17th Artillery Regiment: Lipcani

9th Infantry Division: Constanta
34th Infantry Regiment Constanta: Constanta
36th Infantry Regiment Vasile Lupu: Constanta
40th Infantry Regiment Calugareni: Ferdinand (presently Mihail
Kogalniceanu)
13th Artillery Regiment: Constanta
18th Artillery Regiment: Constanta

10th Infantry Division: Braila
23rd Infantry Regiment Ialomita: Calarasi
33rd *Dorobanti* Regiment Tulcea: Tulcea
38th Infantry Regiment Neagoe Basarab: Braila
3rd Artillery Regiment Franta: Braila
20th Artillery Regiment: Calarasi

11th Infantry Division: Slatina
2nd *Dorobanti* Regiment Valcea: Ramnicu Valcea
3rd *Dorobanti* Regiment Olt: Slatina
19th Infantry Regiment Romanati: Caracal
21st Artillery Regiment: Slatina
26th Artillery Regiment: Curtea de Arges

13th Infantry Division: Ploiesti
7th *Dorobanti* Regiment Prahova: Targoviste
22nd Infantry Regiment Dambovita: Targoviste
89th Infantry Regiment: Brasov
19th Artillery Regiment: Ploiesti
41st Artillery Regiment: Brasov

14th Infantry Division: Balti (moved to Iasi in June 1940)
13th *Dorobanti* Regiment Stefan cel Mare: Iasi
39th Infantry Regiment Petru Rares: Floresti
6th *Vanatori* Regiment: Balti
24th Artillery Regiment: Ungheni
29th Artillery Regiment: Balti

15th Infantry Division: Chisinau
25th Infantry Regiment Maresal Constantin Prezan: Husi
12th Infantry Regiment Cantemir: Barlad
10th *Vanatori* Regiment: Tighina
23rd Artillery Regiment:
25th Artillery Regiment:

18th Infantry Division: Sibiu
18th *Dorobanti* Regiment Gorj: Targu Jiu
90th Infantry Regiment: Sibiu
92nd Infantry Regiment Decebal: Orastie
35th Artillery Regiment: Sibiu
36th Artillery Regiment: Targu Jiu

19th Infantry Division: Turnu Severin
94th Infantry Regiment: Orsova
95th Infantry Regiment Imparatul Traian: Turnu Severin
96th Infantry Regiment: Caransebes

37th Artillery Regiment: Turnu Severin
42nd Artillery Regiment: Lugoj

20th Infantry Division: Targu Mures
82nd Infantry Regiment:
83rd Infantry Regiment Tribunul Solomon Balint:
91st Infantry Regiment Alba Iulia–Regele Ferdinand I: Alba Iulia
39th Artillery Regiment:
40th Artillery Regiment:

21st Infantry Division: Galati
11th *Dorobanti* Regiment Siret: Galati
35th *Dorobanti* Regiment Matei Basarab: Cetatea Alba
24th Infantry Regiment Tecuci: Tecuci
5th Artillery Regiment: Barlad
30th Artillery Regiment: Chisinau

APPENDIX C: German Casualties, Eastern Front

German personnel losses suffered by the army on the Eastern Front from
November 1942 to March 1943:

month	KIA	wounded	missing	sick
November 1942	20,000	75,000	5,000	30,000
December	18,000	80,000	5,000	47,000
January 1943	17,000	71,000	7,000	58,000
February	19,000	100,000	9,000	84,000
March	26,000	57,000	11,000	30,000

About two-thirds of the wounded and all the sick soldiers were calculated to be
returned again ready for service after a reasonable period of time, so that there
were irretrievable losses of 677,000 men in the army in the East over 12 months,
and the *Ostheer* went from 3.1 million men on 1 November 1942, down to 2.85
million a year later.

BIBLIOGRAPHY

BOOKS

Abbott, Peter (and Nigel Thomas), *Germany's Eastern Front Allies 1941–45*, Osprey, 1982

Bauer, Eddy, Lt.Col, *World War II*, Orbis, 1972

Beevor, Antony, *Stalingrad*, Penguin, 1999

Bellamy, Chris, *Absolute War: Soviet Russia in the Second World War*, Macmillan, 2007

Bernard, Denes (and Dmitry Karlenko and Jean-Louis Roba), *From Barbarossa to Odessa: The Luftwaffe and Axis Allies Strike South-East: June–October 1941*, Ian Allan Publishing, 2008

Bishop, Chris, *The Military Atlas of World War II*, Amber, 2005

Butler, Rupert, *Hitler's Jackals*, Leo Cooper, 1998

Butler, Rupert, *Legions of Death*, Hamlyn, 1983

Carell, Paul, *Hitler's War on Russia, Volume 1*, Corgi, 1966 (translated by Ewald Oser)

Carell, Paul, *Hitler's War on Russia, Volume 2, Scorched Earth*, Corgi, 1971 (translated by Ewald Oser)

Cawthorne, Nigel, *Turning the Tide: Decisive Battles of the Second World War*, Arcturus, 2007

Cooper, Matthew, and Lucas, James, *Panzer: The Armoured Force of the Third Reich*, Book Club Associates, 1979

Cornish, Nik, *Armageddon Ost: The German Defeat on the Eastern Front 1944–5*, Ian Allan, 2006

Corti, Eugenio, *Few Returned: Diary of Twenty-eight Days on the Russian Front, Winter 1942–43*, University of Missouri Press, 1997 (translated by Peter Edward Levy)

Davies, Norman, *Europe At War 1939–1945: No Simple Victory*, Macmillan, 2006

Edwards, Robert, *White Death: Russia's War on Finland 1939-40*, Weidenfeld & Nicolson, 2006

Geddes, Giorgio, *Nichivo: Life, Love and Death on the Russian Front*, W&N, 2001

Hamilton, Hope, *Sacrifice on the Steppe: The Italian Alpine Corps in the Stalingrad Campaign, 1942–1943*, Casemate, 2011

Holmes, Richard, *The World At War*, Ebury, 2007

Hooton, E.R, *Eagle in Flames: The Fall of the Luftwaffe*, Arms & Armour, 1997

Levy, Alan, *Nazi Hunter – The Wiesenthal File*, Constable & Robinson, 2002

Littlejohn, David, *Foreign Legions of the Third Reich*, Volume 3, James Bender, 1985

Littlejohn, David, *Foreign Legions of the Third Reich*, Volume 4, James Bender, 1987

Lowe, Keith, *Savage Continent – Europe in the Aftermath of World War II*, Viking, 2012

Matthews, Rupert, *Hitler: Military Commander*, Arcturus, 2007

Munoz, Antonio J., *For Croatia and Christ: The Croatian Army in World War II, 1941–1945*, Europa, 2003

Nevenkin, Kamen, *Take Budapest! The Struggle for Hungary, Autumn 1944*, Spellmount, 2012

Porter, Ivor, *Michael of Romania: The King and the Country*, Sutton, 2005

Rhodes, Richard, *Masters of Death: The SS-Einsatzgruppen and the Invention of the Holocaust*, First Vintage, 2003

Taylor, Brian, *Barbarossa to Berlin, Volume 2, The Defeat of Germany, 19 November 1942 to 15 May 1945*, Spellmount, 2004

Thomas, Dr Nigel, and Szabo, Laszlo Pal, *The Royal Hungarian Army in World War II*, Osprey, 2008

Turner, Jason, *Stalingrad Day by Day*, Windmill, 2012

Ungvary, Kristian, *Battle for Budapest: 100 Days in World War II*, I.B. Tauris, 2005

Walker, Ian W., *Iron Hulls, Iron Hearts – Mussolini's Elite Armoured Divisions*, Crowood, 2003

WEBSITES
www.axis101.bizland.com
www.ehistory.freeservers.com
www.fantompowa.net
www.feldgrau.com
www.feldpost.tv/forum
www.germanwarmachine.com
www.gutenberg-e.org
www.histclo.com
www.nuav.net

INDEX

If you enjoyed this book, you may also be interested in…

Take Budapest
Kamen Nevenkin

Kamen Nevenkin tells the fascinating story of the 'Market Garden'-like operation to knock Hungary out of the war in October 1944, thereby bringing the Red Army as far as Munich, using a number of never before published German and Russian archival documents, including German papers exclusively held in the Russian military archive. The dynamic, detailed text is accompanied by previously unpublished photographs and uses first-person accounts to render a human tale of all-out war.

978 0 7524 6631 6

Hitler's Gauls
Jonathan Trigg

Hitler's Gauls is an in-depth examination of one of Hitler's foreign legions, the Charlemagne division, who were recruited entirely from conquered France. The men in Charlemagne, often motivated by an extreme anti-communist zeal, fought hard on the Eastern Front including the final stand in the ruins of Berlin. This definitive history, illustrated with rare photographs, explores the background, training, key figures and full combat record of one of Hitler's lesser known foreign units.

978 0 7524 5476 4

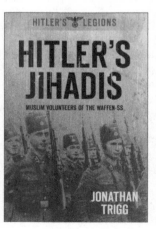

Hitler's Jihadis
Jonathan Trigg

Jonathan Trigg analyses of some of the most intriguing and controversial of Hitler's foreign volunteers – the thousands of Muslims who wore the SS double lightning flashes alongside their erstwhile conquerors. Herein lies an insight into the pre-war politics that inspired these Islamic volunteers, who for the most part would not survive. Using first-hand accounts and official records, *Hitler's Jihadis* peels away the propaganda to reveal the complexity that lies at the heart of the story of Hitler's most unlikely 'Aryans'.

978 0 7524 6586 9

The History Press

The destination for history
www·thehistorypress·co·uk